AF394760

Tove Jansson

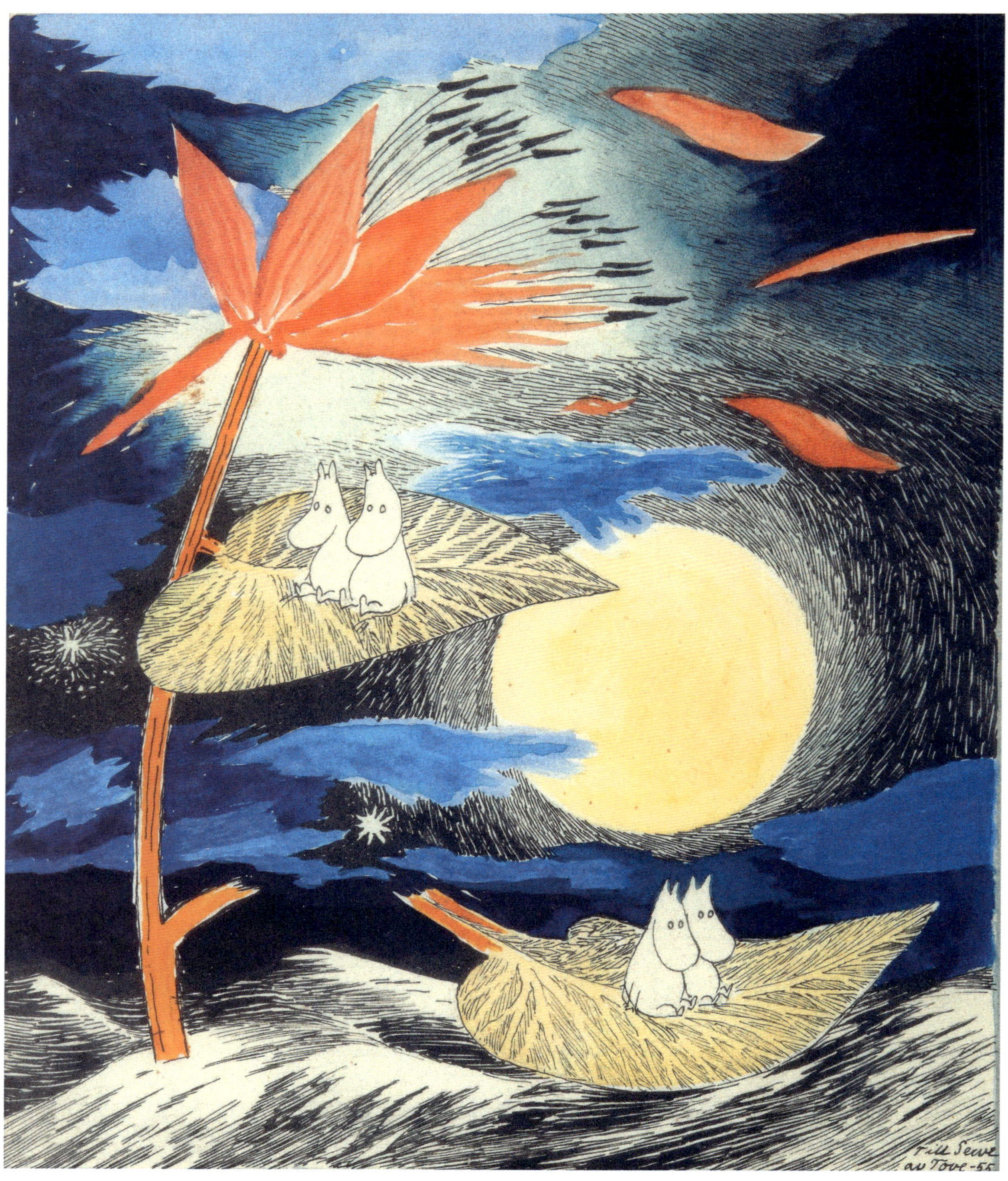

Paul Gravett

THE ILLUSTRATORS

Tove Jansson

SERIES CONSULTANT QUENTIN BLAKE
SERIES EDITOR CLAUDIA ZEFF

106 ILLUSTRATIONS

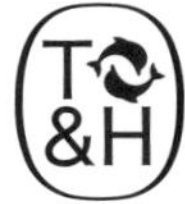

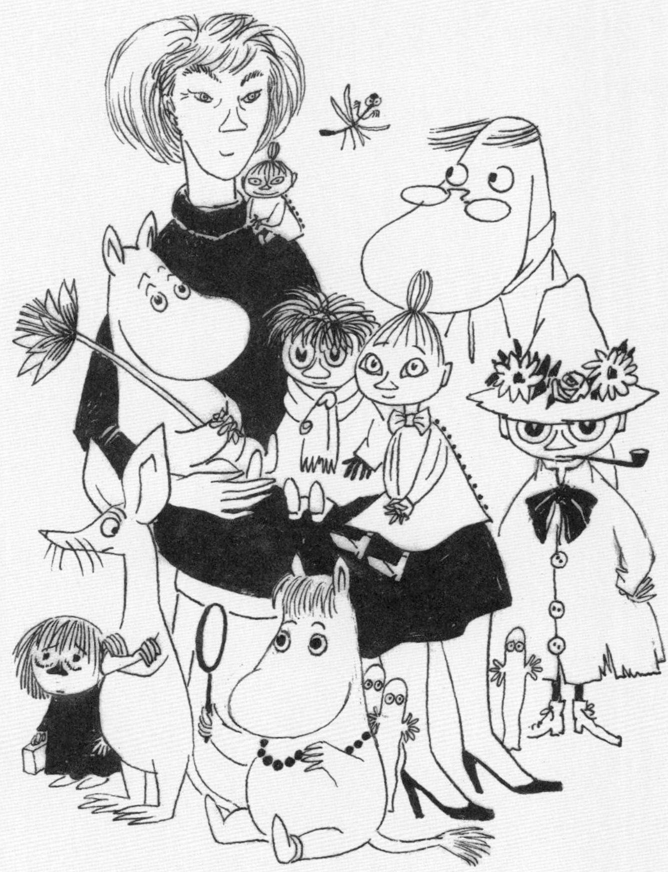

FRONT COVER From the comic *Moominvalley turns jungle*, 1956 © dmg media licensing, London and © Moomin Characters™
BACK COVER Tove Jansson, photograph by Per Olov Jansson © Per Olov Jansson

FRONTISPIECE Private watercolour sketch, signed 'To Serve', 1955.
ABOVE Self-portrait with her cast of characters, 1957.
PAGE 112 Illustration for the Italian colour edition of *Moominland Midwinter*, 1961.

First published in the United Kingdom in 2022
by Thames & Hudson Ltd, 181A High Holborn,
London WC1V 7QX

First published in the United States of America
in 2022 by Thames & Hudson Inc., 500 Fifth Avenue,
New York, New York 10110

Reprinted, with corrections, 2024

Tove Jansson © 2022 Thames & Hudson Ltd, London
Text © 2022 Paul Gravett
Illustrations unless otherwise stated © 2022 Tove Jansson,
Moomin Characters™

Designed by Therese Vandling

British Library Cataloguing-in-Publication Data
A catalogue record for this book is available from
the British Library

Library of Congress Control Number 2021943196

ISBN 978-0-500-09433-4

Printed and bound in China by C&C Offset Printing Co. Ltd

Be the first to know about our new releases,
exclusive content and author events by visiting
thamesandhudson.com
thamesandhudsonusa.com
thamesandhudson.com.au

CONTENTS

Introduction

'You yourself are all ages, from youngest to eldest, and perpetually at the start of your life, which you have already lived many times over.' Tove Jansson's friend, lover and almost-husband Atos Wirtanen understood that she was living multiple lives. A creative force, drawing and writing naturally from infancy with her parents' complete encouragement, the grown-up Jansson was to become a painter, illustrator, cartoonist, stage designer and muralist, as well as an author of memoir, fiction, children's books and plays. The marvel was that she shone at them all. And that was also the problem, because early on she had set her heart on the life of a painter. She was one of only two women in her painting class at art school, and although at times she looked close to realizing this dream, factors including the Second World War, the sexism of an ever-shifting art market and the need to earn a living interfered. But this was no failure. Jansson's many other lives gave us her best-known and loved work, the inimitable Moomins, and more wonders besides.

Swedish-speaking, lesbian and a woman, Tove Jansson lived within three minorities in twentieth-century Finland. She loved women, although she knew her homosexuality was classified as a crime in Finland until 1971 and as a mental illness until 1981, and so upset her parents that they could not let the words pass their lips. More positively, Jansson had both Swedish and Finnish culture to draw upon; women had long been somewhat equal in Finland, working hard alongside men in traditional farming society, a work ethic that Jansson followed. From 1906, eight years before she was born, women in Finland could vote and run for office, and in 1907 the Finnish parliament was the first in the world to appoint women as members, nineteen of them making up almost one-tenth of the country's first governing body.

Tove Jansson is world-renowned primarily for writing and illustrating her Moomin books, evocative, philosophical fantasies that speak to all ages. Their magic was observed by a reviewer in *The Times Literary Supplement*: 'Largely what creates the spell of these Moomin books is that by no trace of explanation or apology does the author mar the

Smoking Girl, a self-portrait in oils, 1940.

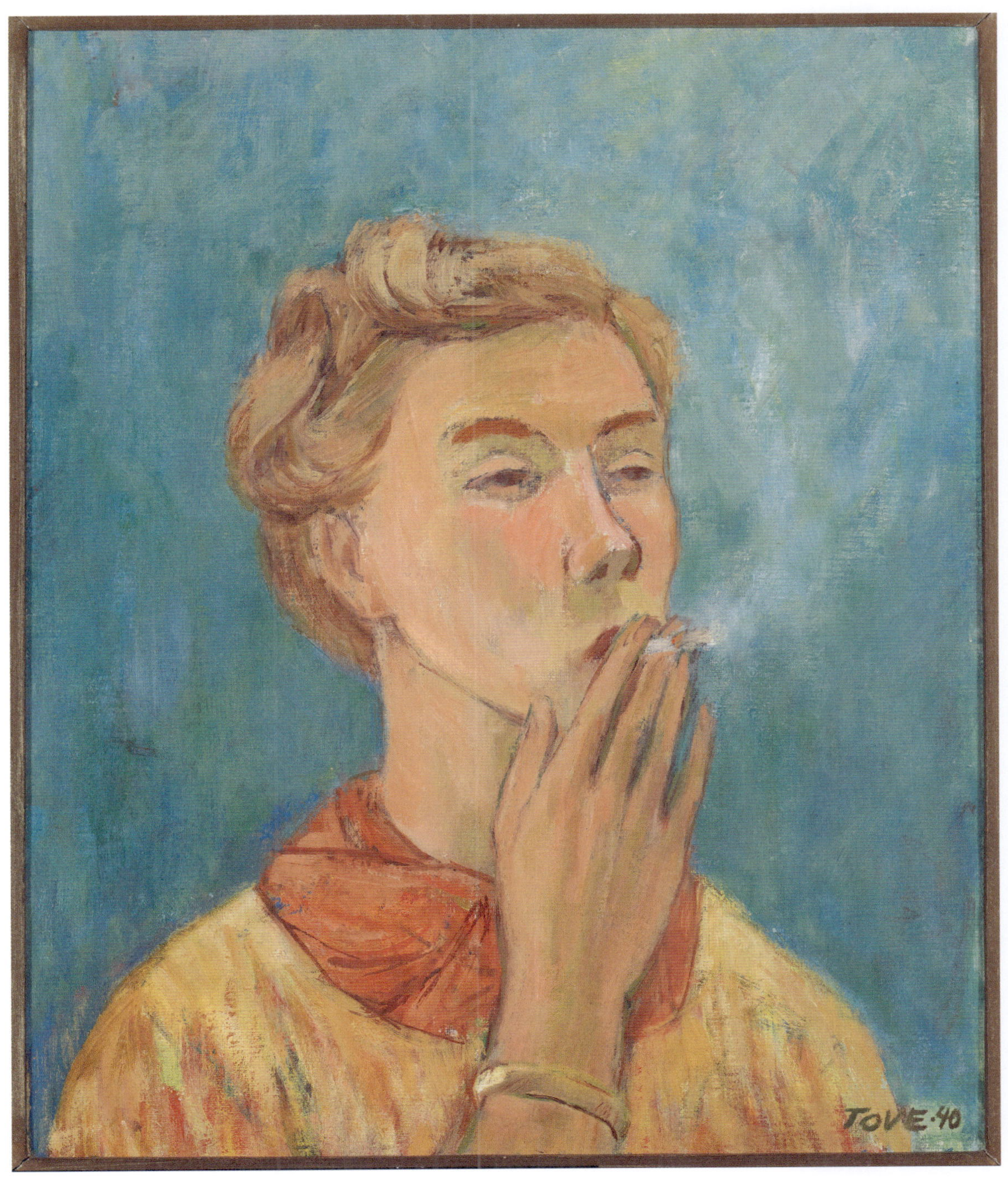

TOVE·40

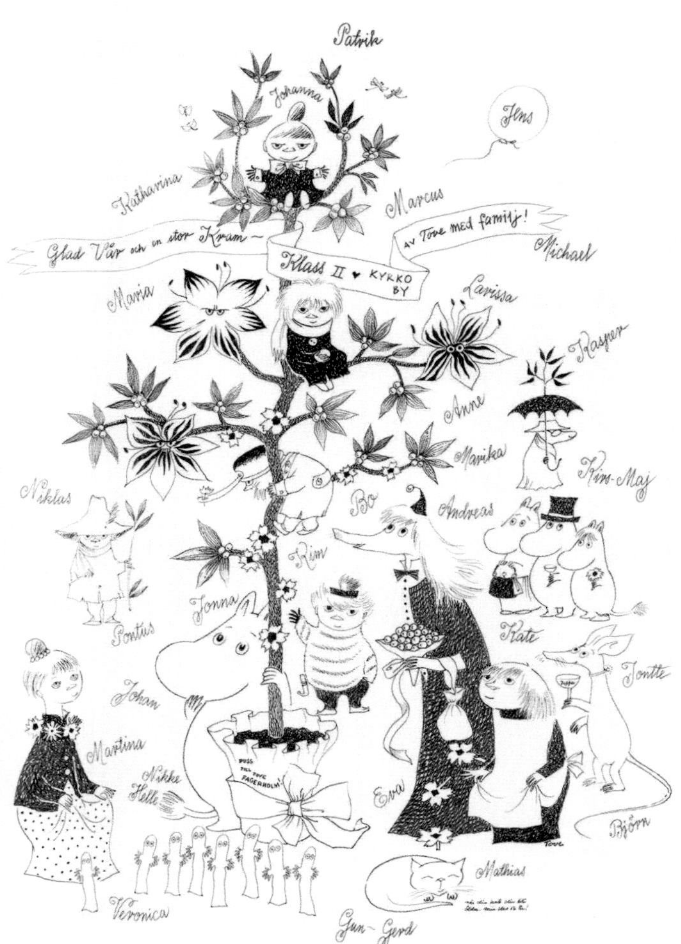

The cast of characters from the Moomin books send spring greetings to a school class.

LEFT

The cast of characters from the Moomin books send spring greetings to a school class.

BELOW

Self-portrait with a small Moomin.

OPPOSITE

Tove Jansson and her mother resting and reading in her studio, photographed by her brother, Per Olov Jansson.

OVERLEAF

Box artwork by Tove Jansson and her brother Lars ('Lasse') for the Moomin Game, which involves a hunt through Moominvalley for items that have fallen from Moominmamma's handbag: seashells, beautiful stones and the key to her store of jam.

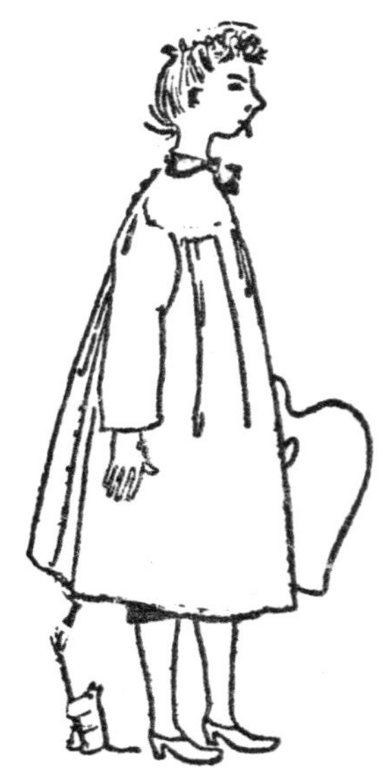

dreamlike possibility of her world.'[1] She was also acclaimed and awarded for her paintings, mainly landscape, interior and still-life and later some abstracts, and her fifteen books of un-illustrated prose for older readers. In fact, Jansson is Finland's most widely translated author, into over fifty languages, although she wrote in Swedish. In posthumous recognition in 2020, she became the second woman to be honoured by the Finnish government with a recommended annual Flag Day on her birthday, 9 August.

From the Moomins' unassuming debut in an illustrated novella in 1945, Jansson would create seven illustrated novels, a short story collection, five picture books and twenty-two comic-strip stories, as well as several plays and a libretto for an opera, for which she often designed their scenery, costumes or both, and images for all manner of promotional 'Moominalia'. Among her artistic expressions, illustration was vital through almost her entire life, extending also to books by other writers, social and political cartoons, public murals and advertising, set and costume designs for theatre, television and opera, and more.

Her mother, Signe Hammarsten, was like a lighthouse throughout her life. An illustrator herself, she instilled in Jansson a passion for drawing and for nature in the

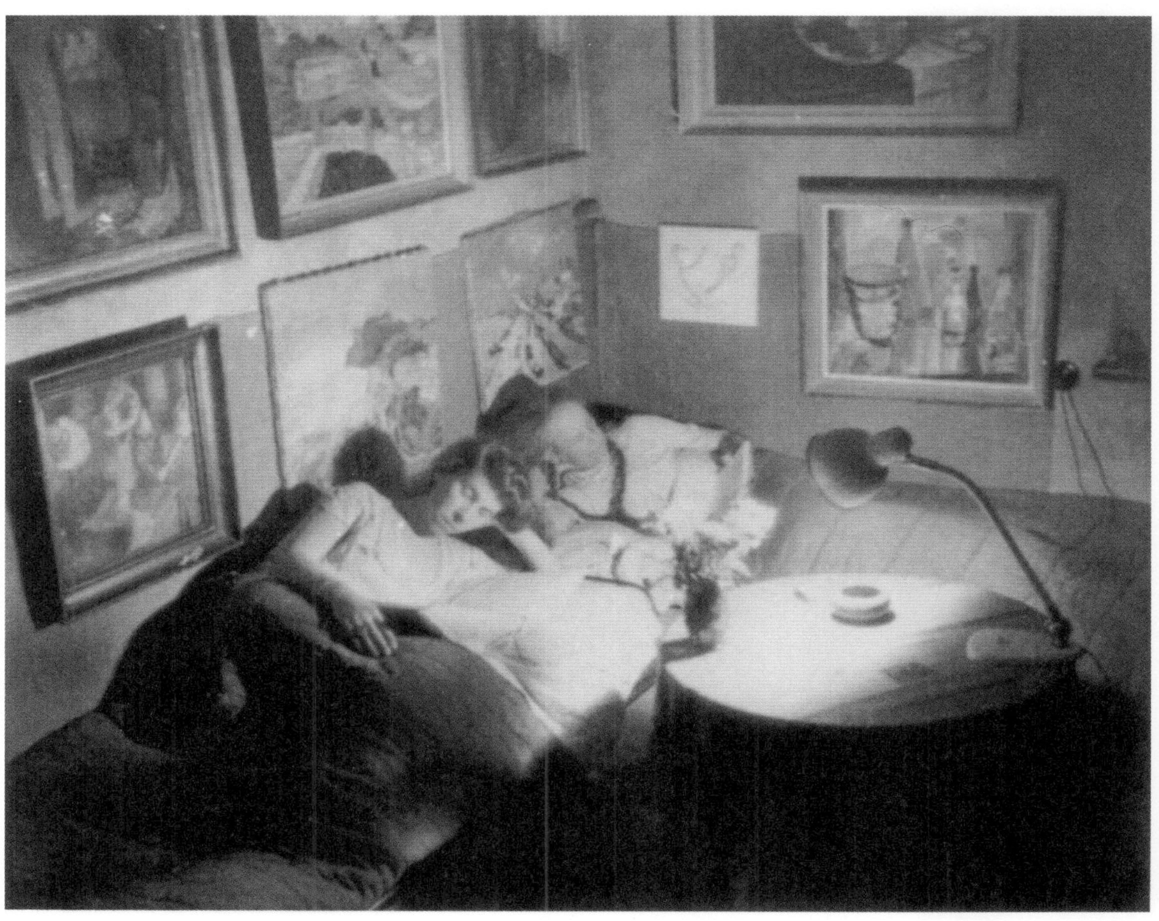

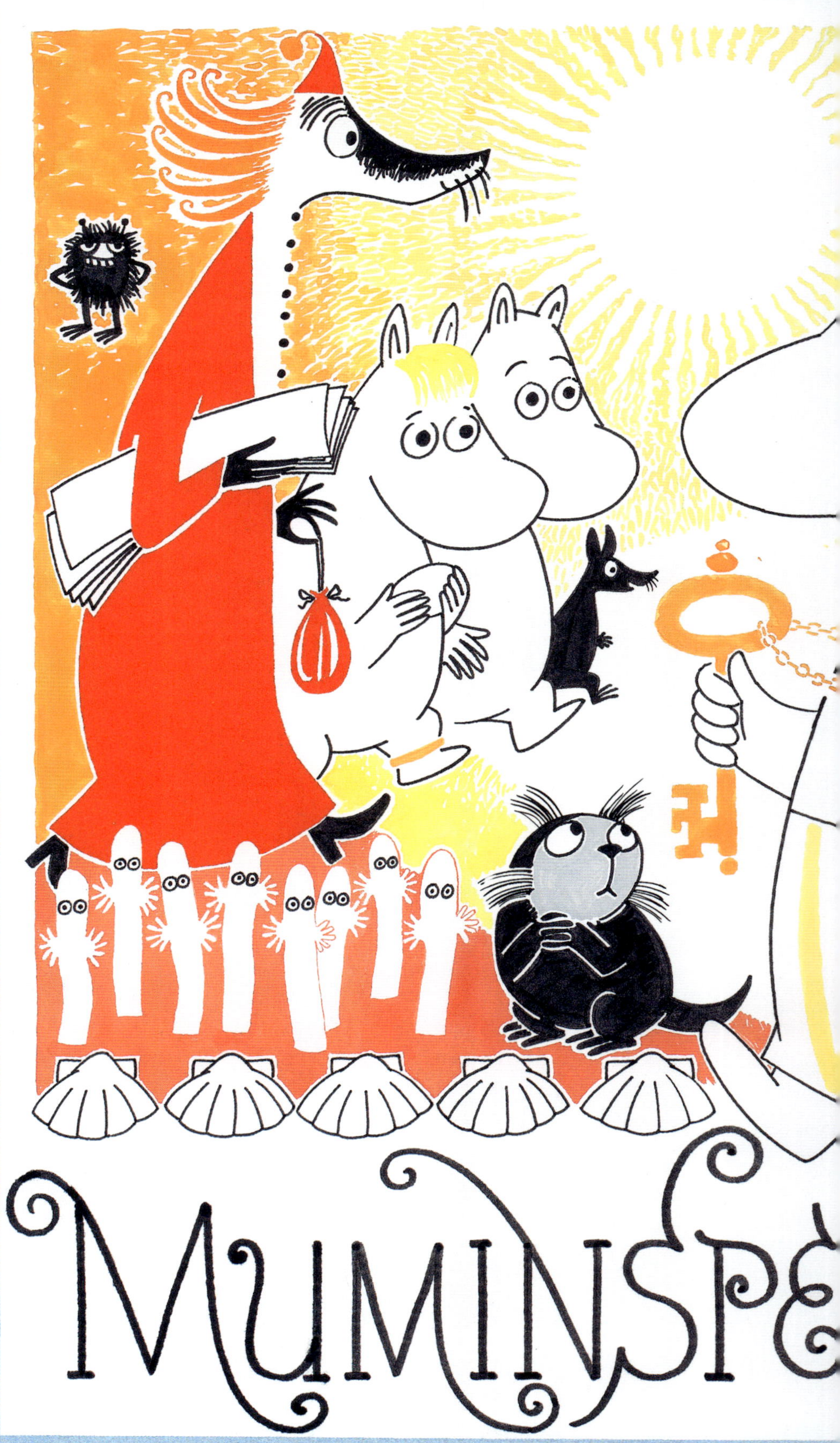

MUMINSP

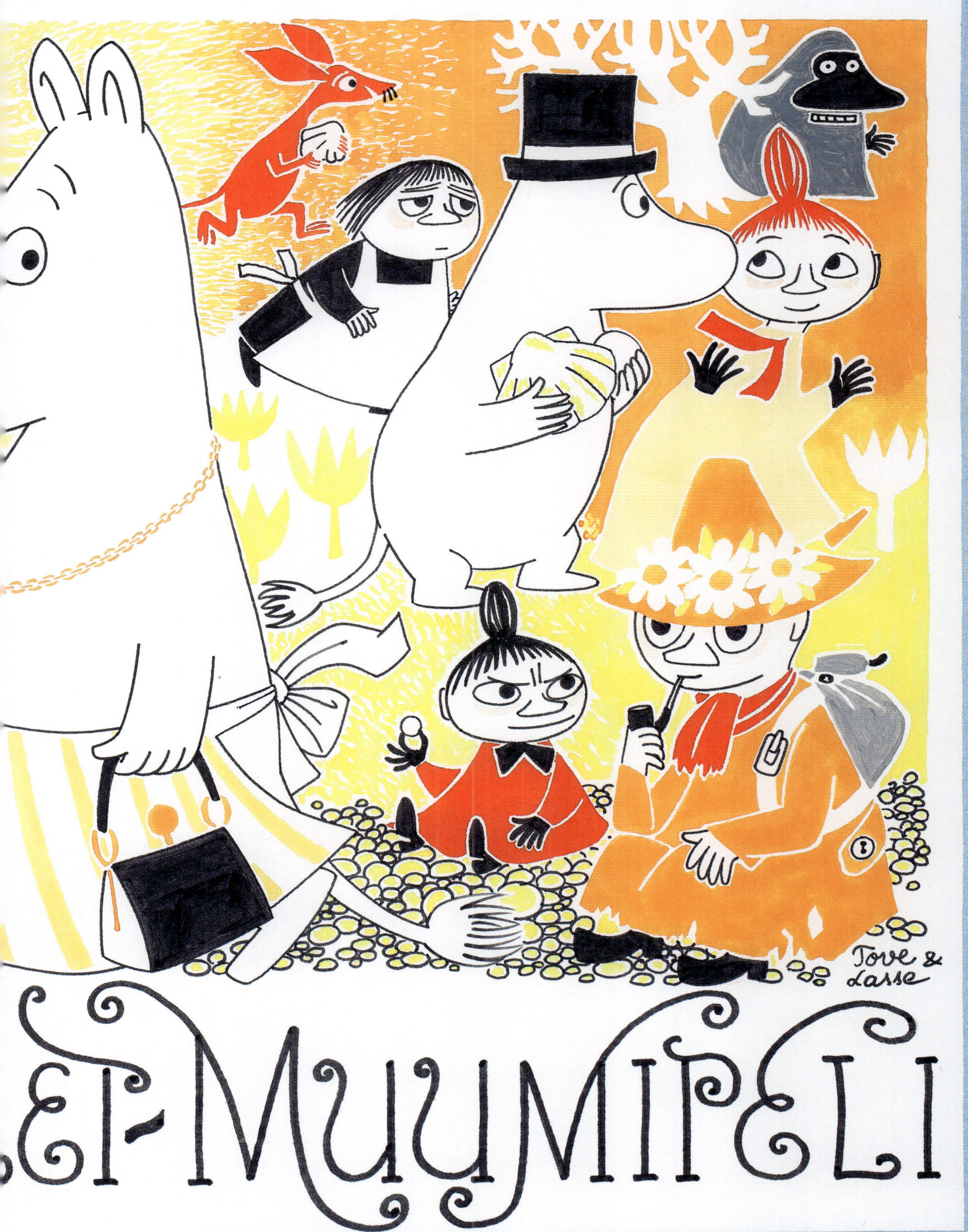

Tove &
Lasse
MUUMIPELI

raw, especially the sea, the stormier the better, and its islands, of which Finland has around 188,000, more than anywhere except Sweden. This love of the wild outdoors was fuelled through adventurous childhood summers in a hired guesthouse on an island in the Pellinge archipelago. It only got stronger as an adult, driving Jansson to move from Helsinki back to the Gulf of Finland and self-build her own *stuga*, the modest, practical cabins commonly used for national holidays, notably in July. Her first was on a small, remote island in the Gulf, before she moved to even smaller, more remote Klovharun, which Jansson made her near-annual personal paradise for eighteen years, staying as long as possible, ideally from spring's thaw to autumn's return.

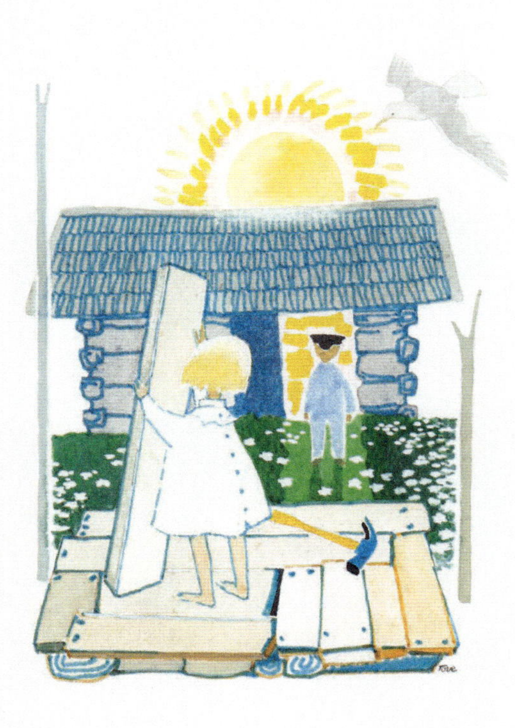

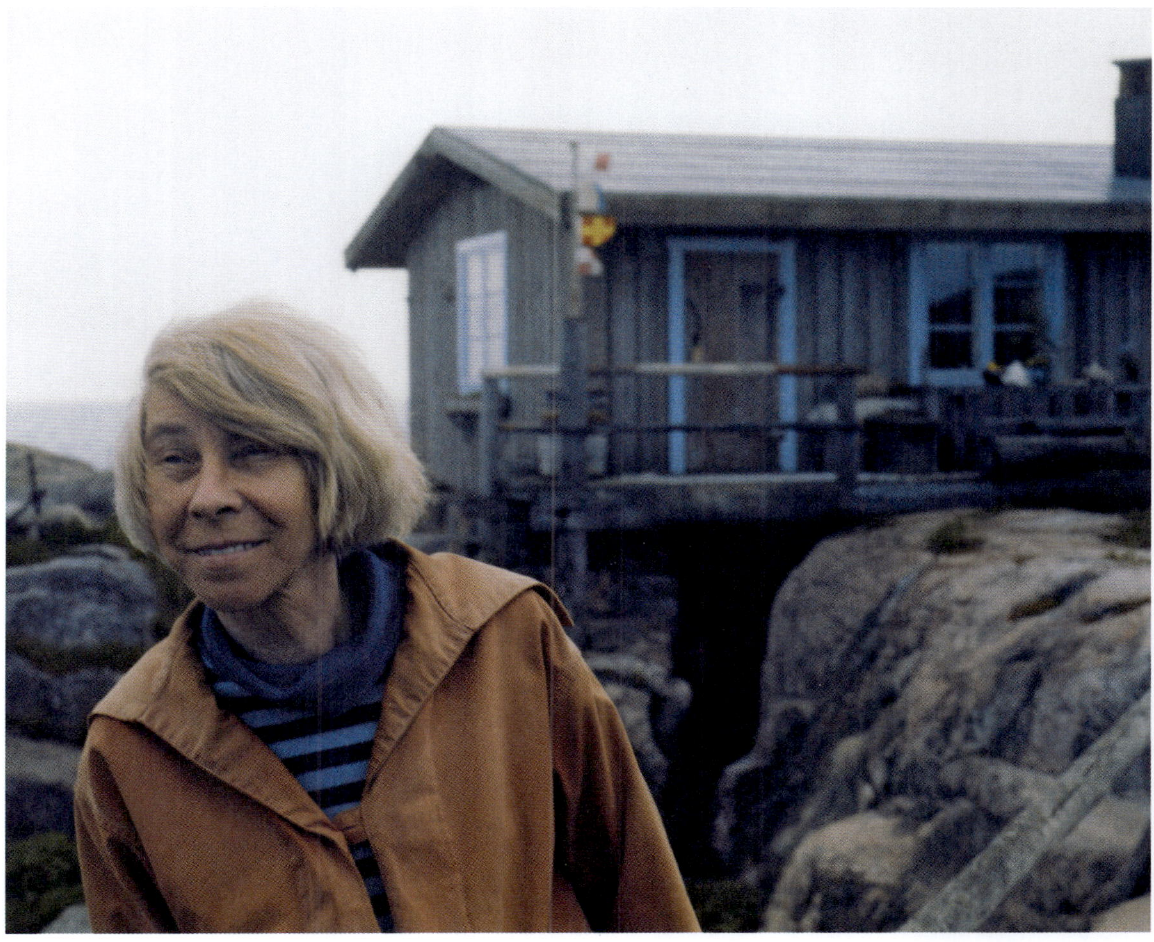

Tove Jansson outside her island cabin, photographed by Per Olov Jansson in the 1970s or 1980s.

Jansson's further lives were spent as an architect, builder and interior designer, defining and designing her environments, whether real or imaginary, from her island retreats and her lofty studio-home in the city, to her drawings, descriptions and scale models of the Moomins' home and idyllic valley, made with her long-term partner Tuulikki Pietilä. Life in Finland, a relatively young country without any earlier independent Golden Age to hark back to, liberated the Finnish to shape their own identity and destiny, something Jansson would do in all of her lives.

First lessons

Jansson was born in Helsinki into darkening times, less
than two weeks after the outbreak of the First World
War in 1914. She was the first of the three children of
Viktor Jansson (1886–1958), a sculptor of mainly public
monuments from a Finnish-Swedish family, and his Swedish
wife, Signe Hammarsten-Jansson (1882–1970), a graphic
designer and illustrator who had moved to Finland after
her marriage in 1913. For their fair-haired newborn, her
parents chose the name 'Tove', derived from the Old Norse
for 'beautiful'. The couple's homes doubled as their studios,
where they worked as dedicated, full-time artists. Little
Tove absorbed her bohemian parents' lesson that making art
was everyday and everything, and as natural and vital as
breathing. Or, as she once put it, 'To paint is to be'.

A family story goes that, almost before she learnt to walk,
Tove Jansson had learned to draw. It was an immediate
love. A photograph shows her mother working at her table,
her daughter seated on her lap and absorbed in witnessing
a drawing come to life before her eyes. When she was only
eighteen months old, her mother sketched her as she drew.
Jansson recalled, 'When I was little, I drew all the time....
You know, a kid is placed on the potty...and so that I would
sit quietly and peacefully, they'd set some sort of footstool

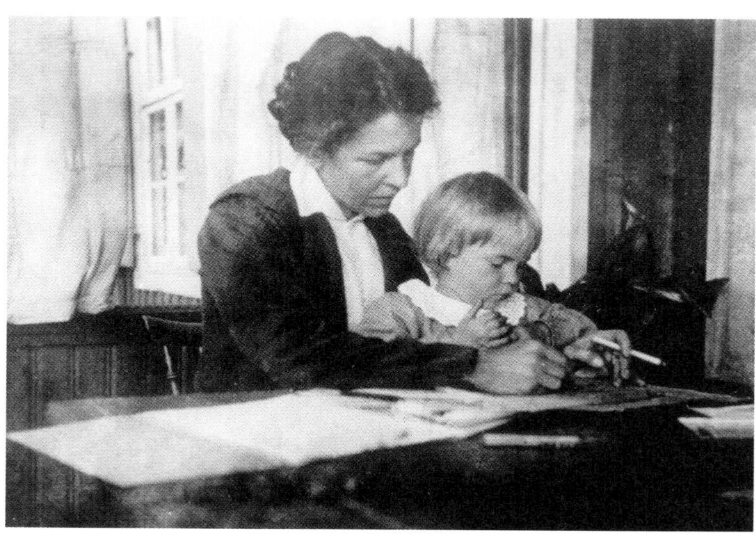

LEFT

A young Tove sitting in her
mother's arms and watching
her drawing, *c.* 1916–17.

in front of me and then I'd draw and draw and draw'. Such an upbringing would make her intent on following in her parents' footsteps, while forging an independent path.

At an early age, her delight in hearing her mother's spontaneous spoken yarns spurred her to learn to read for herself, and to begin making up stories. Jansson enjoyed traditional fairy tales, as well as horror stories (lapping up Edgar Allan Poe when she was nine) and adventures by Jules Verne, Arthur Conan Doyle, Carlo Collodi and Edgar Rice Burroughs. Two Swedish book illustrators also made a lasting impression. John Bauer's seminal Rackham-esque illustrations in the annual anthologies of Sweden's folktales, *Bland tomtar och troll* (*Among Gnomes and Trolls*), were a family favourite. From Bauer, Jansson learned that 'For the forest to appear tall, you have to leave out the treetops and the sky, only straight and thick trunks that rise straight up!' She also studied Bauer's trolls, lanky, long-haired giants with huge noses, a reference for her Moomintrolls' prominent snouts. And in Elsa Beskow, 'the Beatrix Potter of Sweden', Jansson admired how she 'allows the child a wide margin for its own reflections and fantasies' and 'recreated us so that we ultimately did not just see but learned to contemplate and to understand'[2] – effects that Jansson would come to have on her own readers.

At the age of seven, eager to get her own tales published, Jansson began writing and drawing short stories and poems for homemade booklets from the 'Tove Publishing Co.', which she sold to her classmates. Between 1921 and 1925, she printed fourteen of these herself at home on a hectograph or gelatin duplicator, in very limited runs. As the results in purple ink could be faint, she strengthened her illustrations by hand with black ink and extra colouring. Her emerging skills were already evident in such titles as *Julkorven* (*Christmas Sausage*, 1928), and several horror-themed tales such as *Döden* (*Death*, 1924) and *Kakta Knopp* (*Cactus Paper*), the latter reaching a print run of twenty-three copies by its third and final issue. Beginning in 1926, Jansson also kept vividly written diaries, referring to her parents affectionately by their nicknames 'Faffan' and 'Ham' and incorporating observant cartoons, which she captioned underneath. There was much to record, as Jansson had by

then been joined by two brothers, Per Olov and Lars, six
and twelve years her junior.

As their father's public sculpture commissions could
be irregular (politically right-wing, he received twenty-six
commissions over his forty-year career, but none from 1924
to 1927 or 1943 to 1947), it fell to their mother to support
the large family. Luckily, Ham's income from assorted
illustration assignments was bolstered in 1924, when she
was employed part-time by the Bank of Finland to design
their banknotes, and in 1929, when she began designing
stamps for the Finnish Post Office, producing over 200 until
1962. Both required her meticulous draughtsmanship for
the engraving process, working on a large scale in black ink
to build volume and shading out of parallel straight lines,
leaving the white of the paper to convey light. Her young
daughter and protégée learned from this process, developing
her distinct approach to drawing with patterns and textures
in lines of varying weights and densities, not precise and
ruled, but informal and naturalistic. Echoing veins on a leaf,
markings on bark or striations on rocks, Jansson's linear
style also drew strongly on close observation of nature, her
other great teacher.

Ham used a range of styles to suit her almost 300 book
covers and interiors, and the witty cartoons and caricatures
she made for satirical Swedish-language magazines. Her
daughter learned from these, too, as well as from her
favourite Swedish comics. These included Petter Lindroth's
Jocke, Nicke och Majken (1921–1933), weekly six-panel
comedies about two young boys' rivalry for a girl's attention,
which she later suggested partly influenced how she
prepared her first Moomin strips in 1946. She also relished
the absurd, often anarchic humour in Oskar Andersson's
'pantomime' or wordless strips, sketchy, spontaneous-looking
drawings about 'The Man Who Does Whatever Comes to
His Mind'. To Jansson, Andersson's dapper, non-conformist
Swede 'was a bit of a sadistic, strange fellow, who did
whatever popped into his mind. Maybe that helped him get
rid of too much niceness.' Jansson's work would also acquire
this edge.

Early publications

'I look forward to the day when I can help mother drawing', wrote Jansson in her diary in 1928. She had just started to get her work published and paid for, beginning aged only thirteen in the *Allas Krönika* weekly with three cartoons in an Andersson style. These accompanied verses signed 'Totto', enthusing about seeing the military leader and future president of Finland General Carl Gustaf Mannerheim's 16 May parade, marking the tenth anniversary of his victory in the Finnish Civil War. The following year, Jansson's

Mannerheim Parade, Jansson's first published writing and drawing, in *Allas Krönika*, 1928.

Hej, hurra för Mannerheim.

(En mycket ung dam, som kallar sig Totto har blivit begeistrad av Mannerheims person och insänt följande kväde till vilket hon själv tecknat bilderna.)

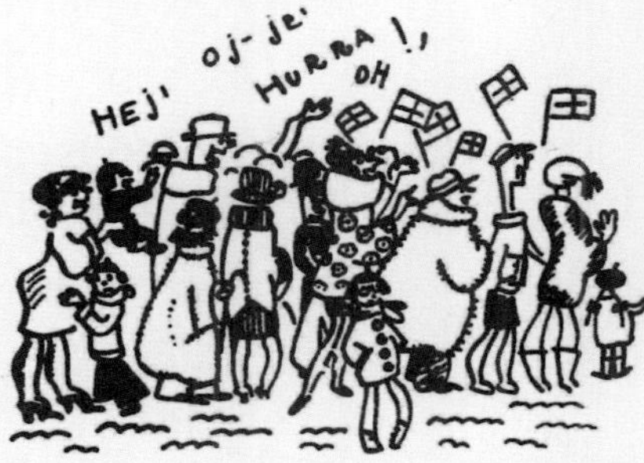

Nyligen kom Mannerheim till H:fors'
strand,
Sen han jagat tigar i Indialand.
Jag var så liten att jag såg honom ej alls.
Fast jag stod på tårna och sträckte på min
hals.

När hans bil genom staden skulle köra,
Man ej sin egen stämma ens kunde höra.
Av människomassan man blev nästan klämd
till mos.
Och om några sekunder var bilen sin kos.

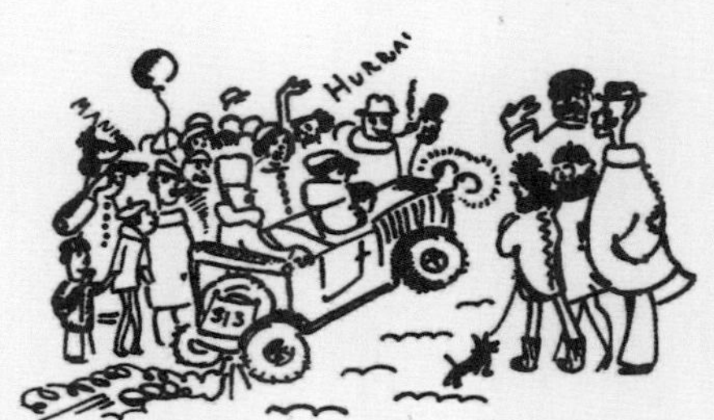

Den store generalen köpte så ett blomster
vitt,
som fästes i medaljers och stjärnors mitt.
Och från Helsingforsares täta mur,
beskådades andäktigt denna procedur.

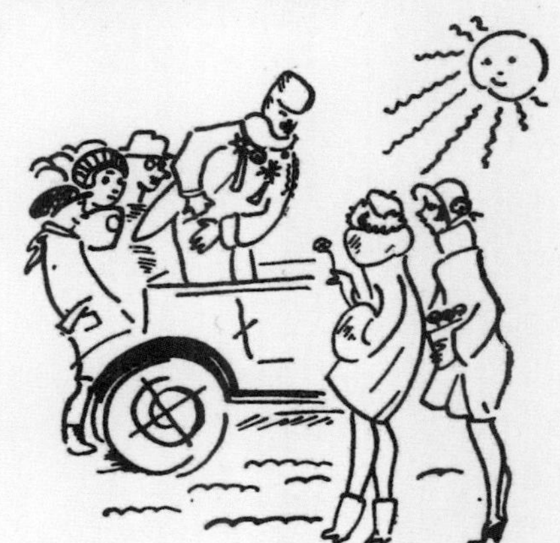

hopes became reality when she suddenly had to stand in for
Ham, who had to leave for Stockholm to tend to her dying
mother. Jansson took over her mother's commissions for
the tenth issue of the children's magazine *Lunkentus*, for
which she nervously prepared the front-cover illustration
and a comic strip for the back cover. Under her *nom-de-
plume* 'Tove', Jansson submitted a cover image of St George
and the Dragon, and the first episode of 'Prickinas och
Fabians äventyr' (The Adventures of Prickina and Fabian), a
charming, simply drawn love story between two caterpillars.
In her diary, she worried, 'so much depends on it, whether
I'll get another commission, if this goes well'. *Lunkentus*
accepted both pieces for the issue dated 30 August 1929,
and agreed to continue her comic for another six episodes,
ending happily if unnaturally with the caterpillar couple
reproducing. Inspired by Lindroth, she told each part in
six equally sized panels, a few with hand-lettered speech

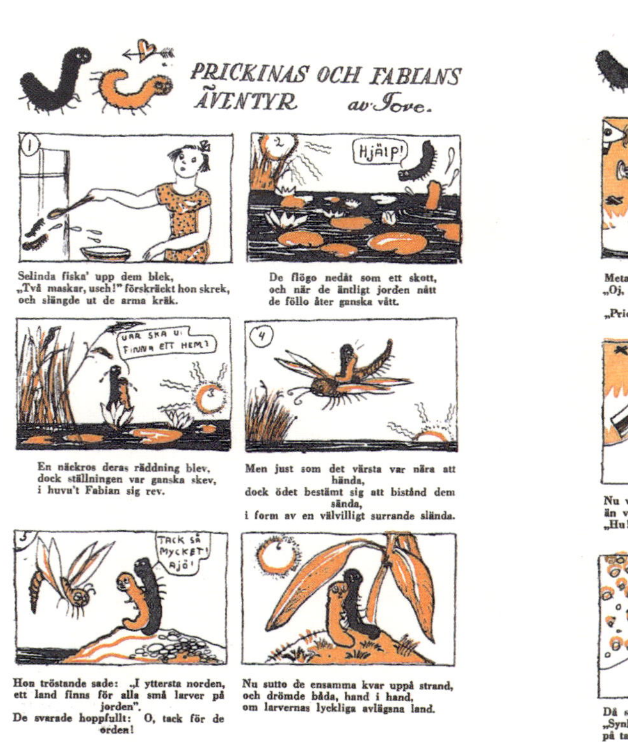

Selinda fiska' upp dem blek,
„Två maskar, usch!" förskräckt hon skrek,
och slängde ut de arma kräk.

De flögo nedåt som ett skott,
och när de äntligt jorden nått
de föllo åter ganska vått.

En näckros deras räddning blev,
dock ställningen var ganska skev,
i huvu't Fabian sig rev.

Men just som det värsta var nära att
hända,
dock ödet bestämt sig att bistånd dem
sända,
i form av en välvilligt surrande slända.

Hon tröstande sade: „I yttersta norden,
ett land finns för alla små larver på
jorden".
De svarade hoppfullt: O, tack för de
orden!

Nu sutto de ensamma kvar uppå strand,
och drömde båda, hand i hand,
om larvernas lyckliga avlägsna land.

Frenckellska Tr. A.-B. H:fors, Anneg. 32.

Skall det lyckas dem att
hitta larvlandet?

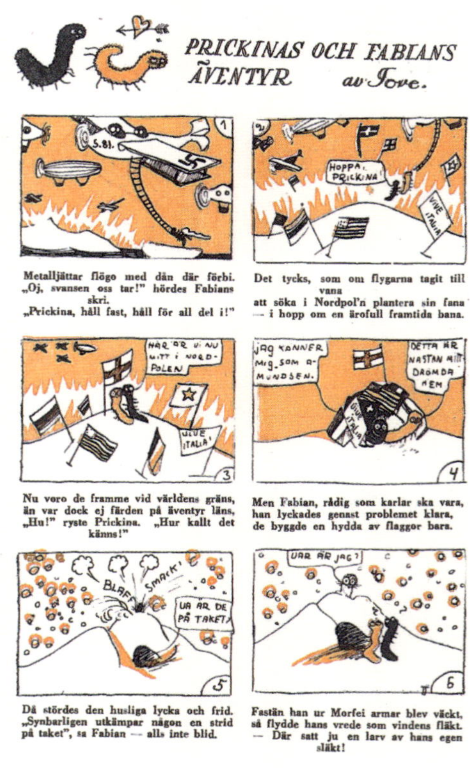

Metalljättar flögo med dån där förbi.
„Oj, svansen oss tar!" hördes Fabians
skri.
„Prickina, håll fast, håll för all del i!"

Det tycks, som om flygarna tagit till
vana
att söka i Nordpol'n plantera sin fana
— i hopp om en ärofull framtida bana.

Nu voro de framme vid världens gräns,
än var dock ej färden på äventyr läns,
„Hu!" ryste Prickina. „Hur kallt det
känns!"

Men Fabian, rådig som karlar ska vara,
han lyckades genast problemet klara,
de byggde en hydda av flaggor bara.

Då stördes den husliga lycka och frid.
„Synbarligen utkämpar någon en strid
på taket", sa Fabian — alls inte blid.

Fastän han ur Morfei armar blev väckt,
så flydde hans vrede som vindens fläkt.
— Där satt ju en larv av hans egen
släkt!

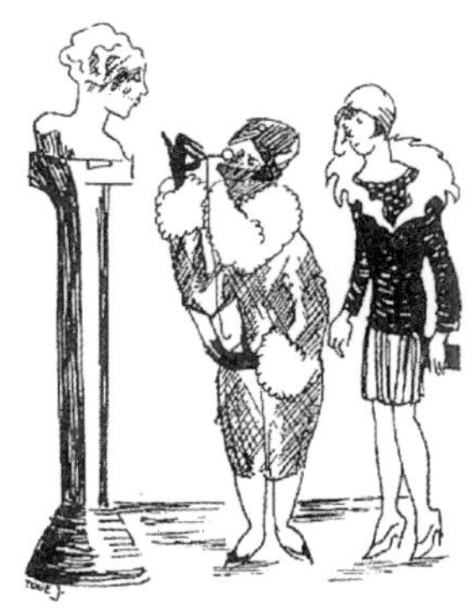

balloons, but with the main text typeset below in her rhyming three-line poems. Though short-lived, this job brought in a welcome 100 marks per page.

Eager to get a book published to boost the family coffers, the proactive thirteen-year-old also submitted her illustrated poems to a publisher, but without success. Then, in May 1928, inspired by Ham's drawings for her 1923 adaptation of a Russian fairy tale, Jansson tried again, proposing a twenty-page illustrated children's story of her own to the publisher Tilmanns, who accepted it. Told in rhymes opposite eight tableaux in simple, appealing lines and bright colours, *Sara och Pelle och Necken's Bläckfiskar* (*Sara, Pelle and the Water-Sprite's Octopuses*) is set in the Finnish archipelago, where a contemporary girl and boy and their dog are captured by a mermaid-like Nordic nymph and forced to tend to her young octopuses on the seabed. The happy ending sees the trio rescued by a passing fisherman in his boat, and the young octopus they bring back with them being cooked by their mother for dinner. Jansson had started fantasizing about octopuses after reading Jules Verne, and the tentacular creatures would recur in her subsequent children's books. But Tilmanns took five years to release her book, by which time she had become intent on making her name as a painter. She chose to replace her credit as author/illustrator with that of a student friend.

Meanwhile, after *Lunkentus*, Ham opened more doors for her teenage daughter, notably introducing her to Finland's Swedish-language satirical magazine *Garm*, to which Ham had been contributing cartoons since it began in 1923. Jansson adopted some of her mother's techniques, and in her first cartoon on 21 November 1929 captured the transformation in women's fashions, contrasting a plump mother's overdressed respectability with her waif-like daughter's liberated modernity. Jansson had seventeen more cartoons printed in *Garm* over the following four years, drawing clearly and economically to convey the jokes, several supplied by the magazine; after 1933 she became a *Garm* regular, devising cartoons of her own, learning and maturing on the job.

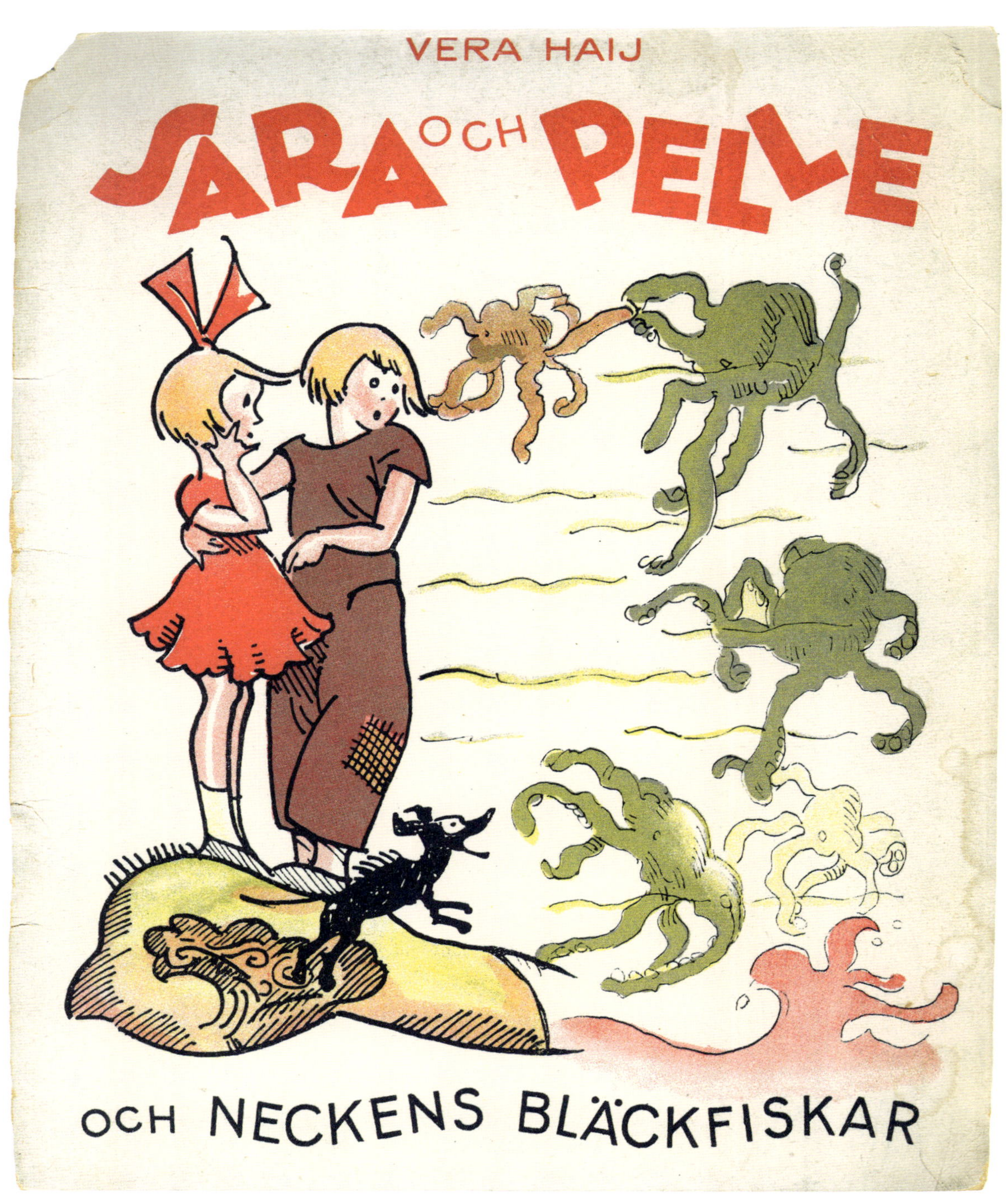
VERA HAIJ
SARA OCH PELLE
OCH NECKENS BLÄCKFISKAR

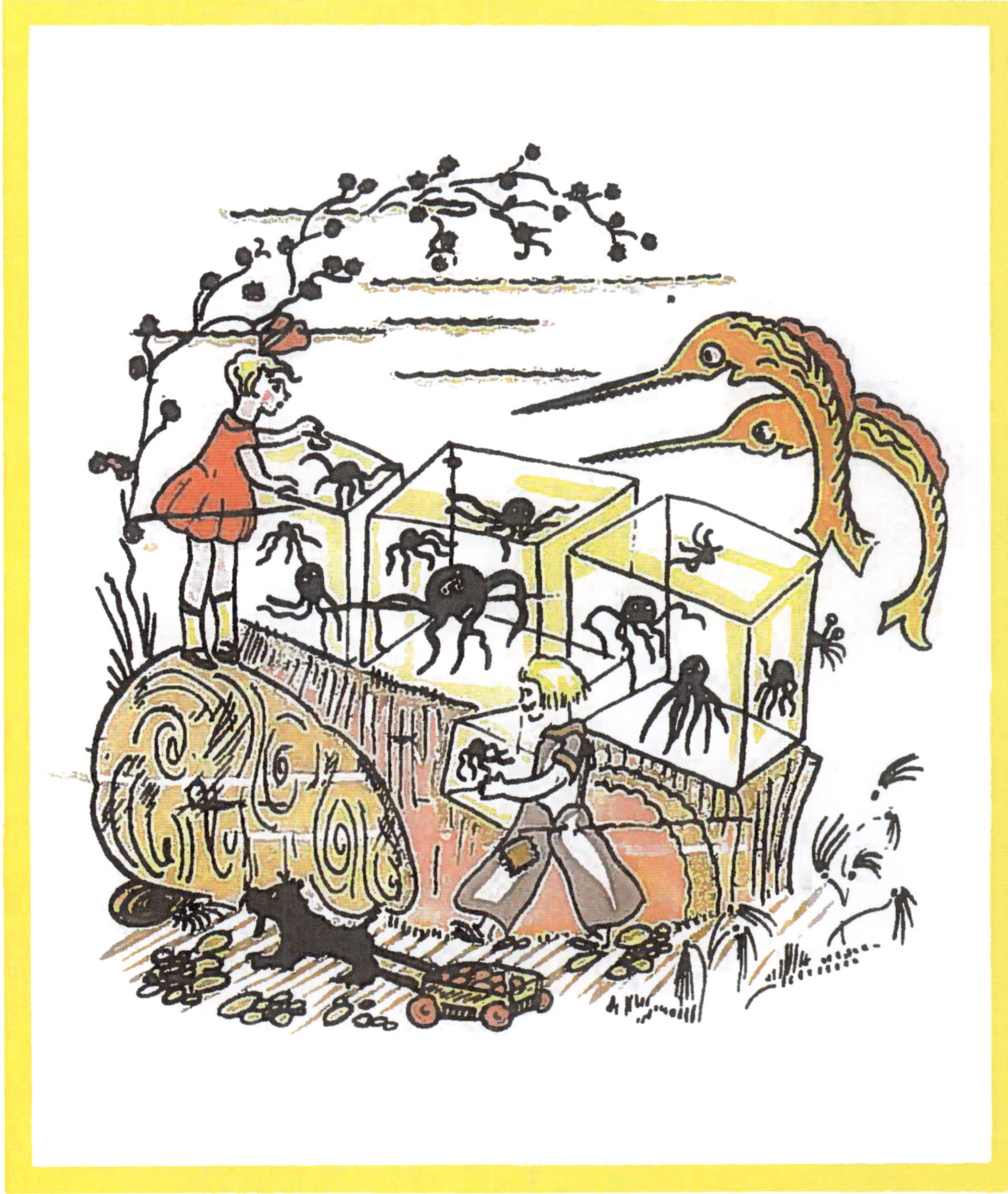

Student dreams

In 1930, Tove Jansson was allowed by her mother to leave
school early. She was to take an affordable three-year
course in arts and crafts, with a vocational focus on book
illustration and advertising design, at Sweden's largest art
college, Tekniska skolan (Technical School) in Stockholm,
where Ham had also studied.

'And now,' enthused the teenager in her diary, 'I shall
begin to live'. Despite her enthusiasm, living away from
home for the first time at sixteen, even if she was lodging
with her uncle Einar, was challenging. She wrote to
her family often, and sent them a hand-drawn booklet,
Hemkomsten (*Homecoming*), about her experiences. One
cartoon pokes fun at her first day in technical drawing
class, where the all-female students had to draw clover
leaves, some using protractors and rulers; one student,
probably Jansson, does not look very engaged. Nonetheless,
she persisted, broadening her knowledge and abilities,
and realized, as she wrote in her diary for 1931, 'I have to
become an artist for the family's sake', probably meaning
a commercial artist like her mother. While studying, she
also took on work, including her first book cover for an
edition of Collodi's *Adventures of Pinocchio* in 1932, and
won a Swedish grant, 'a goodly little sum' of 300 krona,
which she used partly for extra life-drawing classes. Her
strongest subject was decorative painting, a skill that
she later applied to several mural commissions. Always
conscientious and practical, near the end of her course
she wrote home in March 1933 that 'nothing could
be more hateful to me than causing you unnecessary
financial worries'.

Nevertheless, Stockholm had stoked her other goal
and passion to an even greater extent. Tove Jansson
wanted to become a painter. Returning to Helsinki, she
studied painting from 1933 to 1936 at the School of
Fine Arts, where her father had studied sculpture. The
conservatism of certain teachers led to her and other
students protesting, and at times quitting, only to return
and, in her case, finally graduate. Other tutors were more
progressive and inspiring to Jansson, and she took extra

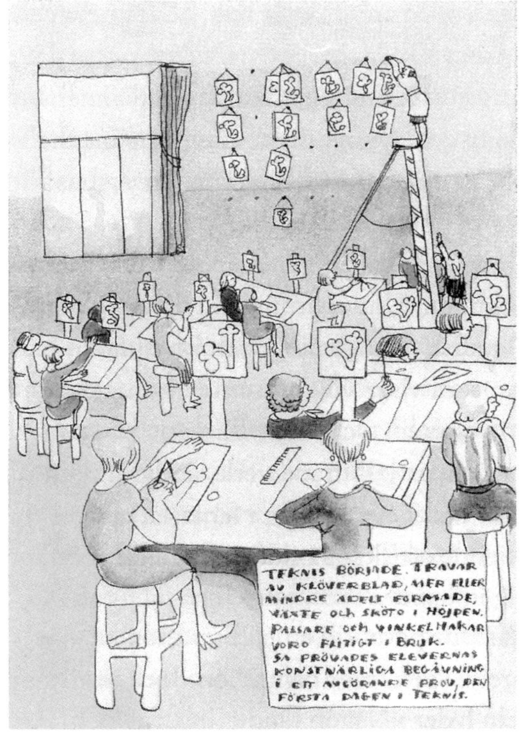

Tove Jansson's cartoon about her first drawing class at college in Stockholm, from *Hemkomsten* (*Homecoming*), a booklet sent home to her family, 1930.

private tuition from Sam Vanni, who became her mentor and lover, and later a champion of abstraction. As the Second World War loomed, her prospects remained hopeful, with exhibitions, awards, study grants and travels to Paris and Italy, studio space and sales of some of her canvases. But Jansson knew from her father's struggles that making a living from her art alone would be difficult. No matter how accomplished her portraits and landscapes might be, she needed critics and gallerists to approve and champion them. The problem was that her painting could not help but interact with her drawing and other visual expressions. In a painful review of *The Family* (1942), a group portrait of the Janssons, Vanni criticized it for being 'graphic'. A year before, a critic had called her paintings 'illustrative', not meant as a compliment, and in 1943 complained about the works in her solo show having too many messages, subjects and narratives. If acceptance meant conforming to such art-world diktats, Jansson resolved 'that a painting should be purely painterly, and that the narrative qualities of graphic art should not be imported at all into the world of painting'.[3] But it would not always be easy for someone so multi-talented to compartmentalize her creativity.

If her graphic acumen risked influencing her painting, such cross-pollination would also work in reverse and bring a painterliness to her illustrations. While at college in Helsinki, Jansson was cartooning for *Garm*, sometimes channelling her mixed feelings about her studies and prospects. In one faux-naively drawn cartoon in September 1935, she lampoons the Nordic 'patriotic' painters lauded by her tutors, showing an artist in search of a landscape, who ignores a verdant vista with deer and a mother and child in favour of a bleak scene, empty of all but a decrepit hut and three fir trees. Jansson addressed her career anxieties in March 1936, mere months before her finals. A ragged, barefoot child, not unlike her young self, asks a painter-father 'What is art?', to which he replies, 'That's a foolish question. Art is everything you can't do. If you can do it, then it is no longer art.' His studio is bare, its windows cracked, unpaid bills on his easel, a female nude underway on his canvas as his model struggles to keep warm by a basic stove. Imagining the other extreme, her detailed full-page cartoon for *Hepokatti* magazine in 1943 shows a large studio abuzz with buyers, the successful artist (a man, again) painting two canvases at once while his wife, who resembles Jansson, welcomes more customers, cradling her fourth child. Money a constant anxiety, Jansson would never make painting the full-time vocation she thought she wanted – especially once her Moomins caught on.

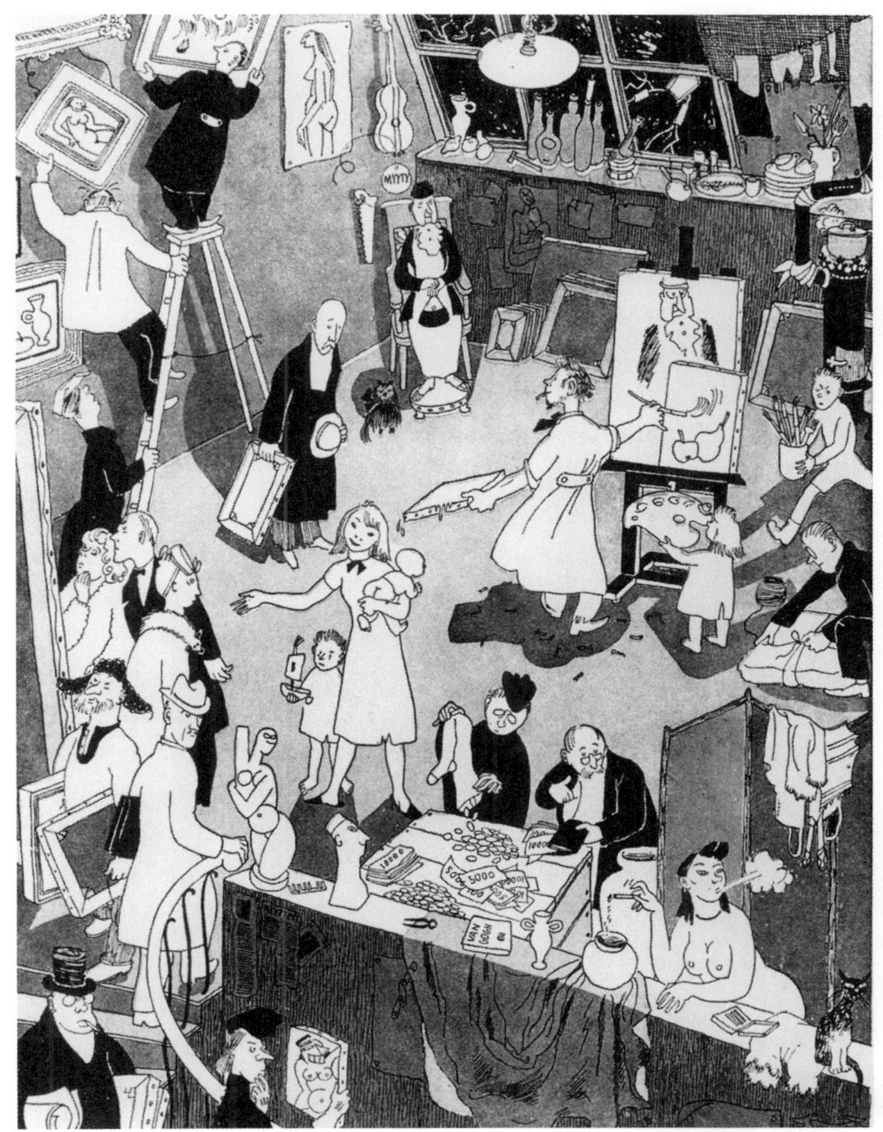

ABOVE

Full-page cartoon from *Hepokatti*,
the annual magazine of the Finnish
Illustrators' Union, 1943.

A working illustrator

Fortunately, Jansson was trained and creatively versatile
enough not to have to survive solely on income from her
paintings. It helped that she was still living at home,
and could contribute towards the costs and rent a studio
with her freelance earnings. In 1935, she drew the first
of around 100 eye-catching front covers for *Garm*, their
crisp pen-and-ink lines often enhanced with one second
colour. She also contributed some 500 cartoons and
numerous illustrations, and the magazine remained a
major client until its closure in 1953 after its founder's
death. This steady platform from which to critique her
times sharpened her skills at caricature and commentary,
and encouraged her awakening left-wing conscience
and opposition to war, fascism and communism. As she
recalled, 'Most of all I liked the fact that I got to be
beastly to Hitler and Stalin', sometimes courting
controversy and censorship on the front cover. She
was a rarity at this time for being such an outspoken
female political cartoonist, and in 1941 was voted the
most humorous in the Nordic region.

Jansson described herself as 'an Indian ink machine', so
prolific was she in a dizzying range of styles, subjects and
media. She worked for many publications, such as *Julen*
(1928–44), for which she provided wartime covers, and
Lucifer (1933–53), and starting in 1934, also wrote and
illustrated around a dozen short stories and reportages
from her travels for magazines. Her first illustrations for
books for adults were published in two titles about sailing,
also a passion of hers. In 1936, she drew the cover to Atle
Welander's *Breaker*, short stories inspired by the author's
sea voyages from the age of fourteen. Then, in 1937, her
uncle, Harald Hammarsten, a keen sailor, commissioned five
interior illustrations for his short story in a book on sailing,
for which Jansson experimented with dynamic washes on her
seascapes of a storm-tossed boat and a young sailor's survival.
Her next, *Jag* (*I*, 1937), was a book by Ella Pilling for parents
to record a baby's growth, for which Jansson and her mother
designed small, simplified vignettes in a palette of red, yellow

A daring front cover for *Garm*
magazine, caricaturing Hitler as
a spoiled child being given many
gifts, including the whole world
as a plum pudding, autumn 1938.

Front cover of the first issue of *Vår
Tid* magazine, including an early
Moomin, 1945.

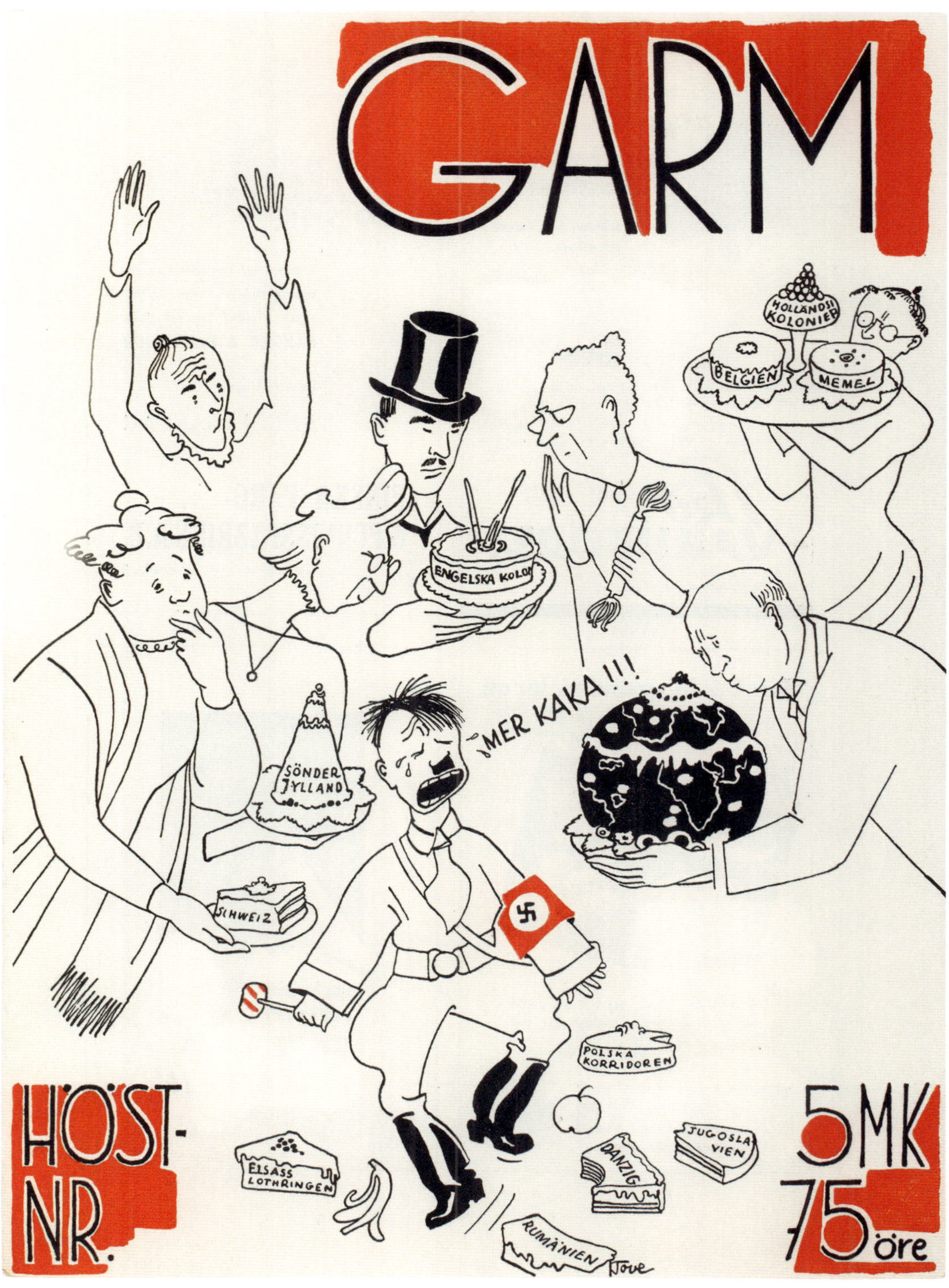
GARM
HOLLÄNDSK
KOLONIER
BELGIEN
MEMEL
ENGELSKA KOLON
SÖNDER
JYLLAND
MER KAKA !!!
SCHWEIZ
POLSKA
KORRIDOREN
HÖST-
NR.
ELSASS
LOTHRINGEN
DANZIG
JUGOSLA
VIEN
RUMÄNIEN
Tove
5 MK
75 öre

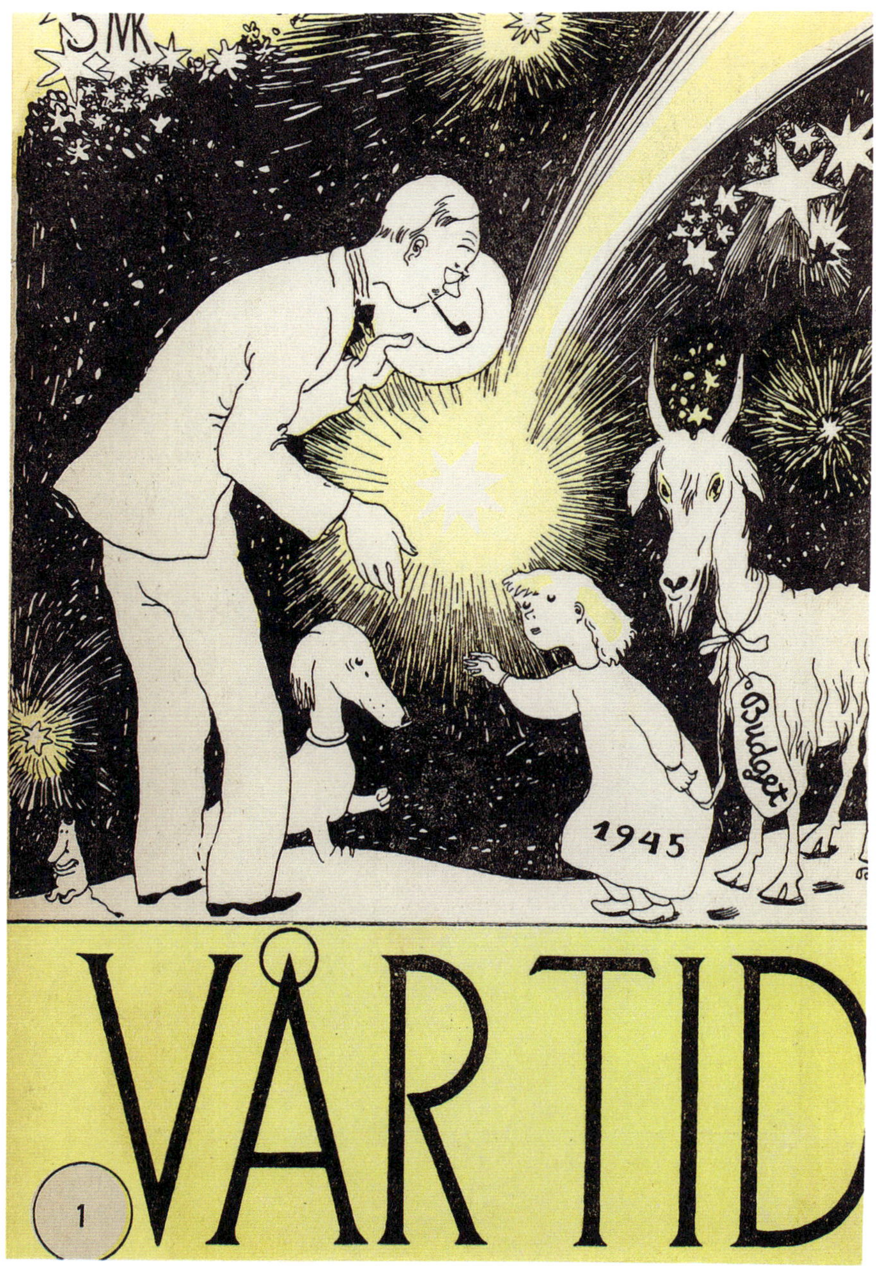

Two earlier cartoons from *Garm*, redrawn and coloured to represent Finland in a survey of the best Scandinavian cartooning in *Folket i Bild*'s Christmas issue, 1941

The captions read:
(Top) — 'Don't you have a doll that says "Momma"?'
— 'No, little friend, our new stock says "Heil Hitler"!'

(Bottom) Apropos Christmas
— 'It was wrapped in white paper with red string…I forgot to put the address on it…'

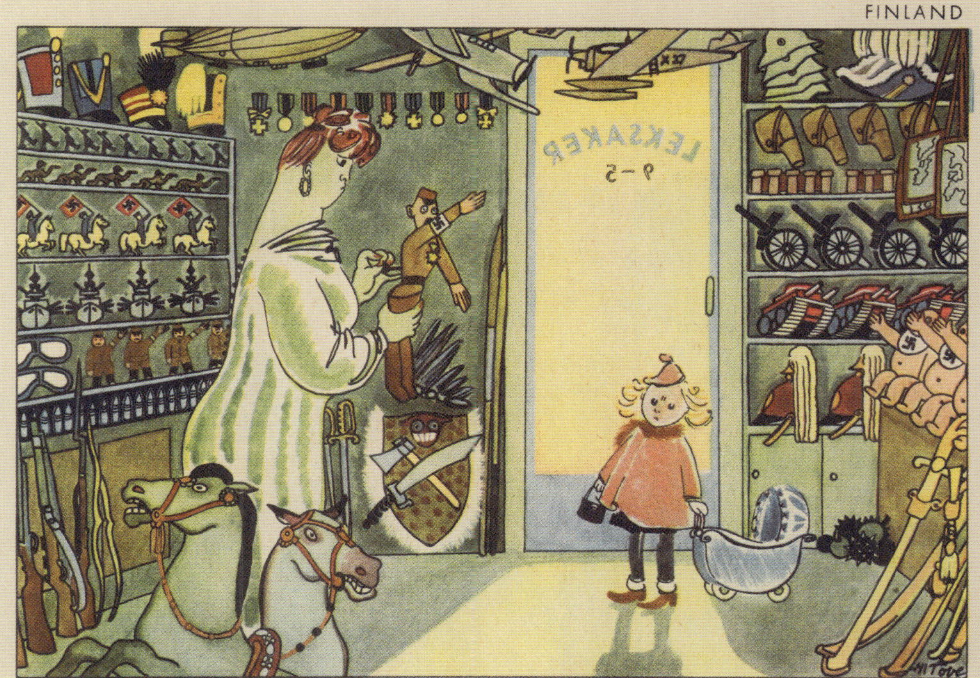

— Har ni inte nån docka som säjer "mamma"?
— Nej, lilla vän, vårt nya lager säger Heil Hitler!

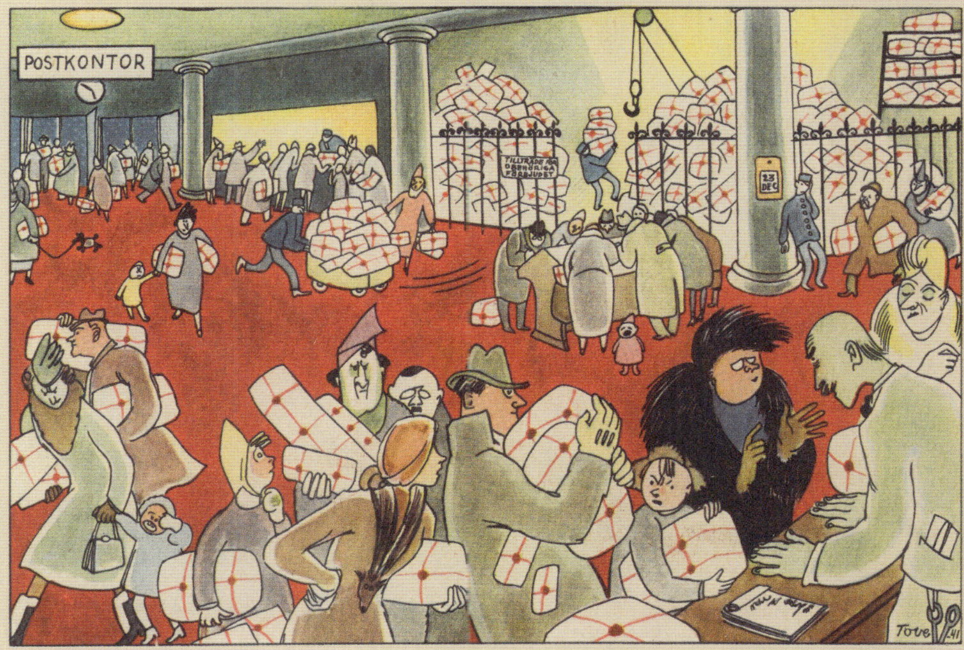

APROPÅ JULEN   — Det vor insvept i vitt papper med rött snöre...
jag glömde sätta adress på det...

Originalteckningar för Folket i Bild
av TOVE JANSSON

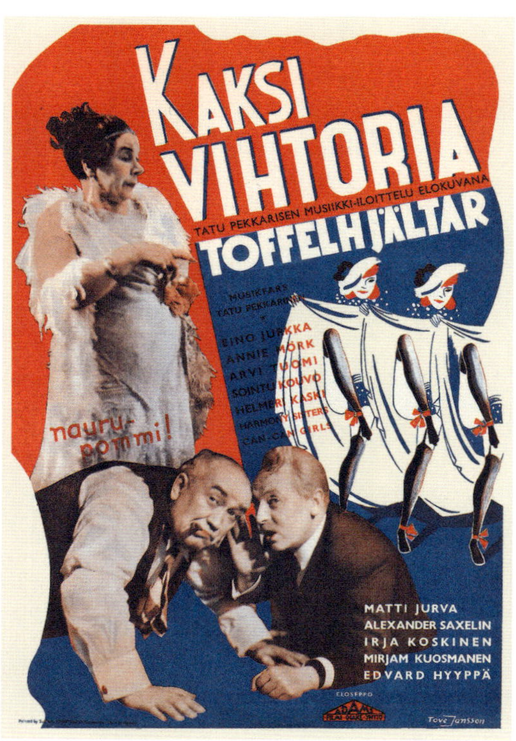

and blue. In 1938, she supplied an elegant cover and eight
illustrations, one featuring a glamorous pin-up, for designer
Kaarlo Karhi's booklet *How do I decorate my home?*, and the
following year, she designed a movie poster incorporating
a trio of Can-Can girls for her friend Veikko Nyyrikki
Tapiovaara's film adaptation of a play by Tatu Pekkarinen,
derived from *Bringing Up Father,* the imported Art Deco-style
newspaper strip by American George McManus.

Throughout wartime the demand for fiction continued
to bring Jansson commissions. For children, she illustrated
Brita Hiort's fable about a smug rabbit's comeuppance,
Lill-Olle och Harpalten (1943), in a picture book of six
pages, each with three unframed images of the amusing
animal cast in pen and ink, spot-coloured in red and
yellow. Solveig von Schoultz reimagined her letters to her
young daughters while they were evacuees in Sweden into
Nalleresan (*Teddies' Journey*, 1944), a *Toy Story*-style tale
about two teddy bears, whose 'mothers', two girls, are sent
away from Finland to Sweden. In sensitive line drawings,

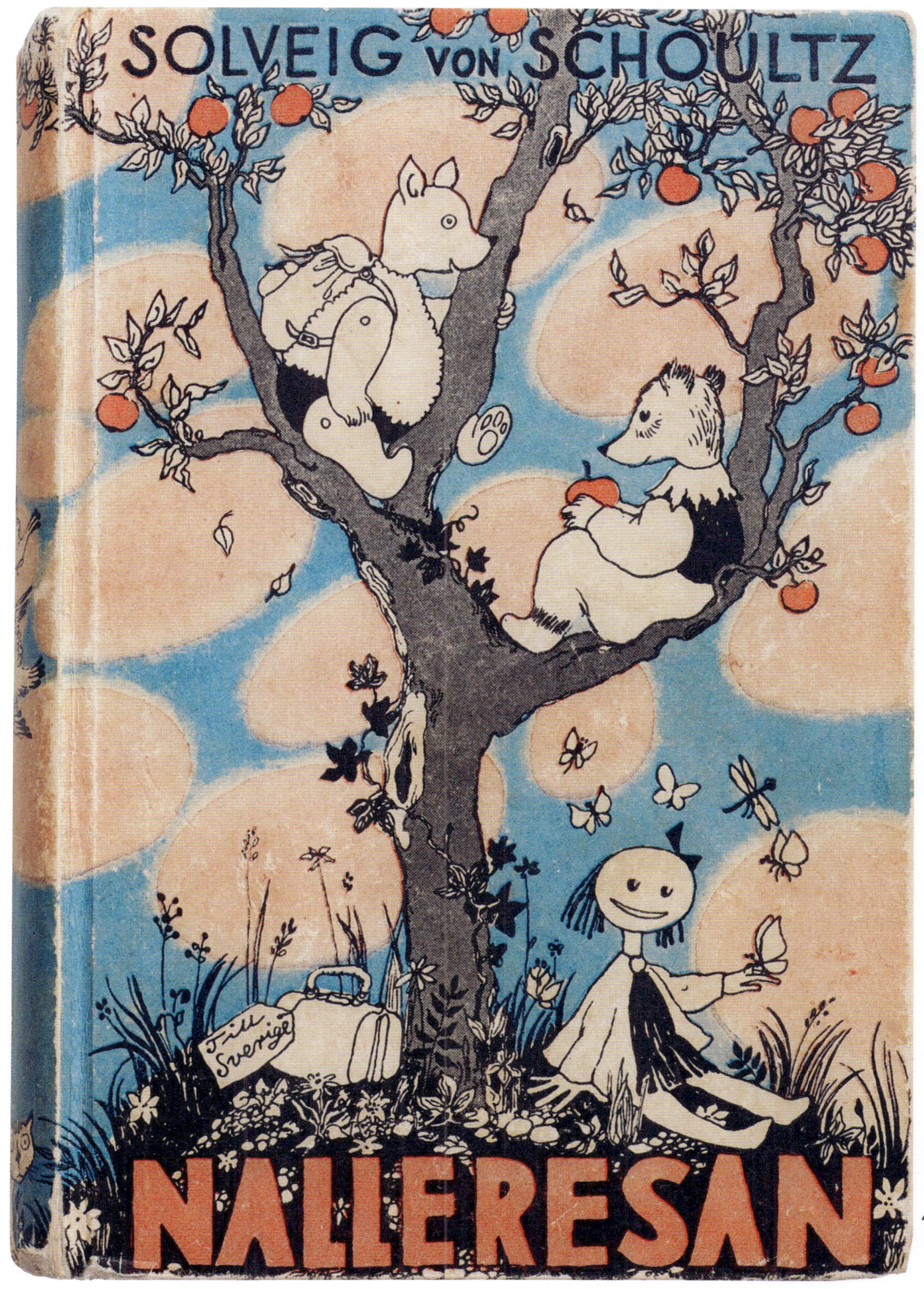

SOLVEIG VON SCHOULTZ
Till Sverige
NALLERESAN

Jansson empathetically conveyed their sadness, fears and
eventual joyful reunion. She also regularly drew covers
for adult titles for the publisher Söderströms, the most
unusual of which was a novel from 1936 by the progressive
Hungarian Jewish author Illés Kaczér. Originally entitled
Pao, it sympathetically related the inequalities experienced
by a young Nigerian, Nangangesi, as he tries to make a
new life in Paris. Despite the Nazis' banning its German
edition in 1938, Söderströms dared to release it in Finland
in 1941 with a cover by Jansson, under what she called 'a
particularly "thrilling" title: *Svart Erotik* (*Black Eroticism*)'.
After working on this title she may have reflected differently
on her experience of Paris nightlife in 1938, when she
spent Valentine's Day evening at the Boule Blanche club
in Montparnasse to 'take a look at Fernanda, rose of
Martinique', a celebrated Black dancer.

ABOVE
Interior illustration for *Nalleresan*
(*Teddies' Journey*), 1944.

OPPOSITE
Artwork for the front-cover
illustration of the novel *Svart
Erotik* (*Black Eroticism*), 1941.

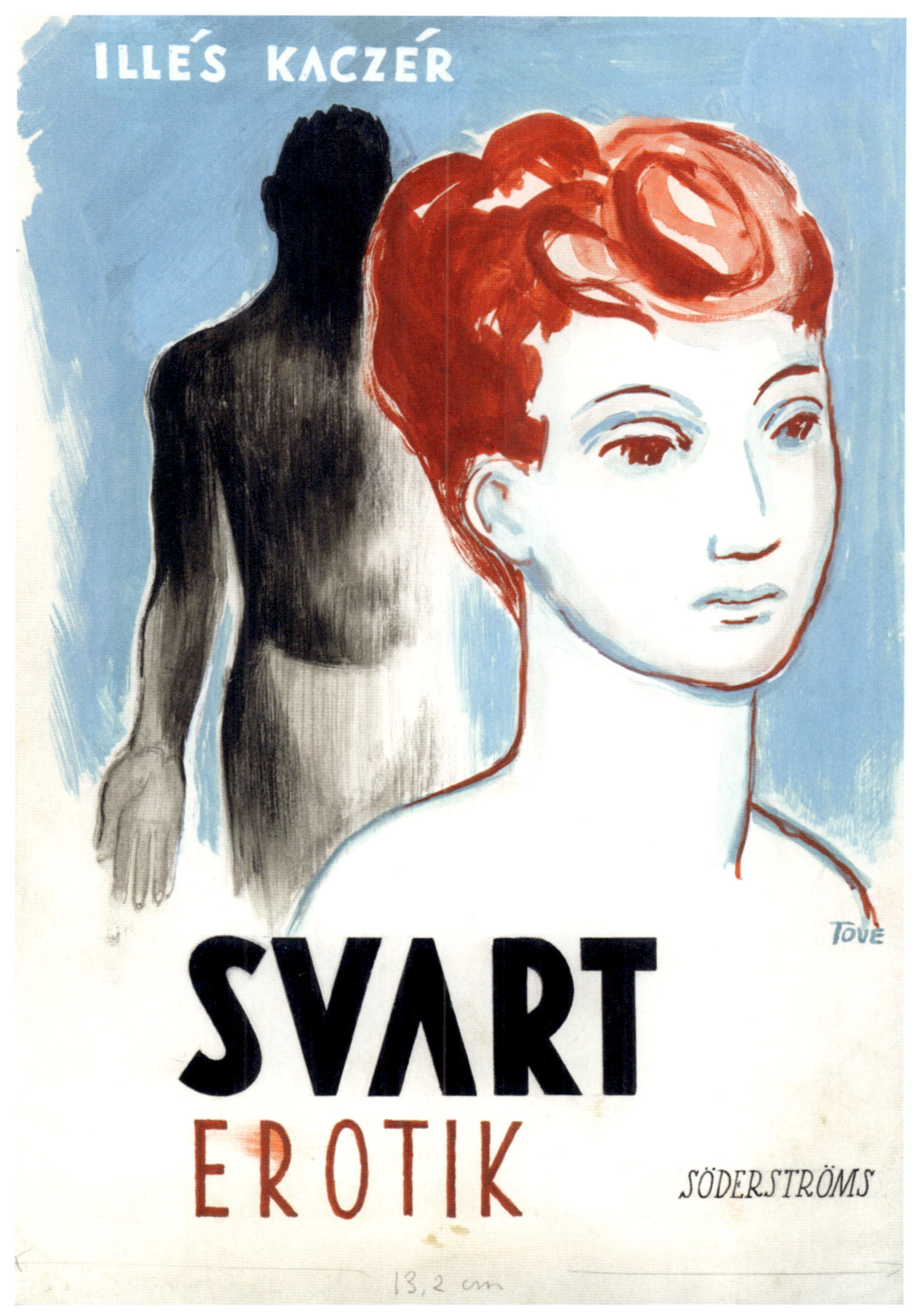
ILLÉS KACZÉR
SVART
EROTIK
SÖDERSTRÖMS
TOVE
13,2 cm

The Moomins emerge

One summer holiday in the 1930s, a young Jansson
produced a deliberately quick, minimal pencil graffito of
a long-nosed, armless, earless, grumpy troll. She captioned
it 'SNORK' in capital letters, like the sound of an irritated
sniff, and added the phrase 'Freedom is the best thing'.
These were her final remarks in a philosophical squabble
with her brother Per Olov over Immanuel Kant, which
they escalated onto the outhouse wall of her parents'
rented island cottage. Thus, the Moomins began to evolve.
Amazingly, the siblings' scrawls have survived.

Jansson recalled that she first got the idea for Moomin's
more spherical snout from spotting a tree stump 'covered
in snow which was hanging down like a big round white
nose', nature providing another of her many sources. As
for the name, she traced this back to her time as an art
student, lodging with Uncle Einar: 'When I was very young
and always hungry and stayed with him in Stockholm, I
used to help myself to snacks from the larder at night. He
did his best to convince me there were "moomintrolls" who
would come out and blow down the back of my neck – they
lived behind the stove in the kitchen.' What began as the
bogeyman in her uncle's scare story, Jansson developed
into representations of her anxieties amid the worsening
pre-war situation. Early examples of trolls lurk as ghostly
presences in her diary sketches; others, black, pointy-eared
and almost demonic, haunt a series of watercolour paintings.
Two little white trolls first caught the public eye in her

The surviving graffiti from the
Janssons' holiday outhouse wall,
where in the 1930s Tove drew a
Moomin prototype named 'Snork'.

Observed from life, this oil painting
shows Helsinki residents crowding
into a basement to shelter from a
Soviet bombing raid, 1940.

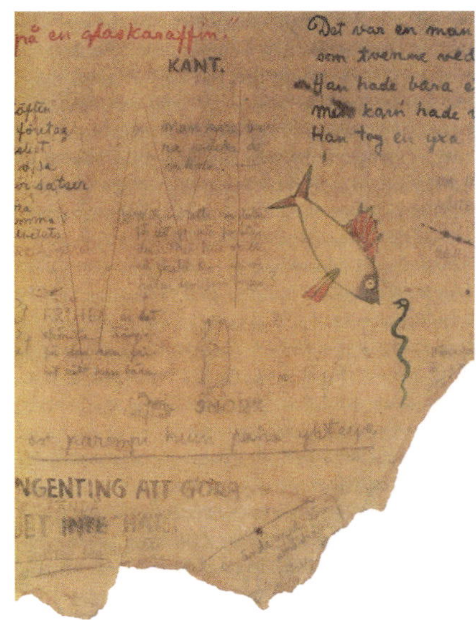

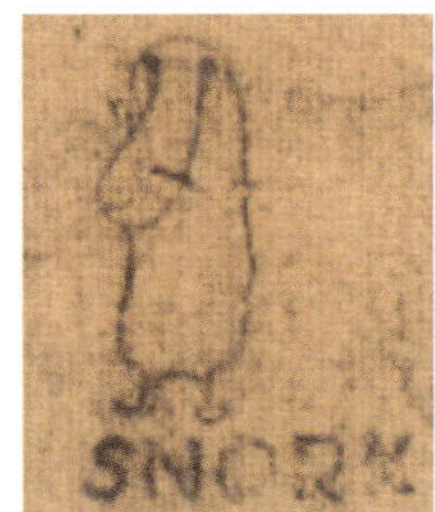

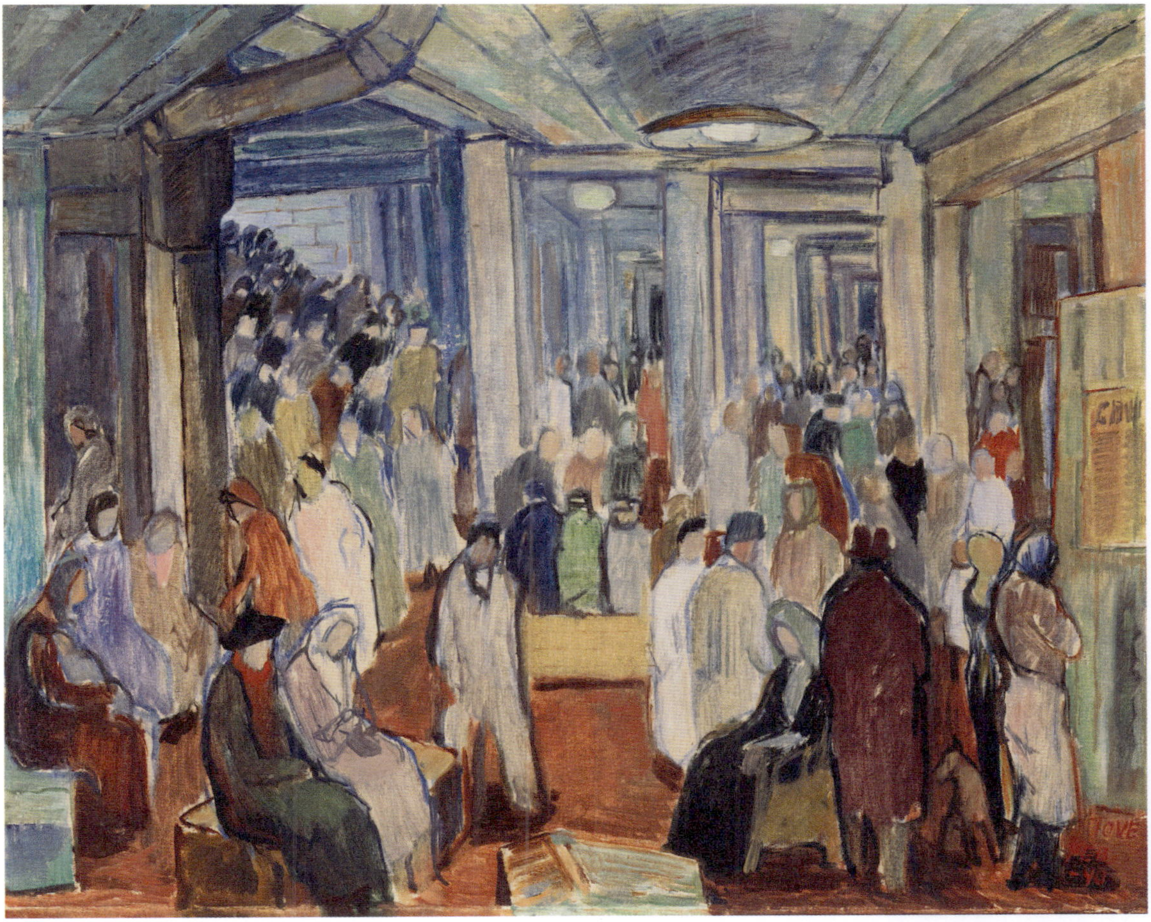

covers and single-panel cartoons for *Garm* from 1943. One of
them, called 'Snork', became her 'angry signature character',
appearing sometimes next to her name or the magazine's
logo, other times within the joke itself, often echoing
or commenting on the main image from the sidelines.
Gradually, this Snork morphed into a more benevolent
and appealing prototype.

In the winter of 1939, with her elder brother away in
the army, the Second World War brought Jansson to a low
point about her painting: 'it felt completely pointless to try
to create pictures'. Jansson, twenty-five at the time, could
only respond to the Soviet Union's first bombings of the
Finns, officially pro-German at that point, with a doom-
laden, monochromatic watercolour street scene of fleeing
civilians, all colour removed with the exception of one tiny
red light signalling the air-raid shelter. To counteract this
artistic block, she turned to hand-writing an unconventional
fairy tale about her Snork creature, and finally gave it a
name: Moomintroll. She wrote only half of the story before
having to put it aside in a drawer to make a living and
help her family and friends survive. In the spring of 1944,
however, with Per Olov home on leave, her enthusiasm
returned and she resumed her manuscript. Also that year,
after renting several short-term studios while still living at
home, Jansson left her family to live and work in the quirky,
high-ceilinged, top-floor apartment that would be her studio-
home for many decades. It was here that she reached her
manuscript's happy ending, and, on a friend's suggestion
that it could sell as a children's book, added illustrations.
Thrillingly, her client Söderströms agreed to publish it, her
first book wholly written and drawn by her and published
under her real name.

Like Jansson, it was time for the Moomins to emerge
from the shadows and sidelines and take centre stage,
under the spotlight. For the book's title, Jansson suggested
Moomintroll and the Great Flood, but Söderström worried
that nobody knew the Moomins; they preferred simply
Småtrollen och den stora översvämningen (*The Little Trolls
and the Great Flood*). When the war's grim final year
delayed publication, Jansson smuggled Moomintroll into
her illustrations for von Schoultz's *Teddies' Journey* and onto

A Moomin makes a cameo
appearance on Jansson's cover
for *The Borg Brothers' Exploits*
by Carolus Sjöstedt, written under
the pen-name 'Don Carlos', 1946.

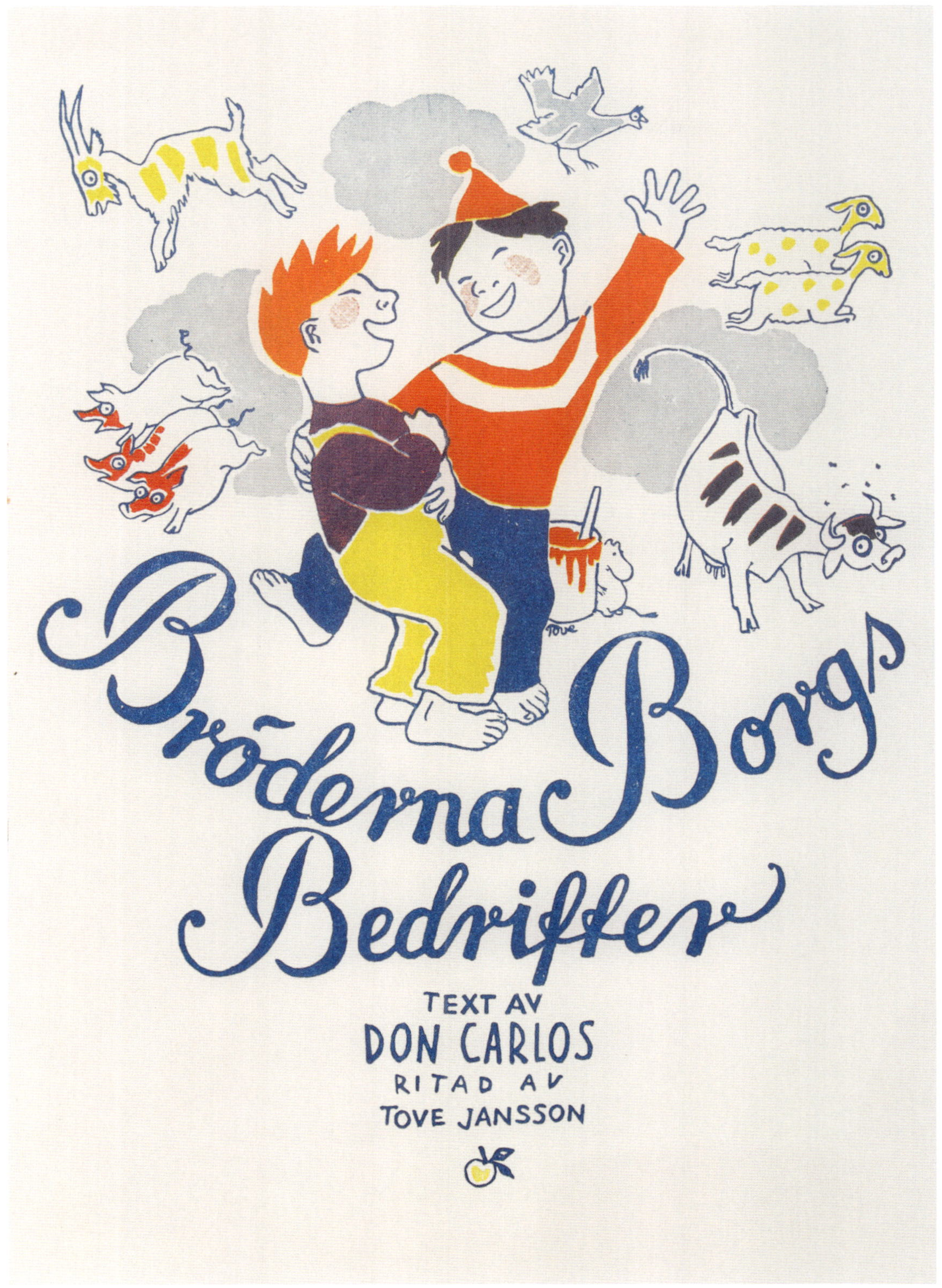
Bröderna Borgs
Bedrifter
TEXT AV
DON CARLOS
RITAD AV
TOVE JANSSON

the cover and opening page of Martin Söderhjelm's *Maya the Fly,* and continued this 'product placement' throughout *The Borg Brothers' Exploits* by Carolus Sjöstedt (1946) and Lilli Forss-Nordström's *Spring Awakens* (1951).

The Moomins' eventual publishing debut in late 1945 introduced much of their 'unbelievable world where everything was natural and benign – and possible' and its initial locations and cast, dropping the names of others to come. Reflecting the tumultuous separation of loved ones endured by Jansson and many families during and after the war, when large areas of Finland were ceded to the Soviet Union, making refugees of some 300,000 Finns, the story follows Moomintroll and his mother on their search for the missing Moominpappa. The resourceful, devoted Moominmamma was a tribute to Jansson's mother, and one of several characters she based on her family, friends, lovers and herself.

In composing *The Great Flood*'s pages and spreads, she applied her reading, training and experience illustrating *Teddies' Journey* to interweave carefully sized pictures, sometimes tall and narrow or L-shaped, around or within typeset text. Her tale grew into a forty-eight-page novella, for which she created thirty-two line drawings in ink, almost all of which float, borderless, on the page. She also painted fourteen more images in atmospheric, if somewhat dark sepia watercolour, five as full-page scenes. For the cover, in eye-catching green and pink, she composed a dense, mysterious forest right out of John Bauer's troll illustrations, adding glowing blossoms that dwarfed her diminutive protagonists. Her early Moomins were outlined with a hand-drawn fragility, less smooth and curvaceous than their later forms, and with their mouths visible. The tale reflected the period's food shortages by imagining a fantasia of confectionary, including 'Fazer' chocolate bars; once the Moomins became popular, they would advertise this brand. But when *The Great Flood* reached the shops, it garnered a single mixed review, and of the 2,800 copies printed, only 219 sold in 1946, sinking to 183 in 1947. Undeterred, even before its release Jansson was already charging ahead on its successor.

Front cover of the first Moomin novel, *Småtrollen och den stora översvämningen* (*The Little Trolls and the Great Flood*), 1945.

Party in the City, the second of two frescos for Helsinki City Hall, 5 x 3.1 m (16⅓ x 10¼ ft), 1947. In 1945, Jansson received her first major commission in large-scale public art, producing two murals for the staff canteen of the Oy Strömberg Ab electromechanical factory. So, when in 1947 she was asked by Helsinki City Hall to provide two modest paintings for the redecoration of their restaurant, she proposed instead to fill the walls with a pair of idyllic frescos. These demanded that she master new techniques, notably painting in dry-powder pigments directly onto freshly laid plaster. After some technical assistance on the first fresco, she worked solo on the second, *Party in the City*. Here she foregrounds herself, nonchalant and smoking, a Moomintroll by her glass, while behind her, in a dress reflecting Christian Dior's 'New Look' of 1947, dances her dark-haired lover, Vivica Bandler.

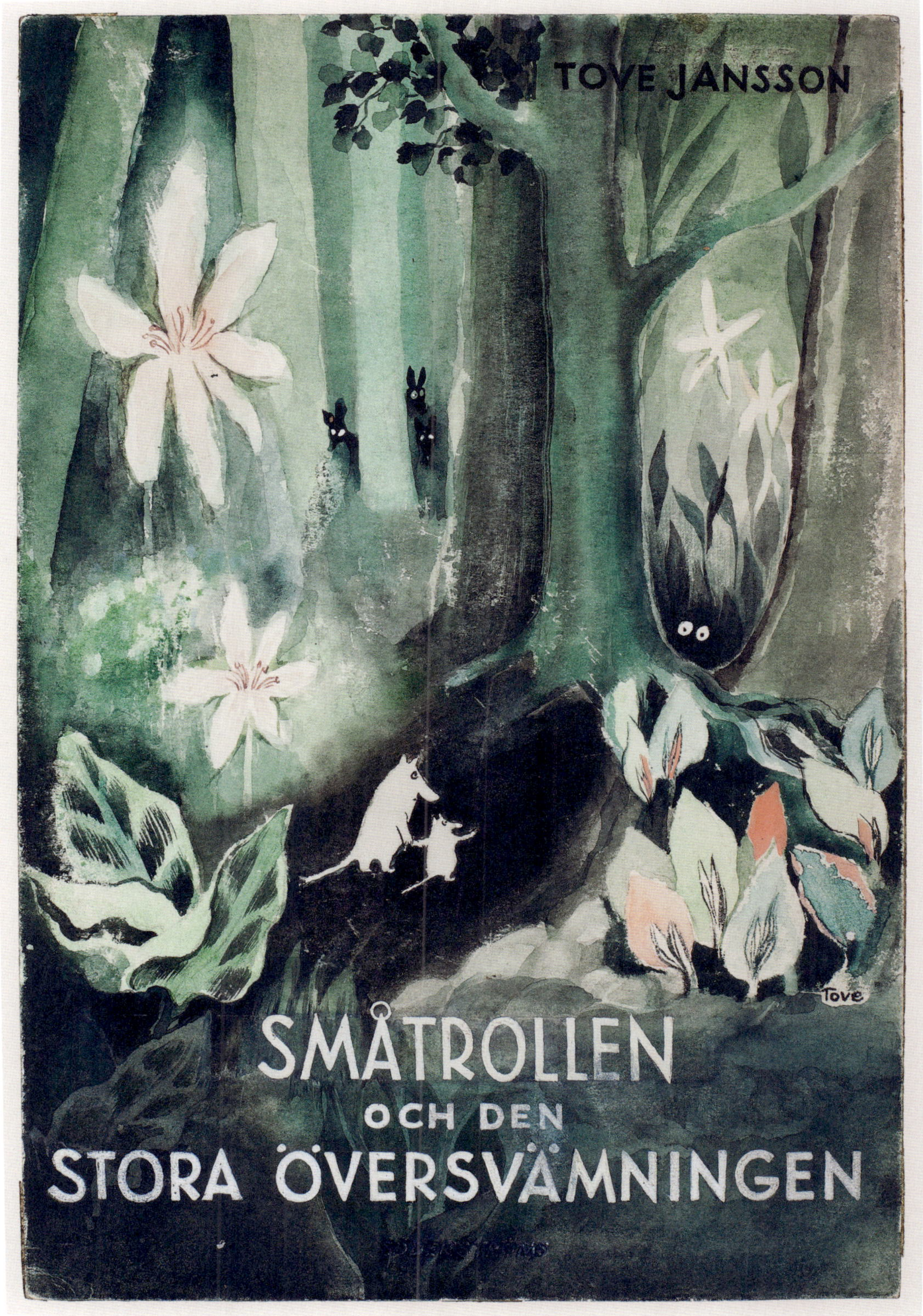

TOVE JANSSON
SMÅTROLLEN
OCH DEN
STORA ÖVERSVÄMNINGEN
Tove

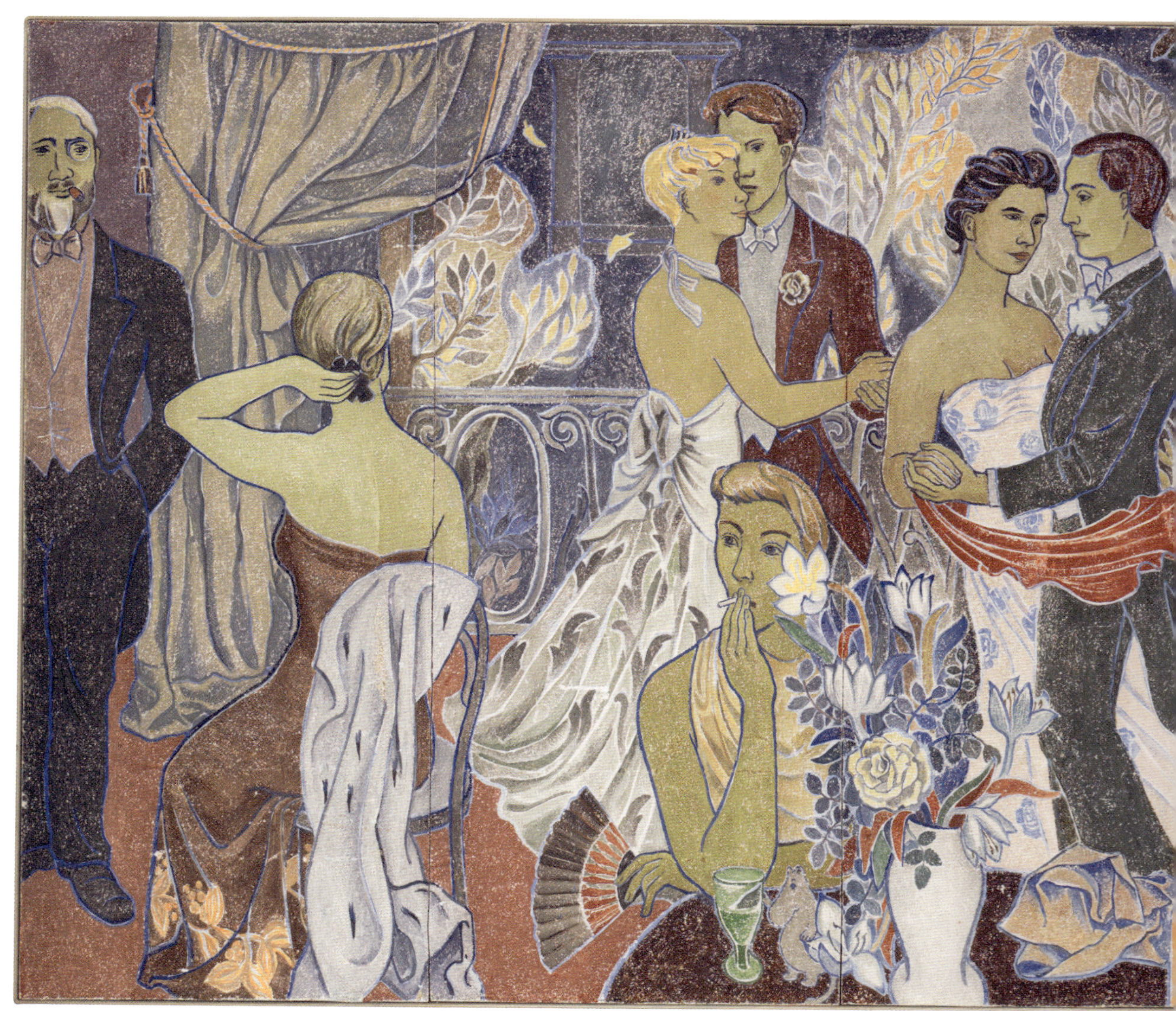

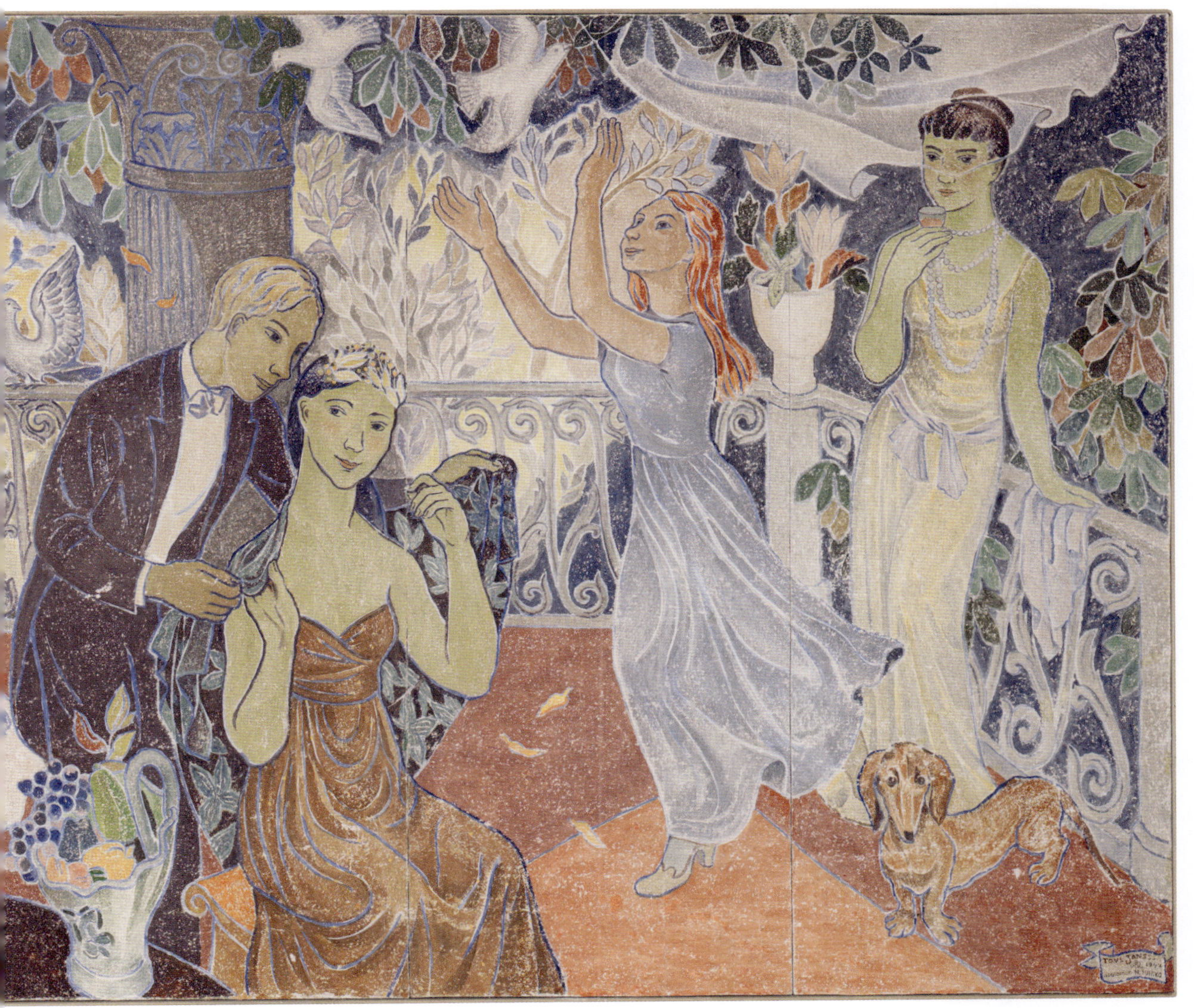

Comet in Moominland

Kometjakten (*The Comet Hunt*; published in English as *Comet in Moominland*) dealt with another natural disaster, this time a scorching comet heading for Moominvalley. Published in 1946, it has been seen as Jansson's response to the air raids she lived through in Helsinki, and to the global news of America's atomic bombings of Japan. Once again, she painted the front cover, a vast surreal landscape, predominantly in green and pink, and made several interior illustrations in ink and muted washes. This book, however, was not another novella but a substantial twelve-chapter novel, the template for a further seven to come. Jansson rarely began with images unless one needed special planning – for example a character's first appearance. She usually wrote first in longhand, carefully refining the story until it was ready to be typeset. Then, when she got the text proofs back, she cut and pasted them into a dummy to lay out each spread, adding a note, title or sometimes a sketch to herself for each

Two interior illustrations made in grey washes for the first edition of *Kometjakten* (*Comet in Moominland*), 1946, and redrawn in line only in 1951 for the English edition.

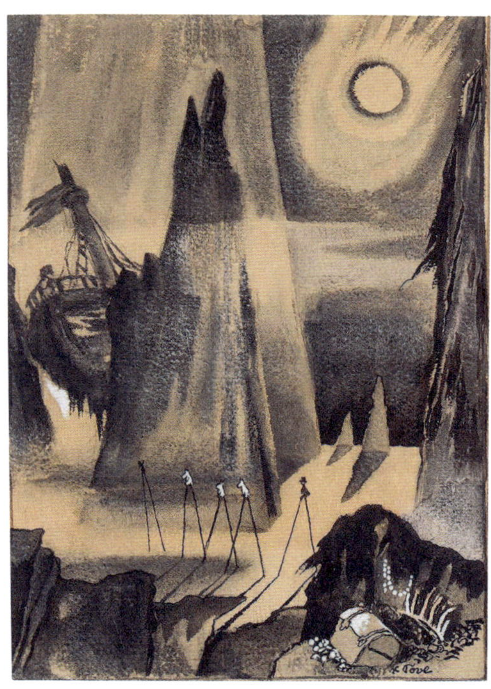

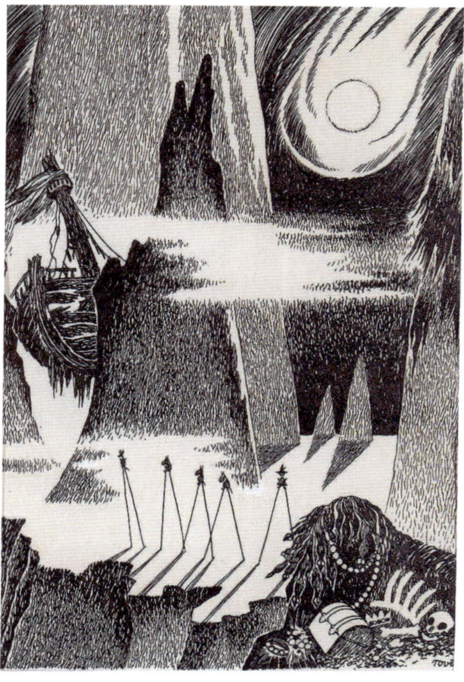

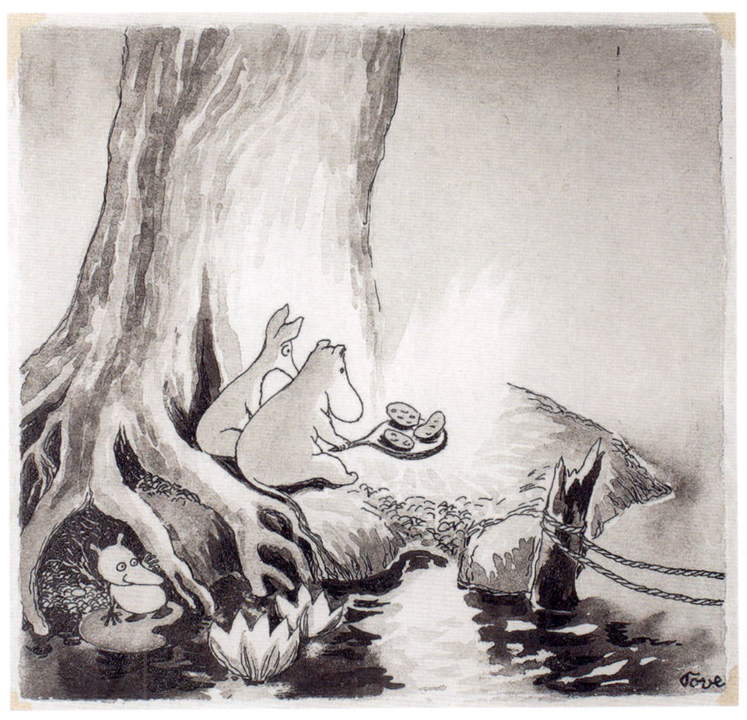

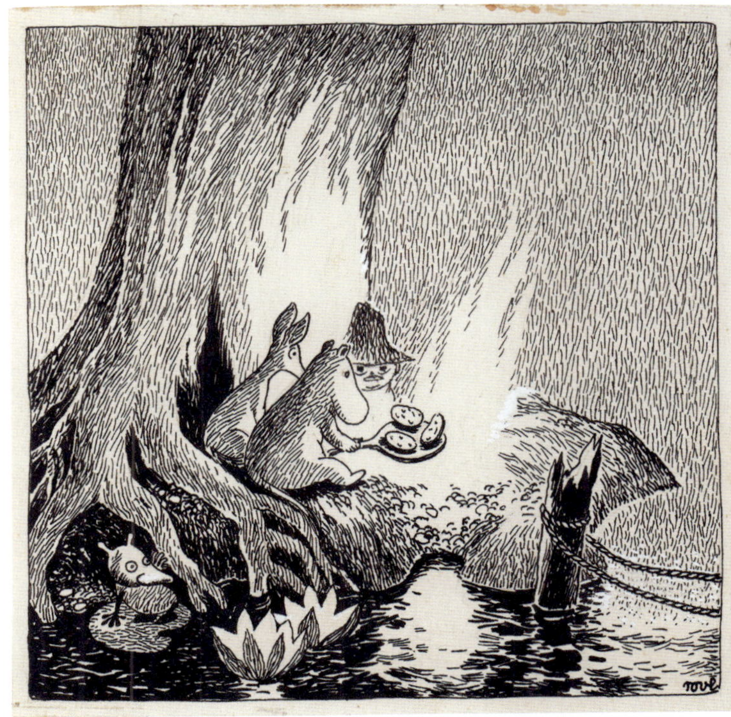

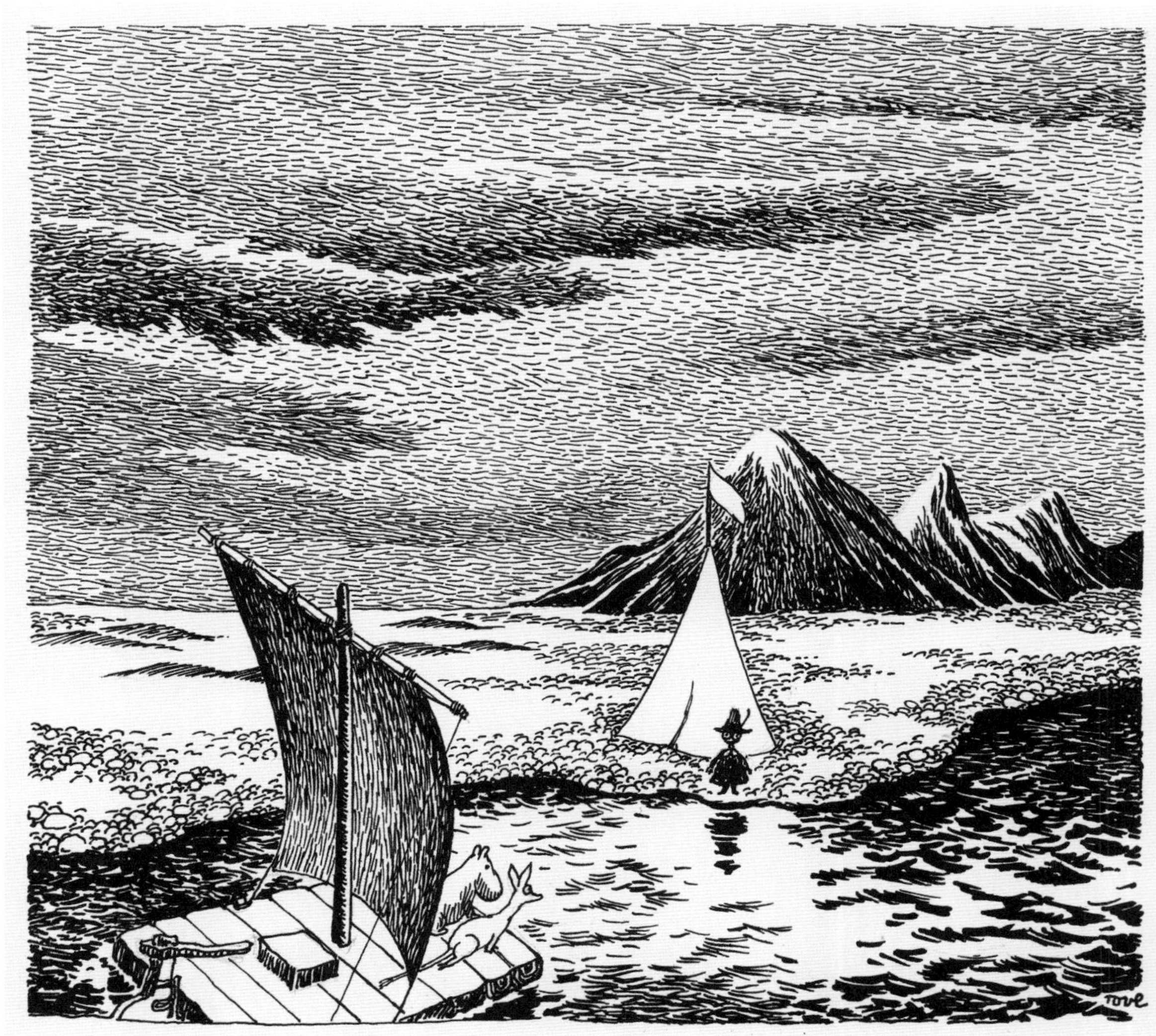

ABOVE

In a distant silhouette, Snufkin
makes his debut in *Kometjakten*
(*Comet in Moominland*).

illustration, its measurements and where it would go.

In this second Moomin book, the comet's apocalyptic threat is overcome, resulting in a world reborn. Jansson punctures the gendered clichés of masculine heroes like Burroughs's Tarzan, a favourite of hers. She portrays Moomintroll saving his friend Snorkmaiden from a poisonous bush, only to have her cleverly rescue him from a giant squid. Snorkmaiden reflects Jansson's feminism, and her vision of how practical and capable women can be. Also introduced here is Snufkin, the unmaterialistic

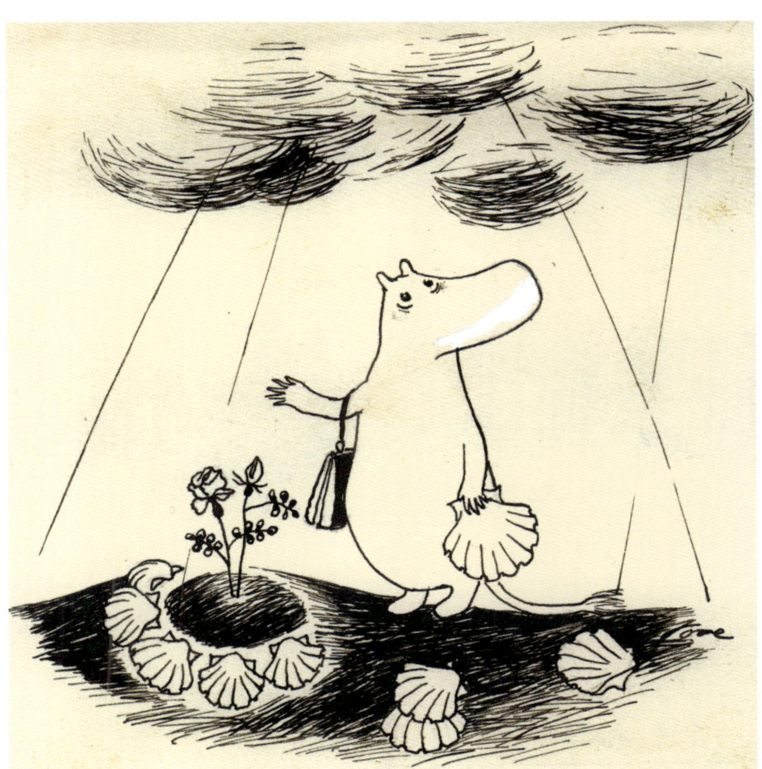

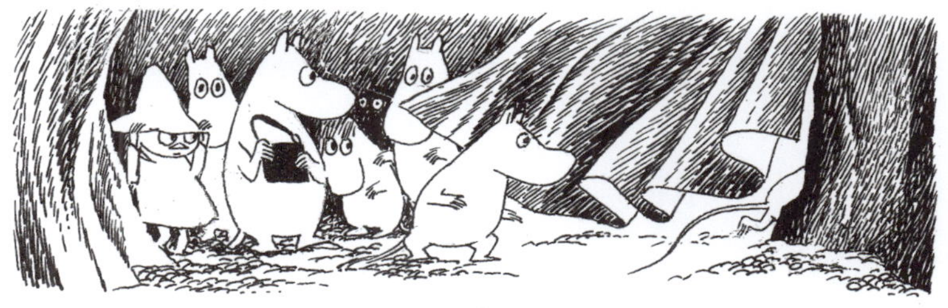

Moominmamma arranges sea shells around the flower-beds in *Kometjakten* (*Comet in Moominland*).

Sheltering from the comet in a cave, reminiscent of wartime air raids, in *Kometjakten* (*Comet in Moominland*).

vagabond with his pipe and green hat, partly inspired
by Jansson's friend and sometime lover, the left-wing
intellectual Atos Wirtanen.

On the back cover, the publisher's blurb announced, 'the
author herself has illustrated her story and the book thus
becomes a very small work of art'. It garnered scant reviews,
mainly favourable, and sluggish sales of only 246 copies by
early 1948. Still, it became Jansson's first Moomin book to be
republished outside Finland. When it premiered in Sweden in
1947, she drew a threatening cover in line, showing the comet
about to strike fearful creatures fleeing with their belongings
into a cave, a clear reference to refugees displaced by the war.
She designed a less distressing jacket and redrew her interior
wash images in pen and ink for the English edition from
publishers Ernest Benn, published as *Comet in Moominland*
(1951), and in 1956, she drew a bolder cover for the book's
Swedish-language re-release in Finland, its red background
pierced by a jagged, *trompe l'oeil* hole, all the characters
leaping through it as though to escape the comet.

In 1947, Wirtanen, then the editor-in-chief of the Swedish-
language Socialist daily newspaper *Ny Tid* ('New Time'),
invited Jansson to make a comic strip for its Friday children's
page. Working to a tight deadline, Jansson adapted her *Comet*
tale. After some teaser announcements and images, the first
six panels of 'Moomintroll and the End of the World' ran on 3
October 1947 as one long, horizontal strip. For her serial, she

Muskrat, the inconsolable
philosopher, reclines on
Moomintroll's cake, in *Kometjakten*
(*Comet in Moominland*).

New cover for the re-release in
Finland of the Swedish-language
edition of *Kometjakten* (*Comet in
Moominland*), 1956.

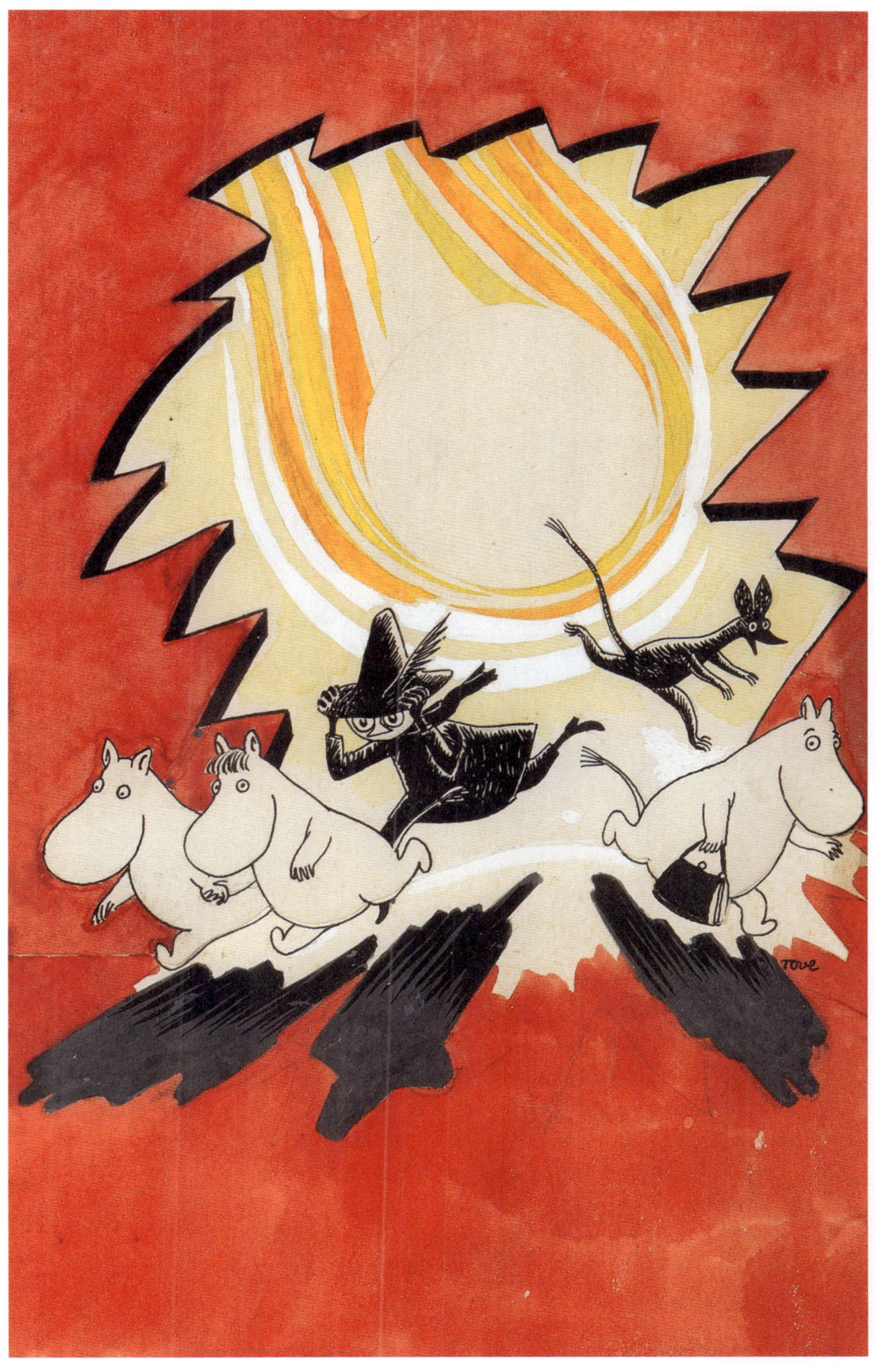

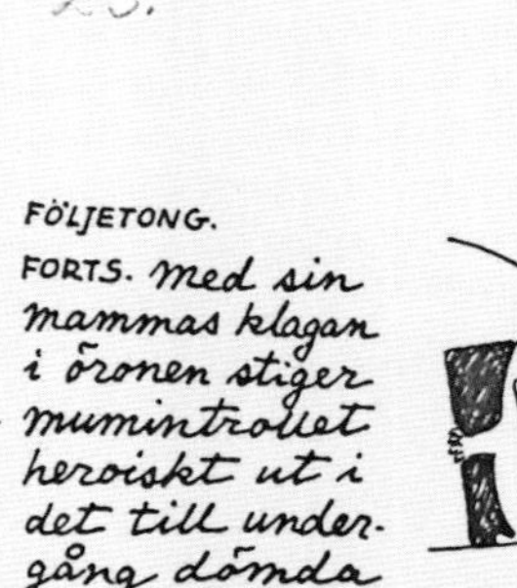

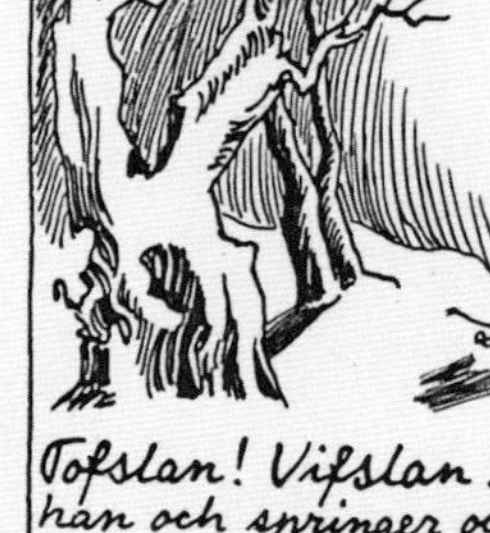
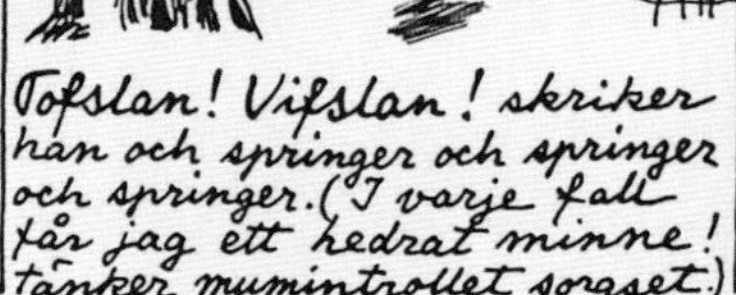

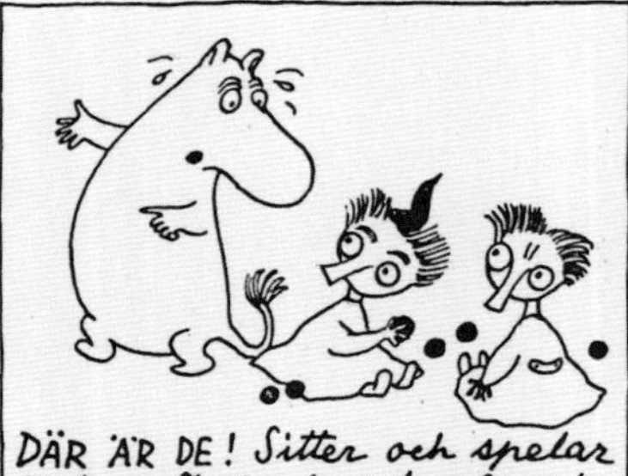

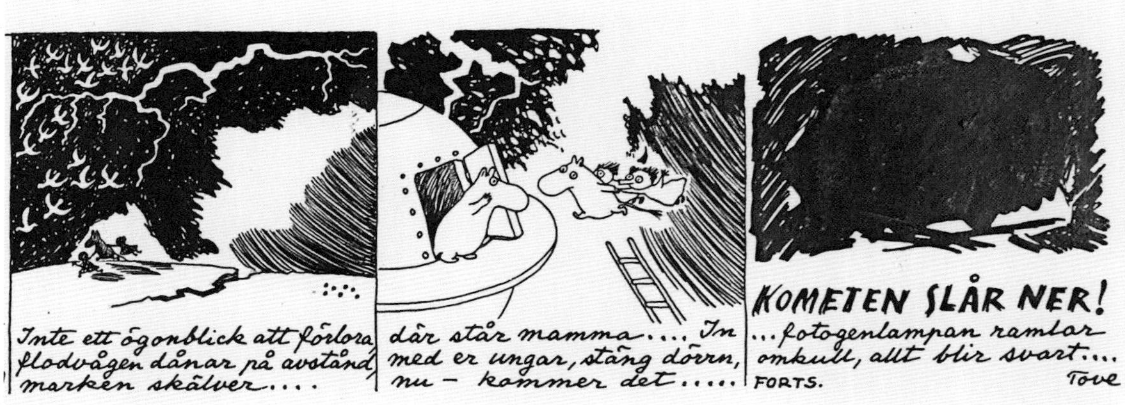

stuck to placing text beneath her images, this time lettered in by hand, adding greater expression and changing size to convey volume. The text becomes more ornate when female characters speak, and flies about when the Cyclone strikes. In the strip for 5 December 1947, she introduced the twosome of Tofslan and Vifslan (Thingumy and Bob in English), after their brief debuts earlier that year in a *Garm* cover and advertisements for bottled drinks. This inseparable pair and their peculiar language were based on herself and her first female lover, the theatre director Vivica Bandler, and their word games. Until homosexuality was legalized in Finland in 1971, Jansson maintained discretion about the women she loved, referring to her sexuality in coded terms as 'the spook side'.

Jansson also first wrote in these strips about the giant, gloomy, glacial Groke, though she was heard but not yet

ABOVE

ABOVE

A six-panel strip from the weekly serial in *Ny Tid*, showing the new characters Tofslan and Vifslan (Thingumy and Bob in English), based on Jansson and Vivica Bandler, 5 December 1947.

Stage set design for the three-act play *Mumintrollet och Kometen* (*Moomin and the Comet*), 1949.

seen. When some prickly *Ny Tid* readers complained about the strip's politics, especially showing Moominpappa reading a pro-Royalist newspaper, Wirtanen felt compelled to ask Jansson to wrap it up sooner. On 2 April 1948, after twenty-six weeks, Jansson resolved the strip abruptly and very differently from her *Comet* novel. *Ny Tid* promised Jansson would return by the autumn, but it would be four years before she would embark on newspaper strips again.

Also in 1948, Jansson retold her *Comet* story afresh as a play. The idea had come from Bandler, who proposed it to the Svenska Teatern in Helsinki. Their board had misgivings about the project's unconventional, unmoralizing and sometimes dark themes, considered inappropriate for a young audience, but a year later agreed to give it a chance. Jansson plunged into the demanding production, drawing detailed colour designs for its costumes and sets. She also painted the poster and contributed twelve black-and-white

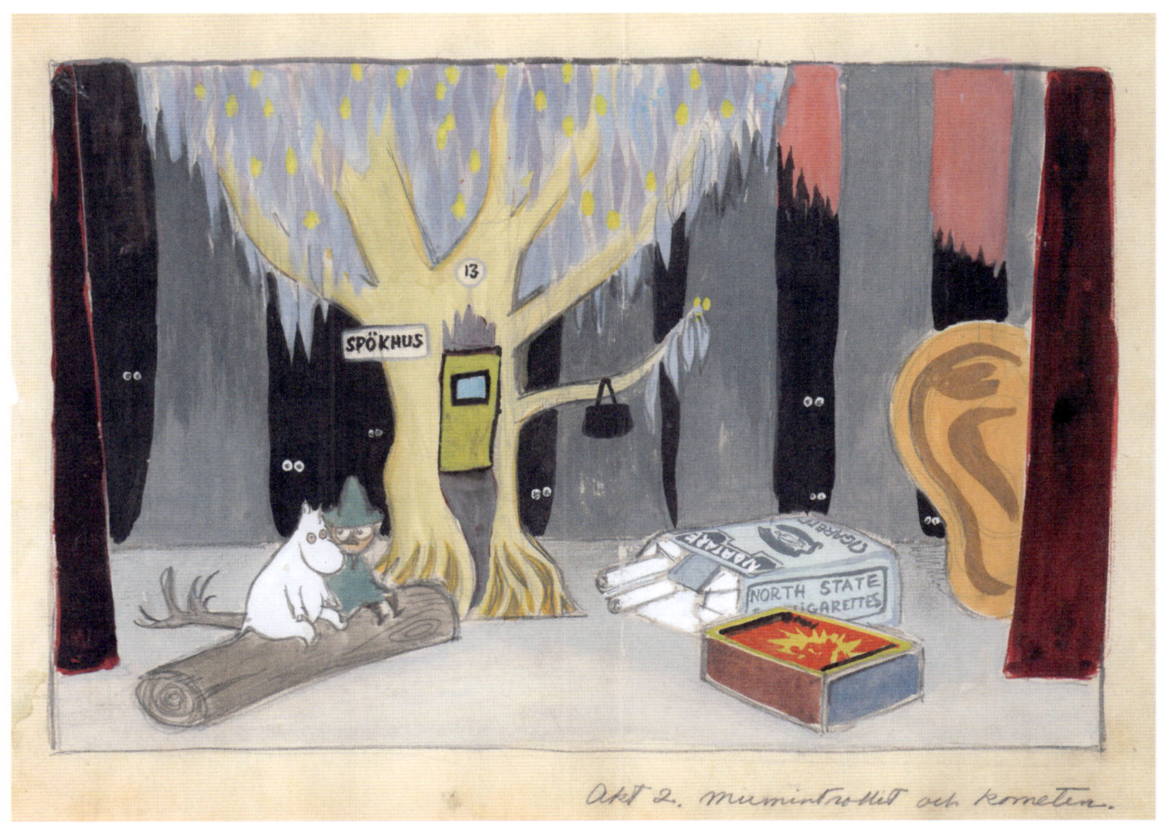

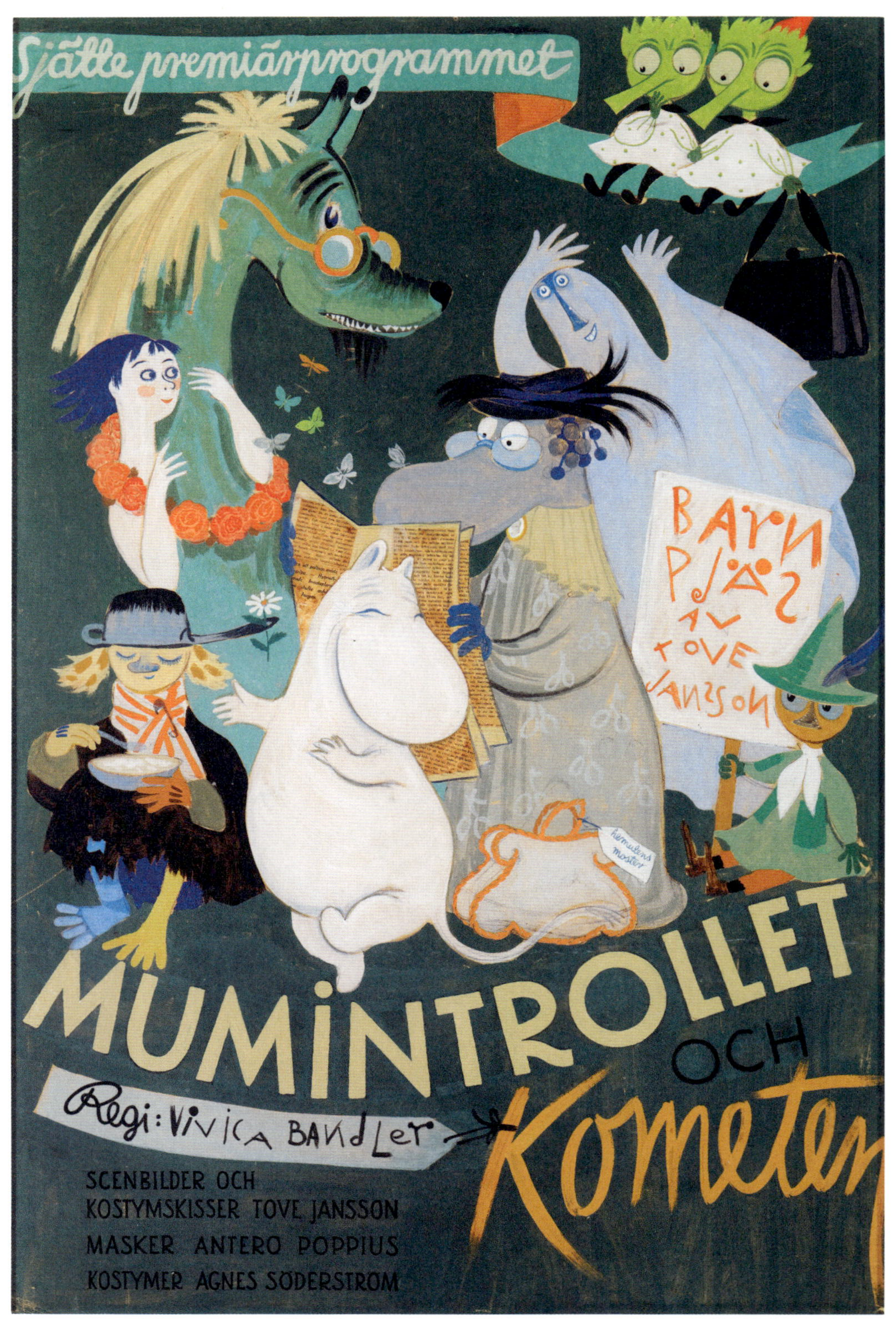

Sjätte premiärprogrammet
BARN PjÄS AV tOVE JANSSON
hemulens moster
MUMINTROLLET
OCH
Kometen
Regi: VIVICA BANDLER
SCENBILDER OCH KOSTYMSKISSER TOVE JANSSON
MASKER ANTERO POPPIUS
KOSTYMER AGNES SÖDERSTRÖM

portraits of the cast and a one-page illustrated 'interview' with Moomintroll to the programme. Her 'children's play in three acts' premiered on 28 December 1949, sparking positive reviews and vigorous debate among newspaper readers, with one 'confused father' misinterpreting her characters as 'mares and marsupials from Hell'. The publicity helped the play run for nineteen performances and led to later tours to other Nordic cities. So began Jansson and Bandler's collaborations in the theatre. In all, Jansson would pen eighteen works for the stage, several more of them Moomin-themed.

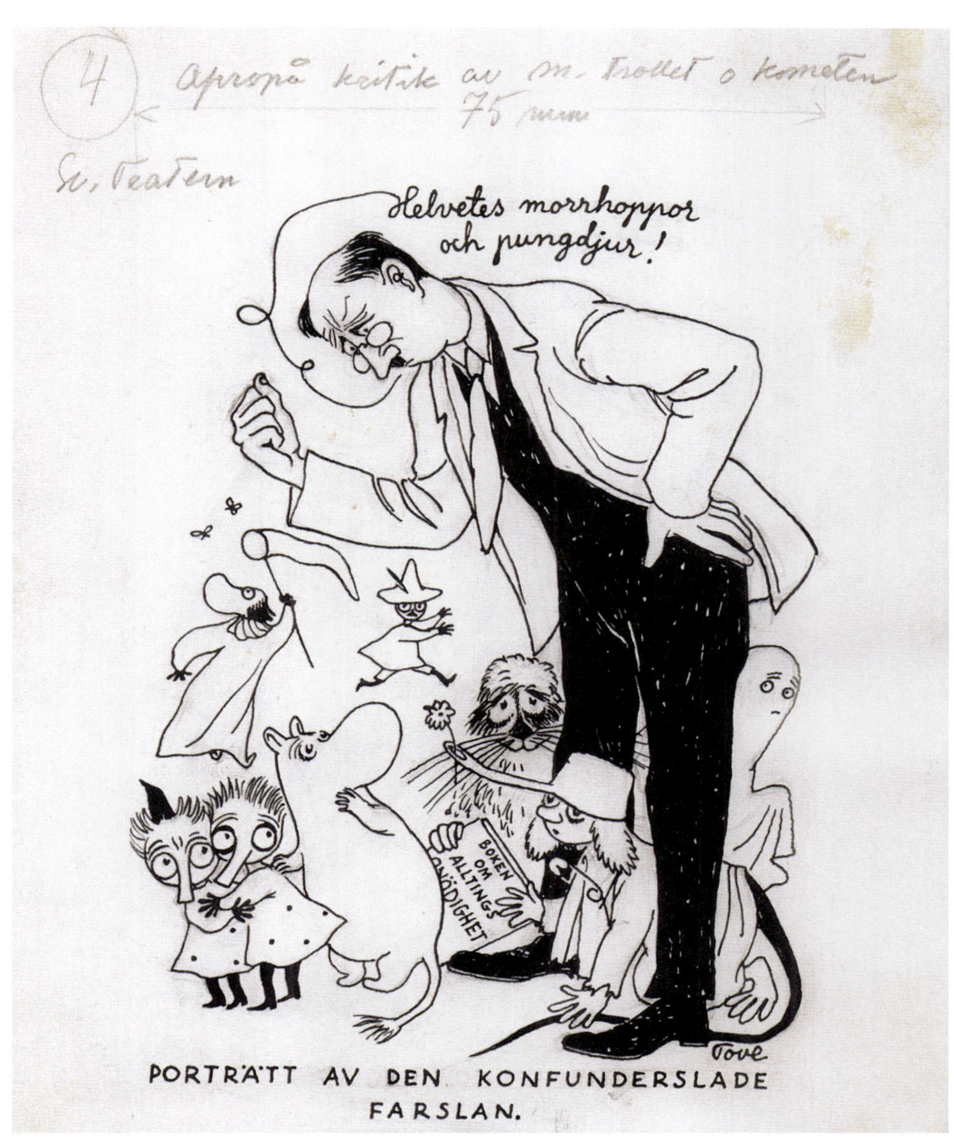

Finn Family Moomintroll

Undaunted by low sales of the *Comet* book, in 1948 Jansson
was swept up into the full creative flow of her third novel,
adapting to a different format set by her new publisher
Schildts, which offered more pages but at a smaller size.
In *Trollkarlens hatt* (*The Hobgoblin's Hat*), she brought the
Moomin ensemble and their world into crisp focus, out of the
war's shadows and into brighter prospects. She also adopted
what she called 'a new technique' for her illustrations: 'They
are better than the ones in *Comet* – nothing tinted, only
black and white.' She abandoned washes and embraced the
rich range of shading achievable by varying the density of
multiple strokes of constant width, typically in two different
thicknesses of Rapidograph technical pens, one thin, the
other a broader no. 2. As an imaginary world-builder, she

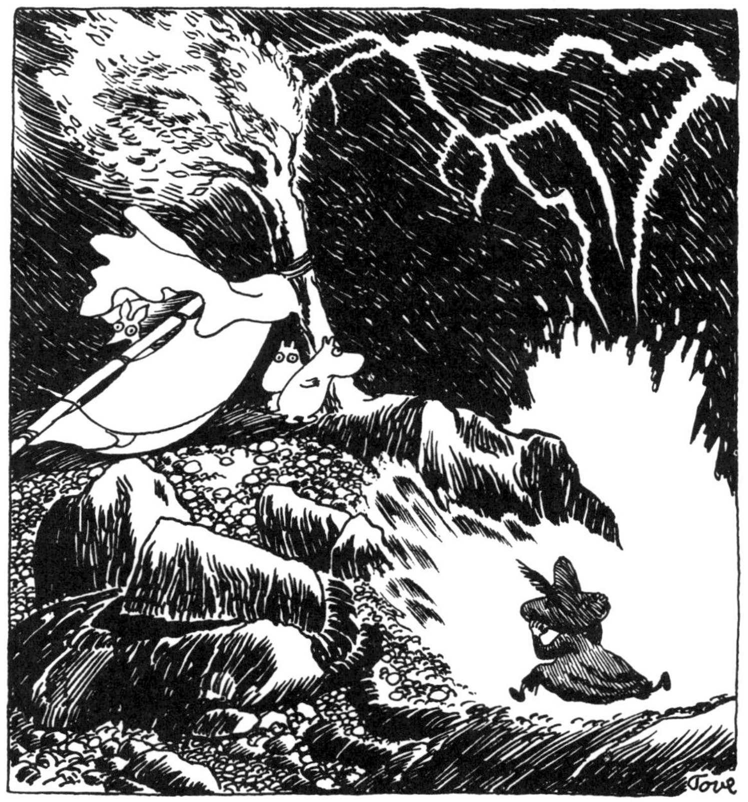

LEFT

Jansson's more intense and
contrasting line work heightens
the drama in *Trollkarlens hatt*
(*The Hobgoblin's Hat*), 1948.

OPPOSITE

One of several striking full-page
illustrations in *Trollkarlens hatt*
(*The Hobgoblin's Hat*), 1948.

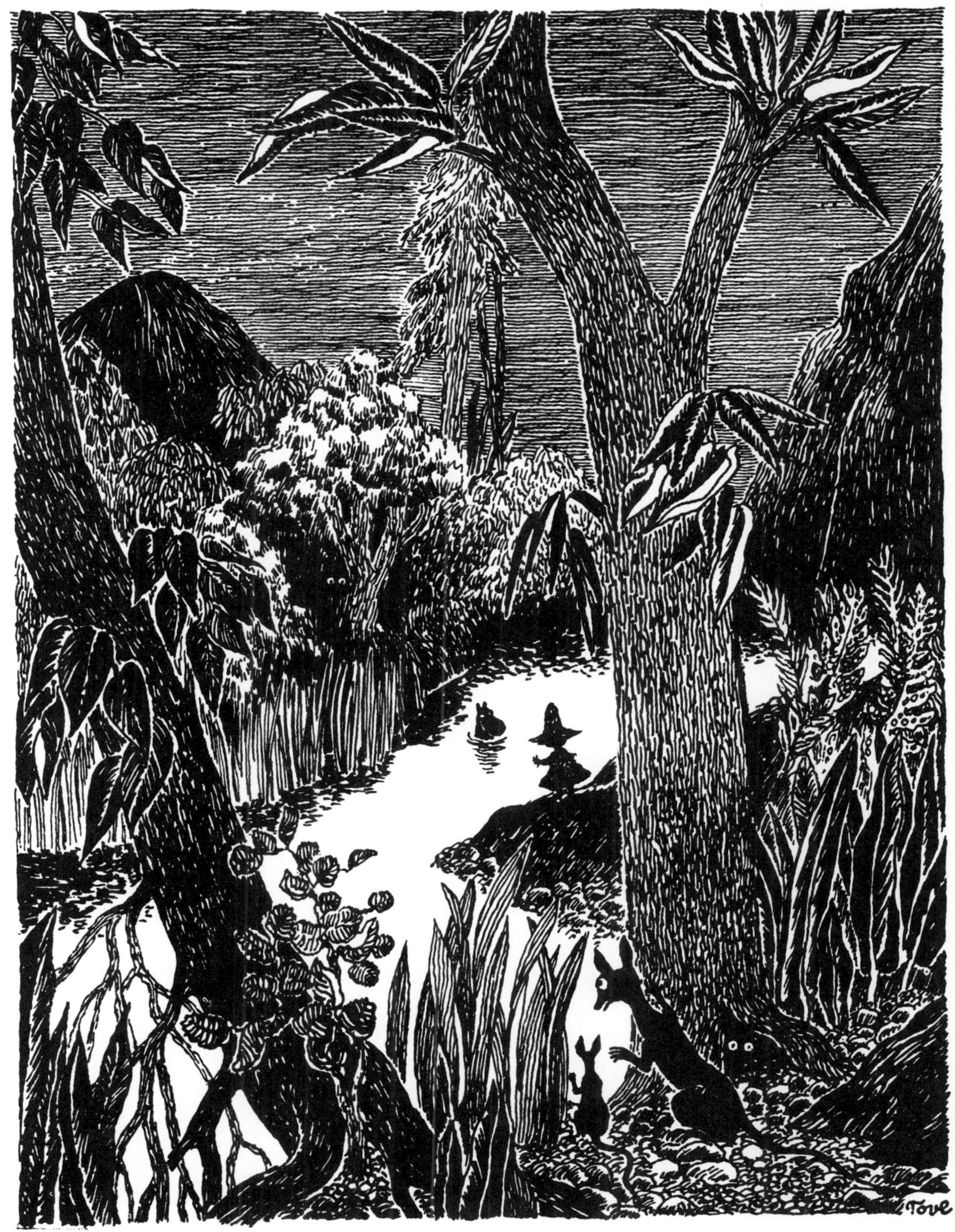

Tove

could draw on her sketches of landscapes, sea and skies
to harness storms of lines, short and long, into intense
impressions and almost tactile forms. For all her evocative
writing, she knew that sometimes 'lines and surfaces can
say more than words'. Some of her images grow so carved
with lines that they resemble a metal-plate etching, yet
her mastery of rendering and contrast means their focal
points are always clear and the characters stand out, framed
by solid black or the white of the page. Japanese experts
Dr Asano Shugo and Kana Murase have speculated that
Jansson's approaches to depicting ever-changing nature
and weather may also have been influenced by those in
traditional *ukiyo-e* or 'floating world' prints.[4] Jansson never
expressed this inspiration, but she owned some examples,
notably by Hokusai, and these intriguing affinities may help
explain the Moomins' appeal in Japan.

The Hobgoblin's Hat established the format of the rest
of the novel series and, as her first book to be more widely
translated, saw the Moomins bring Jansson some much-
needed earnings. It was published in English in 1950, its
title wittily changed to *Finn Family Moomintroll* to include
both the characters' names and as a nod to one of Jansson's
childhood favourites, Johann David Wyss's *Swiss Family
Robinson*. Thereafter, a new novel would appear every
three to five years, from the next, *Muminpappans bravader
skrivna av honom själv* (*The Exploits of Moominpappa*,
1950), to the last, *Sent i November* (*Moominvalley in
November*, 1970), each more successful than the last. On
the books' painted covers, Jansson reduced her use of
hard black outlines in preference for areas of colour, often
distinguishing characters and other elements from the
background with thin white contours, as if aglow. While she
had to define the all-white Moomins in black, she also made
them stand out by adding this 'aura'.

Over the summer of 1951, Jansson prepared her first
children's picture book, *Hur gick det sen? Boken om Mymlan,
Mumintrollet och Lilla My* (*What Happened Next? The Book
about Moomin, Mymble and Little My*), adopting the genre's
double-page spreads to make twelve generous images, like
stage sets, to tell the story of Moomintroll and Mymble's
quest for Little My and reunion with Moominmamma.

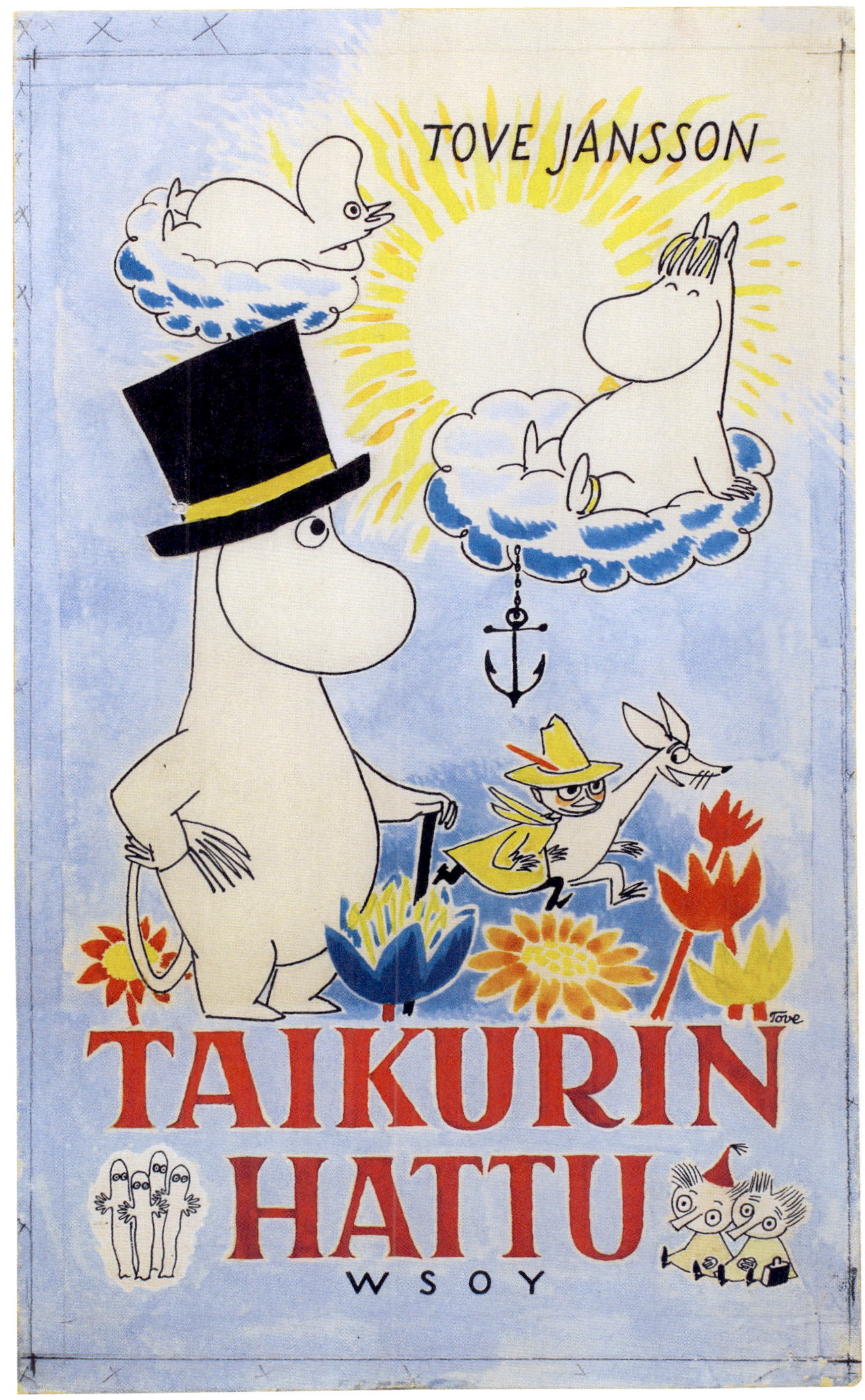

TOVE JANSSON
TAIKURIN
HATTU
WSOY

Inspired by the cut-paper art of Henri Matisse, she drew bold shapes and lines in flat colours, and heightened the transformative appeal of turning the page by designing the front and back covers and each page inside to be missing either a different die-cut hole (actually two out of the first page) or a corner on the right. Peeking through these puzzling apertures fires the readers' anticipation for *What Happened Next?* As she explained, 'looking through each hole (backwards and forwards through the book) you catch a glimpse of something tempting and strange that when you turn the page turns out to be not at all what you expect.' Holes had been used in children's books before, but not with such varied and tantalizing results. Rather than typeset her rhyming narrative couplets, she hand-lettered them, representing words visually to make every spread fully drawn. Her picture book's reception was rapturous, bringing her wider attention and the first of many awards.[5]

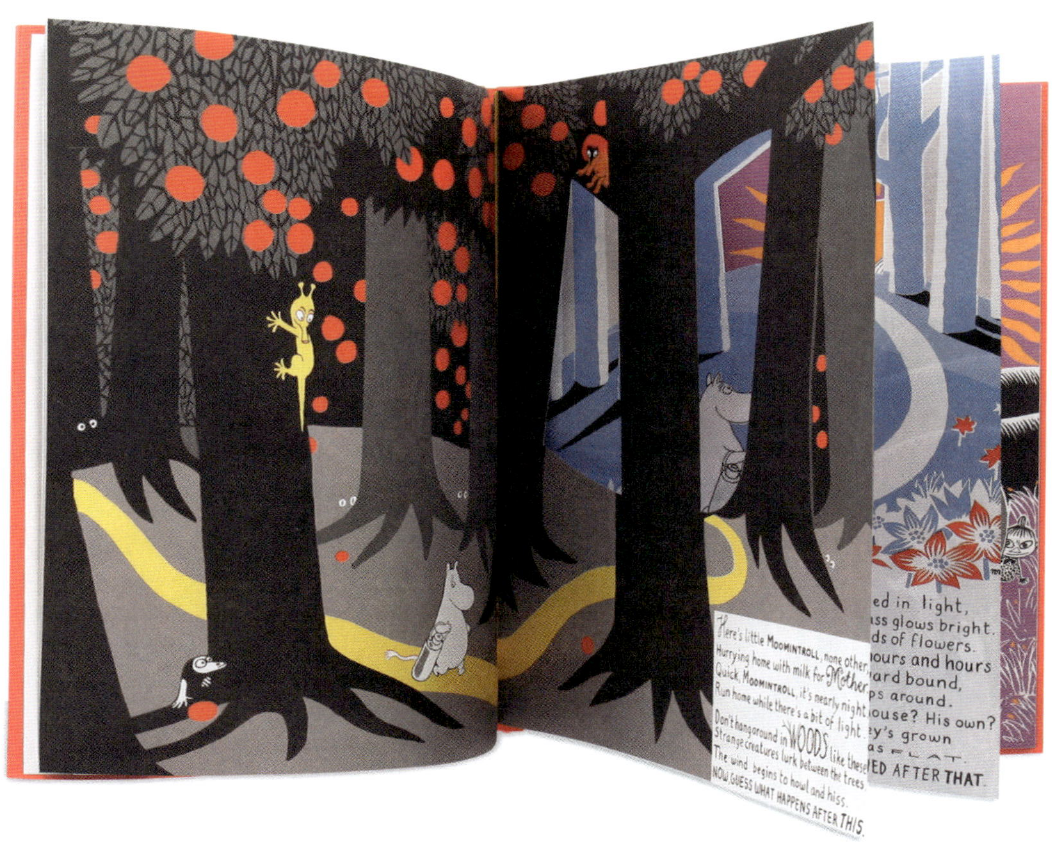

The daily comic strips

On 29 January 1952, a life-changing letter arrived from London. Charles Sutton, head of syndication at Associated Newspapers (AN), had written to suggest that Jansson's 'Moomin Family might make an interesting strip cartoon' for the *Daily Mail*, 'not necessarily for children', but 'to satirize our so-called civilized way of life.' Jansson saw the opportunity, and a flurry of letters over three months led to Mr Sutton (or 'Sister Mutton', as she nicknamed him) coming to Helsinki to approve her proposals for the introductory eighty-episode story and finalize the contract. Sutton arrived on 30 April, the eve of the May Day holiday in Finland, and joined Jansson and her circle in her studio for an all-night party, followed by a boisterous breakfast nearby. They also had serious business to attend to. Jansson had sought advice about the contract, which resulted in Sutton adding a vital clause to pay an additional percentage for her strips being syndicated to other newspapers. These earnings would prove considerable. Once she signed the seven-year deal, Jansson, approaching thirty-eight, began enjoying a regular salary and 'permanent employment – the first time in my life'.

It would take more than another two years of constant correspondence between Sutton and Jansson before her Moomin strip could debut in September 1954. It is hard to think of any other instance of a newspaper syndicate financing such a lengthy, costly development period – it proves the strength of AN's commitment and expectations. Jansson, still a relative novice, responded well to guidance, as she grasped the specific requirements of the modern serial comic strip to engage readers from Monday to Saturday, in no more than three or four panels at a time. At first Jansson placed her text beneath the panels, but Sutton insisted that she use speech balloons, which she had tried occasionally, as early as her self-printed school booklets, but never so consistently. Remarkably, one rejected draft has recently resurfaced, damaged and coffee-stained, rescued by the late AN cartoonist David Myers. Labelled '2', it became strips eighteen and nineteen of the first story. At this point, Jansson had yet to outline her balloons, instead defining them only by a thin, broken line and colouring around them in non-reproducing blue, which the print

Early pencilled drafts for the first three Moomin daily newspaper strips. Tove Jansson writes in Swedish inside the panels, which her brother Lars translates into English beneath.

Drafts of strips 12, 13 and 14, also from the first story, 'Moomin and the Brigands', 1954.

Tove Jansson also drew sample character and costume sheets to show how her finished inked artwork would look. These are for her first story.

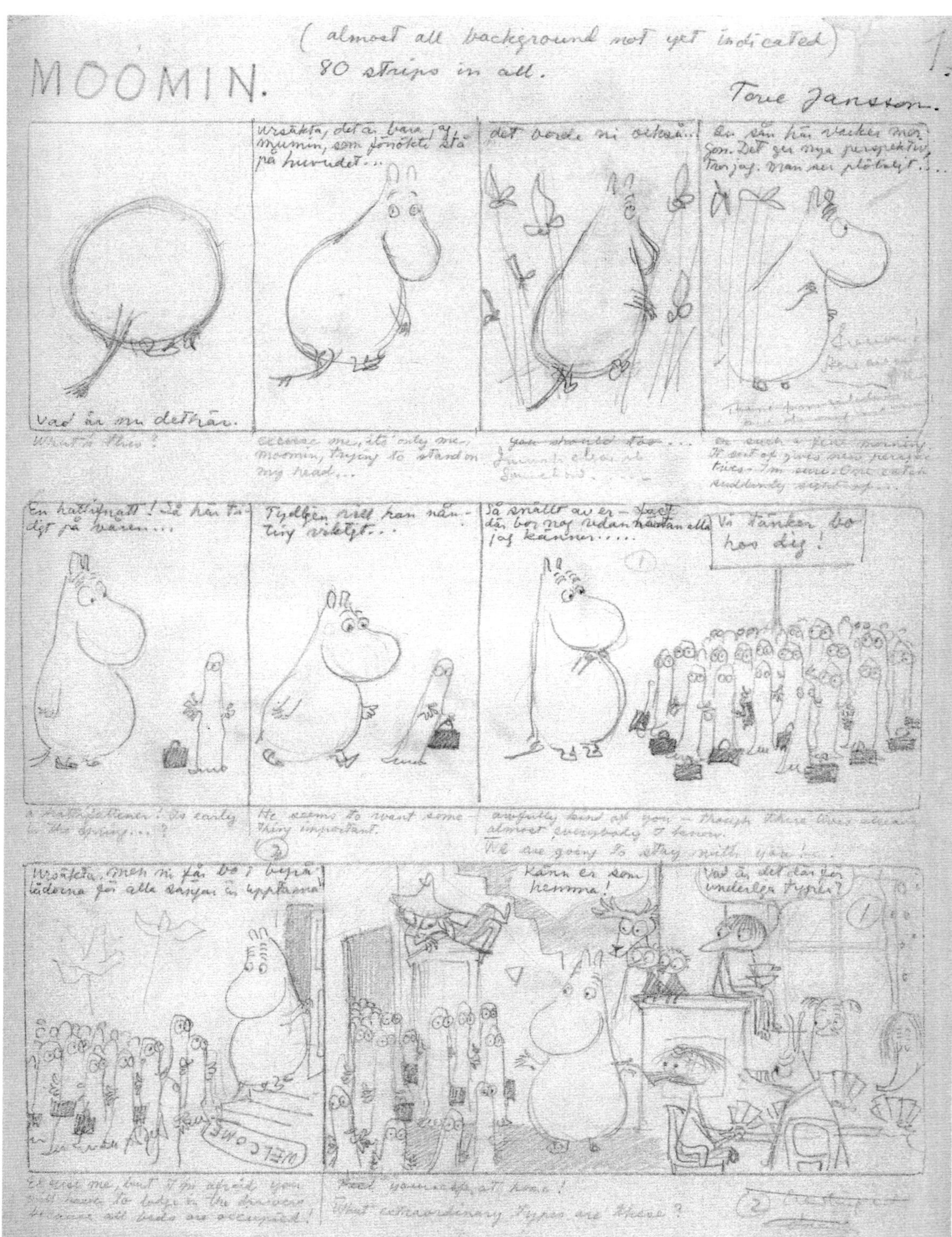

MOOMIN.
(almost all background not yet indicated)
80 strips in all.
Tove Jansson.

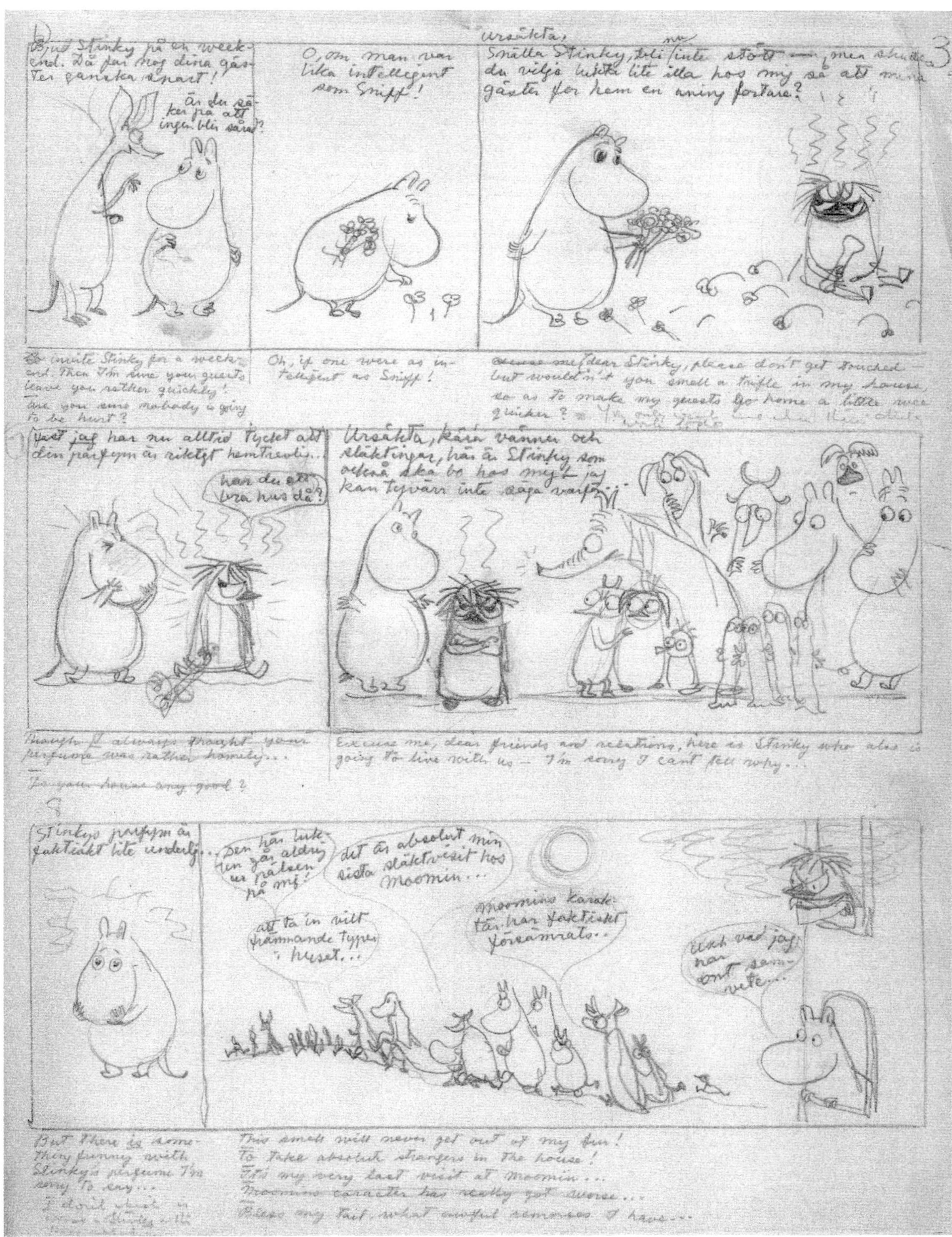
To invite Stinky for a week-end. Then I'm sure your guests leave you rather quickly!
Are you sure nobody is going to be hurt?
Oh, if one were as intelligent as Sniff!
Excuse me, dear Stinky, please don't get touched — but would'nt you smell a trifle in my house, so as to make my guests go home a little more quicker?
Though I always thought your perfume was rather homely...
Is your house any good?
Excuse me, dear friends and relations, here is Stinky who also is going to live with us — I'm sorry I can't tell why...
But there is something funny with Stinky's perfume I'm sorry to say...
This smell will never get out of my fur!
To take absolute strangers in the house!
It's my very last visit at Moomin...
Moomins caracter has really got worse...
Bless my tail, what awful remorses I have...

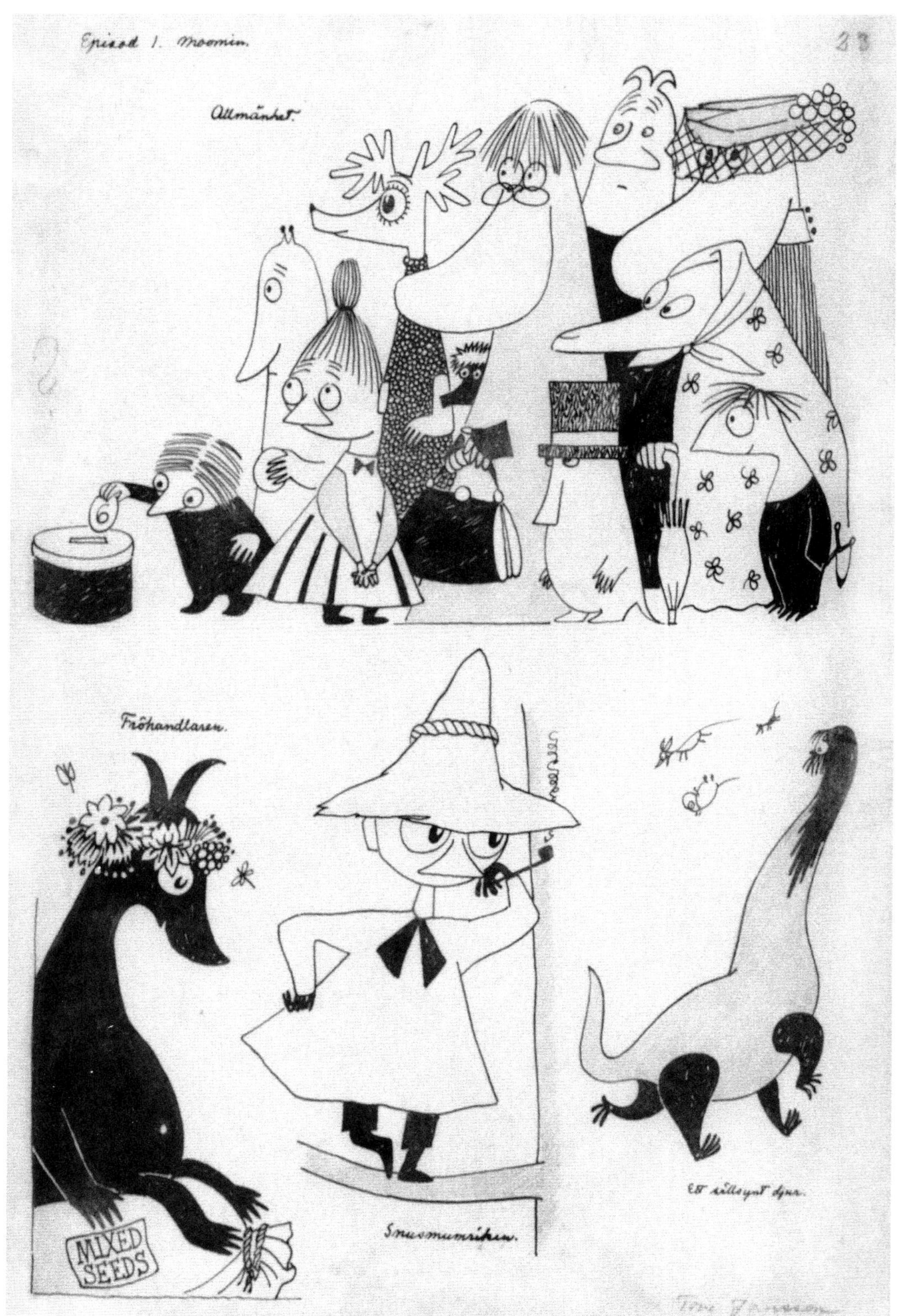

Episod 1. moomin.
28
Allmänhet.
Fröhandlaren.
MIXED SEEDS
Snusmumriken.
Ett sällsynt djur.
Tove Jansson

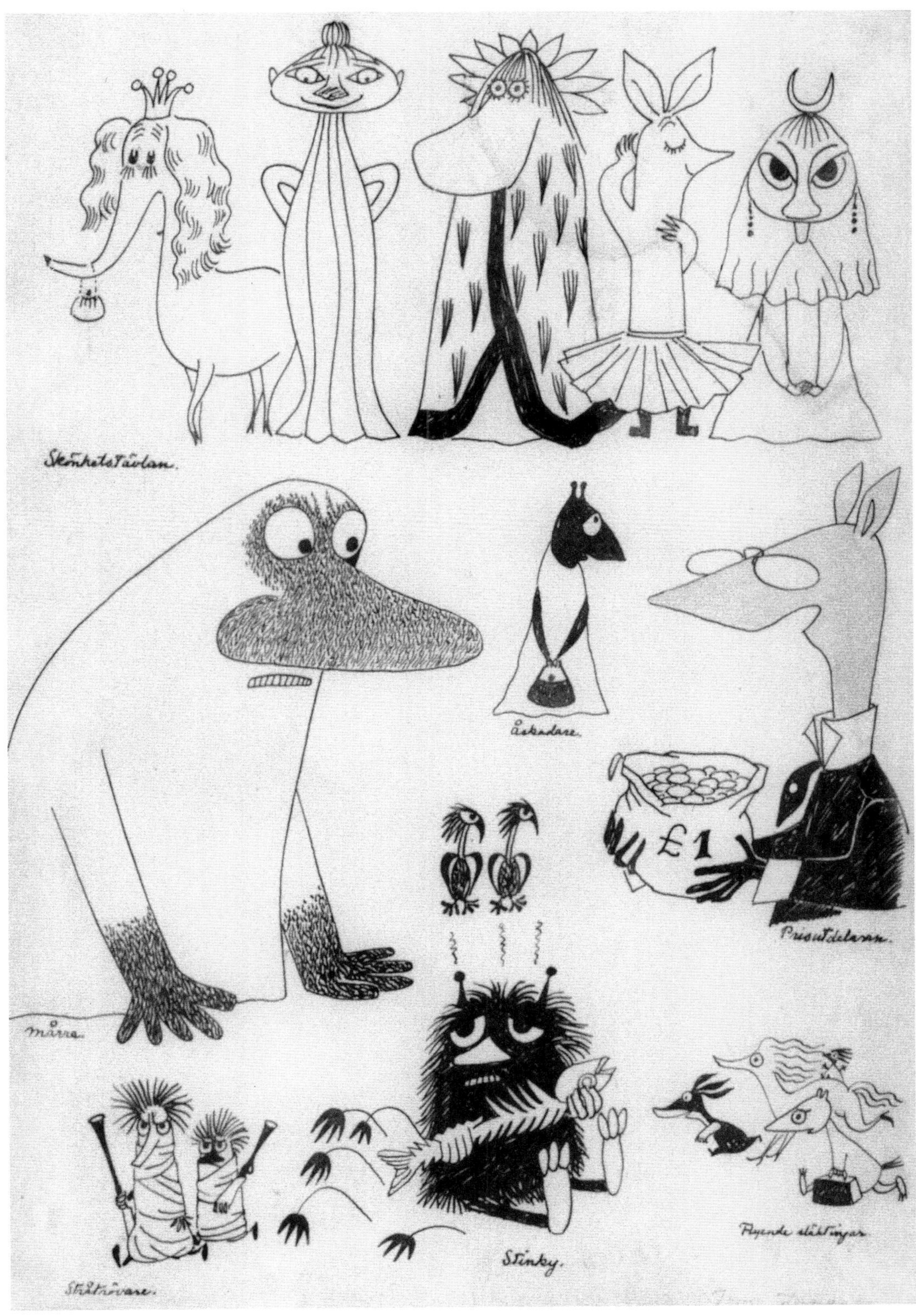

SkönhetsTävlan.
Åskådare.
Prisutdelaren.
Mirra.
Stinky.
Stöttrivare.
Flyende släktingar.

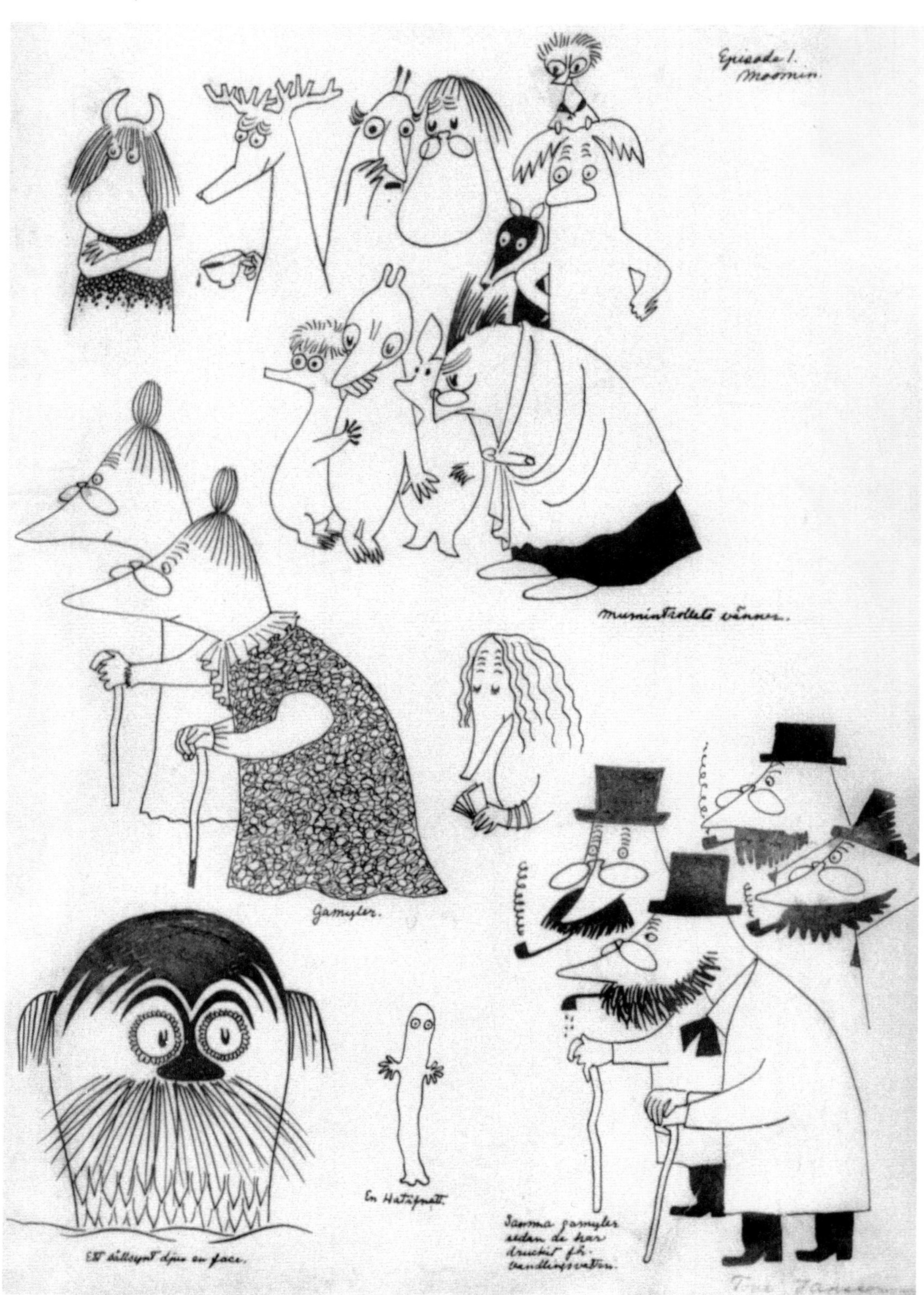

Episode 1.
moomin.

mumintrollets vänner.

Gamyler.

En Hattifnatt.

Ett sällsynt djur en face.

Samma gamyler
sedan de har
druckit för-
vandlingsvatten.

Tove Jansson

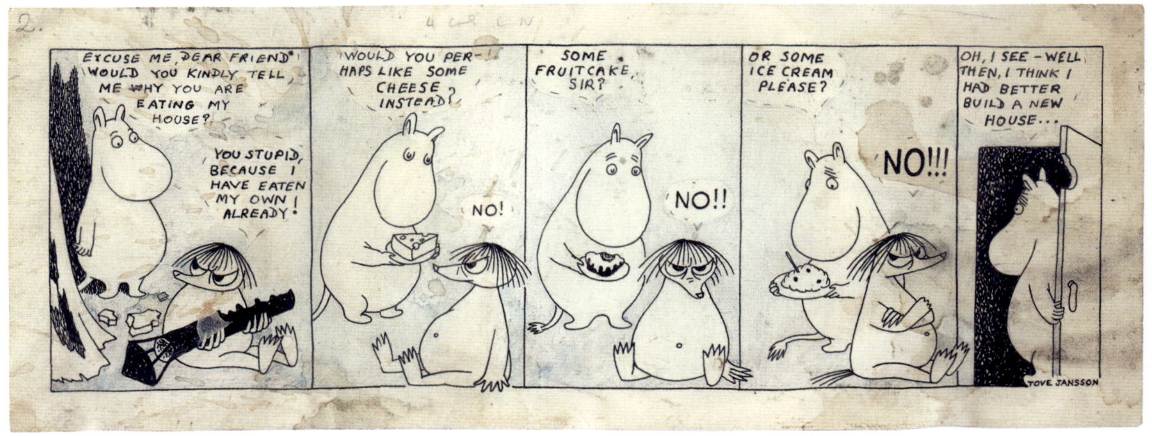

process would turn into grey areas of mechanical dots. While sometimes she would add the hand-drawn textures she used for her Moomin novels' illustrations, faced with having to draw six strips a week, bigger, quicker and for fuzzier newsprint reproduction, she wisely also used this uniform screen tone.

In 1947, Jansson and her brother Lars had rented a small island in the Gulf of Finland, and built a simple home named Vindrosen or 'The Wind Rose', the thorny blossom a symbol of beauty and resilience that recurs in her drawing. During the warmer months, she worked there, and despite distractions found that 'It's good to have the strip cartoons to work on sometimes, I can cope with those however lively my surroundings.' Nevertheless, Jansson found the process protracted, as AN 'keep changing things and raising objections'. When the *Daily Mail* deferred on the strip, Sutton placed it with another paper in the group, the *Daily Sketch*, only for that to fall through too. Finally, an opening came at the London *Evening News*, the world's biggest-selling evening paper. In early March 1954, Jansson was invited to London for two intensive weeks to finalize her strips with Julian Phipps, head of AN's strip department.[6] She wrote to Bandler: 'Any action in them has to be reacted to with "sobs", "oomph", speed lines, sweat and tears.' While Jansson avoided sound effects, she included occasional symbolic 'emanata', such as drops of sweat for worry or wavy lines for aromas. Fortunately, any misgivings she had about having to cut, re-paste and re-draw episodes were calmed by her feeling 'a strong and reassuring sense that it's my stories they want....'

'Moomin every day'

Much fuss was made by the *Evening News* to promote the
launch of the Moomin strip on Monday 20 September 1954.
Jansson designed a banner proclaiming 'Moomin Every
Day' for the top of the paper's fleet of delivery vans, and
throughout the preceding week the paper ran front-page
announcements with teaser panels. On the Friday, a large
interview with Jansson ran on page four. Instead of placing
the first serial with the other strips, it was given pride of
place on page six, surrounded by the much-read classified
job adverts. 'Moomin and the Brigands' opens with a simple
circle of Moomin's posterior, a trick Jansson would use to
begin every story. Her second and third panels are divided
not with a dull vertical line, but an appropriate pictorial

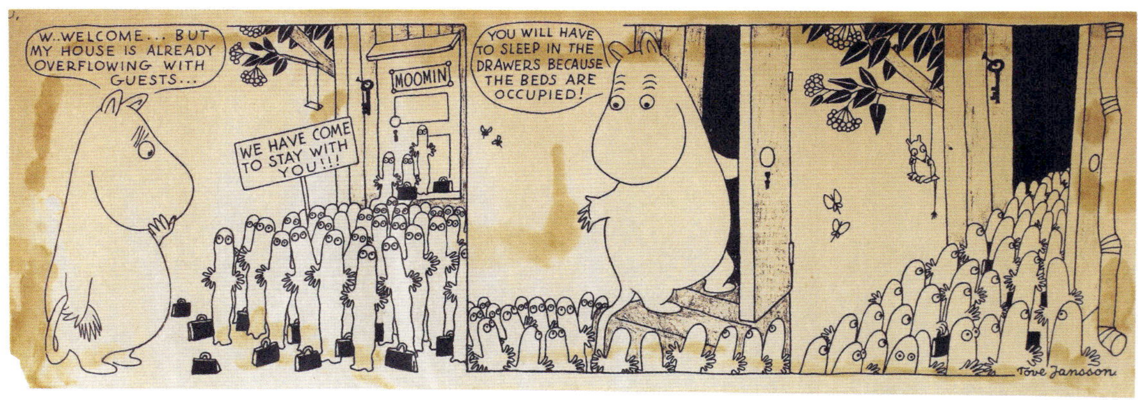

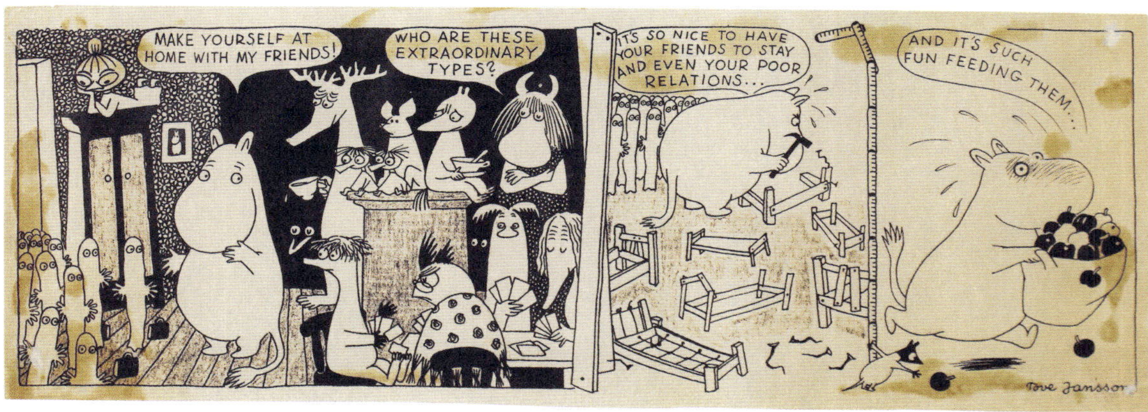

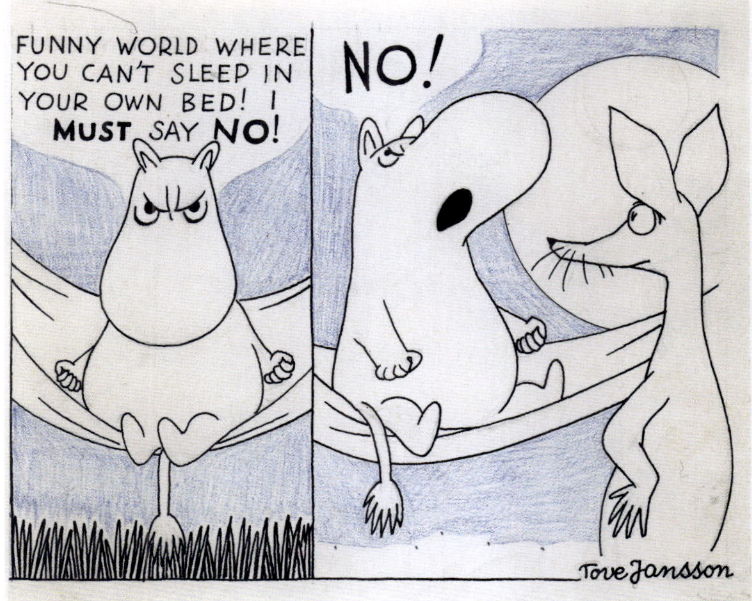

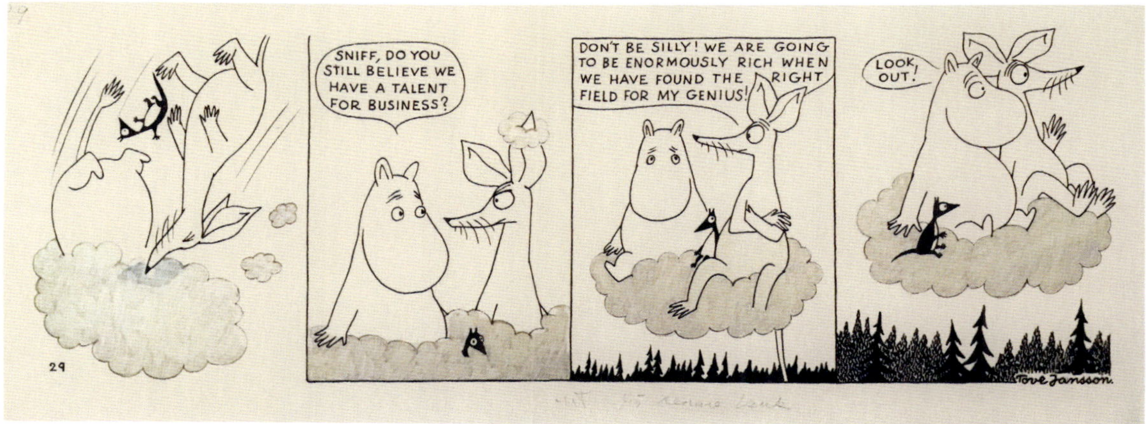

element, in this case tall reeds, the first of many playful graphic panel borders whose technique Jansson invented. In the fourth panel, she introduced Sniff. More of her cast would join them, although Moomin was left parentless until Jansson's second story reunited Moominpappa and Moominmamma with their 'long-lost son'.

One newspaper convention, used to lend immediacy to the strips, was to avoid captions and drive the story through dialogue. This removed Jansson's novels' evocative narration

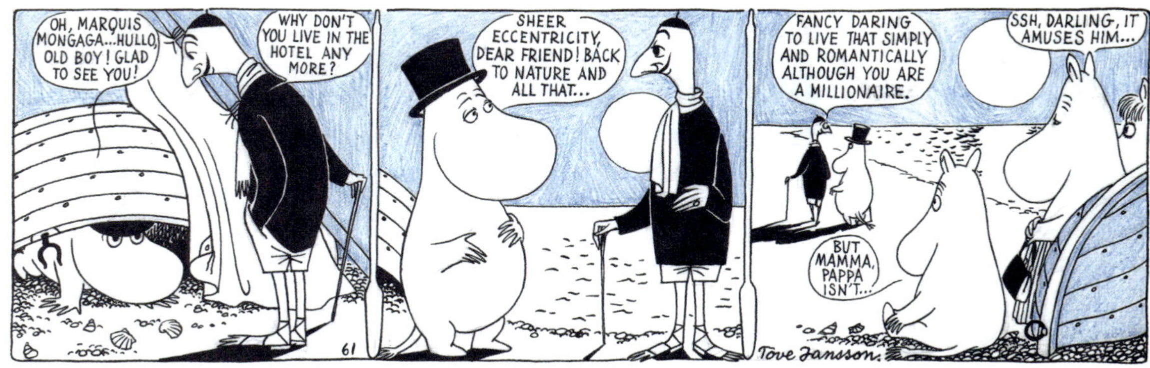

and description, and while aspects of the novels did surface through the strips, the demand for fresh stories and satire pushed Jansson to devise new subjects and locations, from the Wild West to a Martian invasion. Jansson took inspiration from a holiday with her mother on the Riviera and sent the Moomin family there, to experience the glamour and excess of wealth and meet a frustrated, Dalí-like millionaire, who sculpts only elephants and dreams of a poor bohemian artist's freedom. A seven-strip sequence from this tale are among only a dozen or so remaining original finished strips by Jansson, after AN disposed of the rest. Another episode survived only because Jansson withdrew it for possible later use. Luckily, she preserved her preliminary sketches and final, precise layouts in pencil, as well as some thirty 'synopses', proposing a new story's cast, costumes and other designs. The strip swiftly proved popular and foreign syndication took off, reaching 120 newspapers, forty countries and millions of readers. Jansson never doubted that it was her comics which first endeared her Moomins to their most international audience yet.

Jansson had signed up for the daily strip expecting that it would leave her time to do more painting. But the pressure to keep supplying serials of around sixty to 100 episodes was constant. There was no rest, not even for the Moomins, who normally hibernate through winter. On the strip's first anniversary, Jansson interviewed Moomin for the paper, who revealed that he would be engaging in winter sports in the next story. Moomin also announced a following story introducing Moominmamma's maid, Misabel. Jansson

ABOVE

One of the very few published artworks for the strip to have survived, from 'Moomin on the Riviera', in which Jansson comments on the contradictions of the contemporary art world, 1955.

OVERLEAF, LEFT

A character sheet, made as part of Jansson's planning for her eighth story, 'Moomin Begins A New Life', 1956.

was clearly keeping ahead of the production schedules. She kept a tally, counting each panel from draft to publication, totalling '10,252' by late July 1956. Additionally, there were many decisions and designs for the Moomin merchandise boom she had so wished for, and the accompanying media and public appearances. She also felt it her duty to answer every reader's letter personally and by hand.

By the end of her thirteenth published story in April 1957, Jansson had crafted 900 uninterrupted solo strips. She intended her fourteenth story, 'Moomin and the Golden Tail', to be her farewell, but that meant breaking her contract with some two years to go. Jansson's brother Lars, who had long been translating her Swedish dialogues into English, stepped in to write a new fourteenth story with her, titled 'Moomin Goes Wild West'. Thereafter, Lars scripted a further seven stories for his sister to draw, the first four signed 'Jansson', the last three unsigned, bringing the total to twenty-one, told in 1,584 strips. Jansson reached her very last panel in July 1959, published without ceremony on New Year's Day, 1960. It shows Snorkmaiden pouring Dr Hatter's antidote for his shrinking pills onto a vanishing Moomintroll, wishing, 'Oh if he'll only be the same when he appears again.' He would be. Jansson's contract gave AN carte blanche to hire whoever they wanted to continue the strip, and the cartoonist John Jensen drew some samples. But ultimately, Lars had mastered enough of his sister's style to take over the drawing and keep it in the family. Signing his full name, he continued single-handed from 2 January 1960 to 16 April 1975, over three times Tove's printed output.

Jansson compared working in strips to 'a toothache' and 'a two-edged sword', but this 'dreadfully threadbare marriage' would live on in a series of book compilations. Bizarrely, the first of these to be published in English, in 1957, remained a one-off until 2006, when Canadian publishers Drawn & Quarterly began releasing the entire series, prompting more translations than ever. Jansson reconciled her personal regrets in the short story 'The Cartoonist' (1978), in which the creator of a fictional daily strip called 'Blubby' gets 'very tired', deserts his job and vanishes. When his successor tracks him down, they bond, and despite it all, the creator ends by offering to 'do a couple of strips. Sometime. If you'd

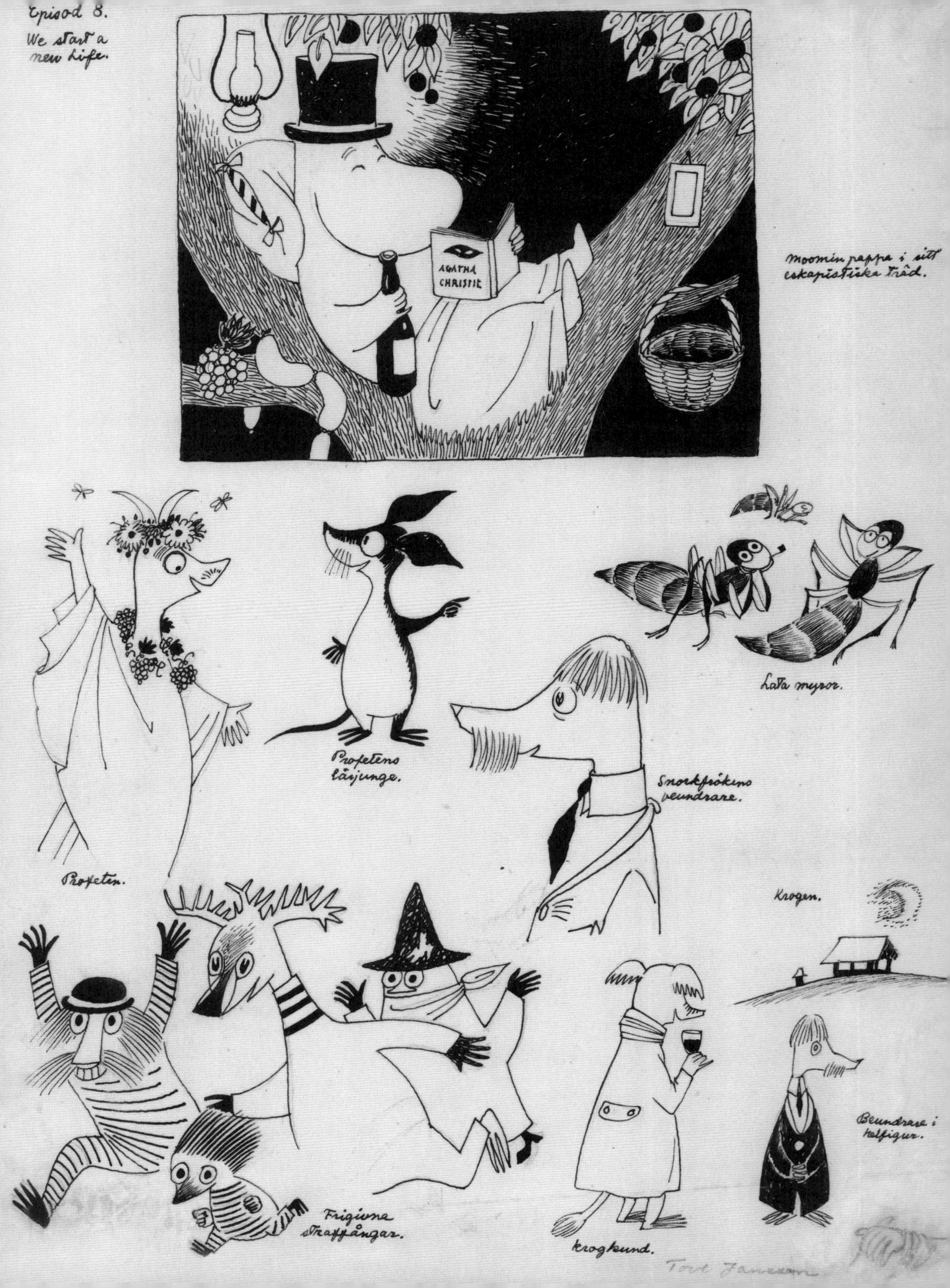

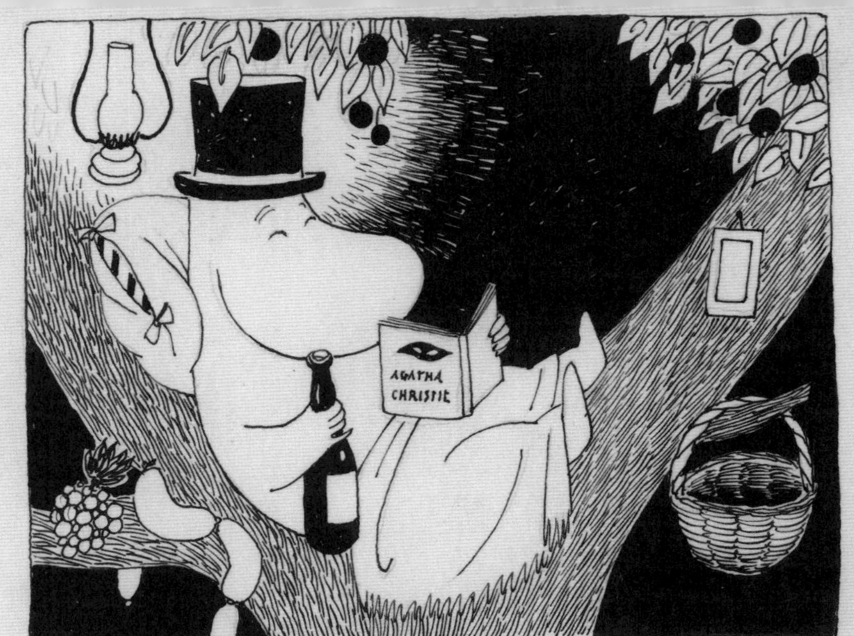

moomin pappa i sitt
eskapistiska Träd.

Profeten.

Profetens
lärjunge.

Lata myror.

Snorkfrökens
beundrare.

Krogen.

Frigivna
straffångar.

krogkund.

Beundrare i
helfigur.

Tove Jansson

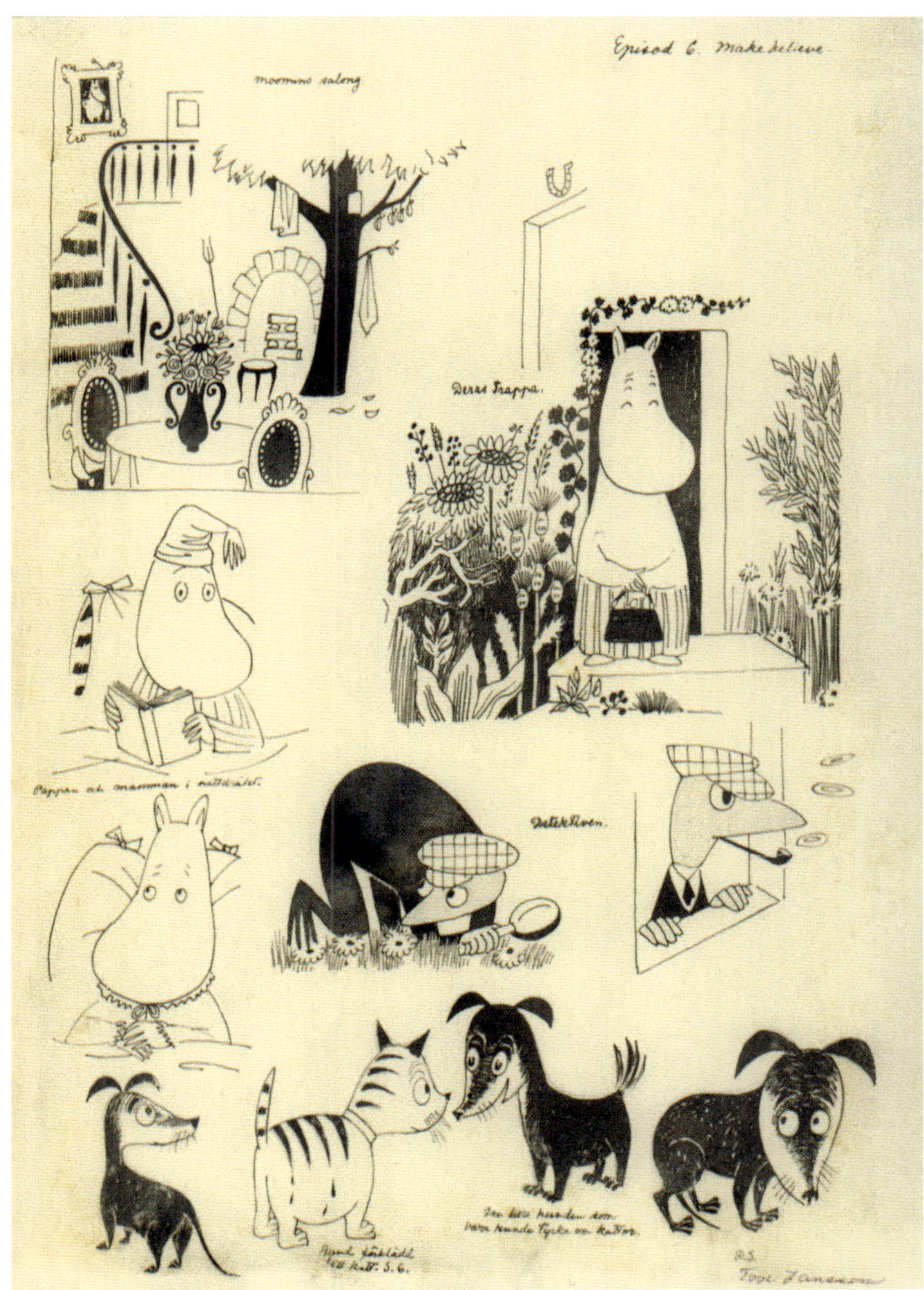

ABOVE

More preparatory designs for the sixth tale, re-titled *Moominmamma's Maid*, 1956.

like….' In contrast, Jansson never returned to the medium; one wonders what gems she might have created had she realized the opportunities of the authorial graphic novel.

Other opportunities

Even at her busiest, Jansson made time for other projects, not least her fifth and sixth Moomin novels, *Farlig Midsommar* (*Dangerous Midsummer*, 1954; published in English as *Moominsummer Madness*) and *Trollvinter* (*Trollwinter*, 1957; published in English as *Moominland Midwinter*). She also took up opportunities that came through Vivica Bandler. In July 1952, Bandler involved Jansson in an exclusive party for dignitaries visiting Helsinki for the Olympic Games, held in the Handelsgillet or private Trade Guild, their Bridge Room converted into a chic pop-up nightclub called 'Le Club de Sauna'. Among the guest performers was the Creole chanteuse and pianist Moune de Rivel, born in Bordeaux of Guadeloupian parents, whom Bandler interviewed in Jansson's studio for the women's magazine *Eeva*. Jansson befriended de Rivel, and at the soirée captured her performance in a drawing for Bandler's report in the Guild members' magazine. The article disclosed that 'The Duke of Edinburgh arrived late and wanted to go on partying till after 3am'.

A reportage drawing from an exclusive musical party at Le Club de Sauna, from the Handelsgillet's house magazine, 1952. The singer Moune de Rivel is shown in profile with a glass of wine in her hand.

Snufkin with Little My on his hat and little Woodies at his feet from *Moominsummer Madness*, 1954.

Character sketches of Snufkin and Little My for a Stockholm production of *Moomintroll in the Wings*, 1982.

Moomin meets an absent-minded squirrel in *Moominland Midwinter*, 1957.

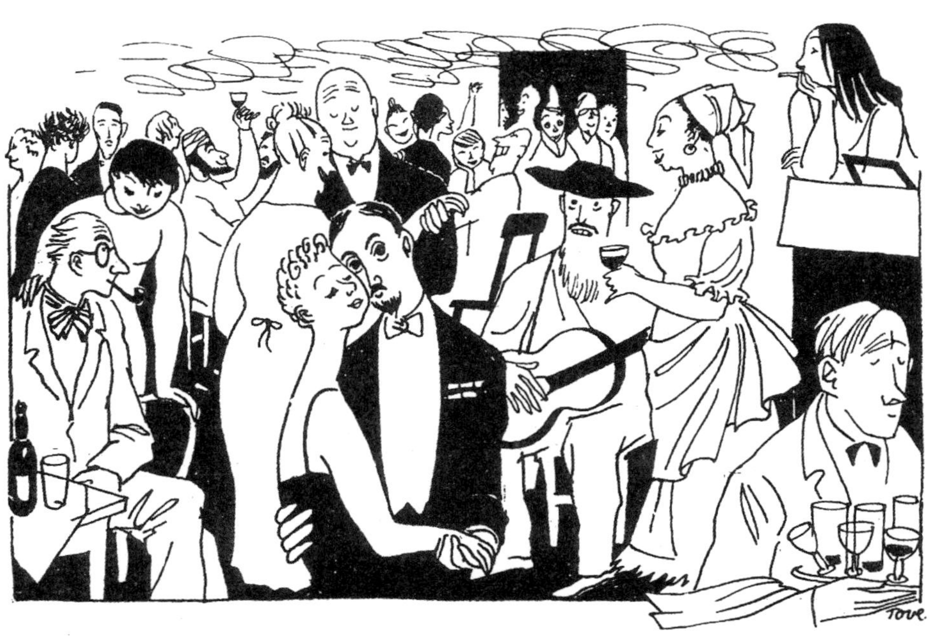

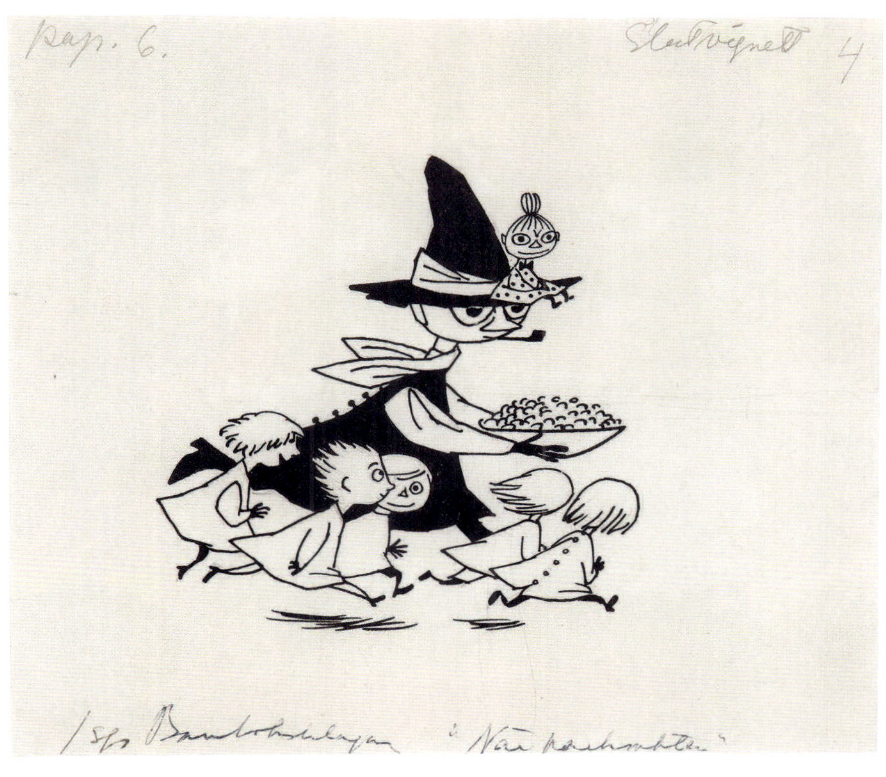

pap. 6.
Slutvignett   4

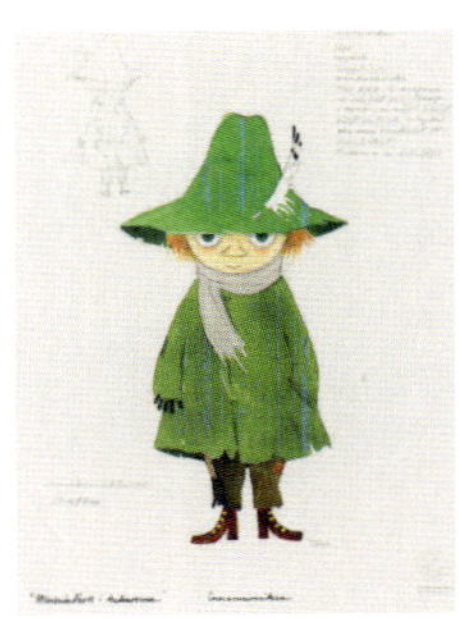

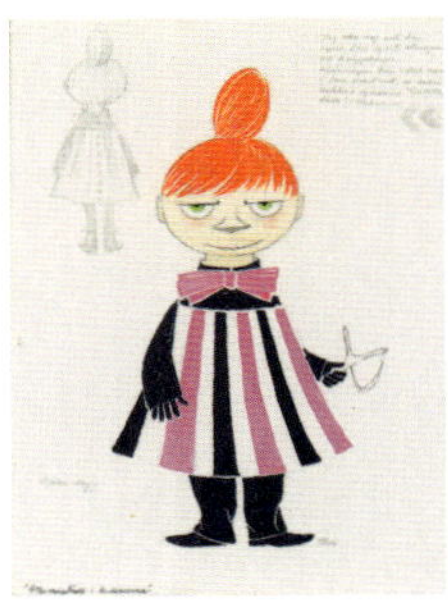

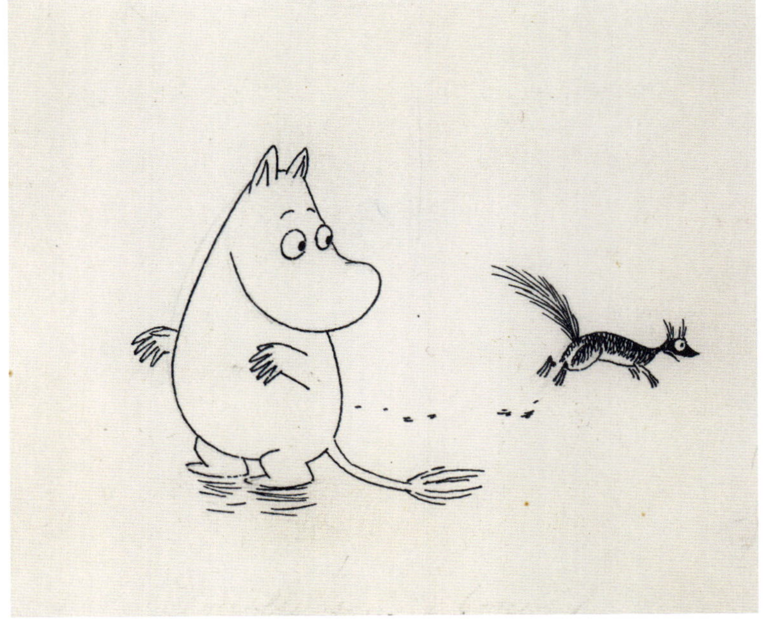

Jansson entrusted Bandler to proof drafts of every
Moomin novel and revised them based on her feedback,
dedicating the theatrical *Moominsummer Madness* to
'Vivica'. The partnership returned to the stage in 1958, when
Jansson wrote another play, *Troll i kulisserna* (*Troll in the
Wings*), again designing the costumes. Jansson juggled a
startling amount, in both her work and her love life. Bandler
had been her first, fiercest flame, followed by other female
'mymbles', a codeword in Jansson's circle for former lovers of
either sex. But in 1952, she fell for the goldsmith Britt-Sofie
Fock, who moved in. For several years they lived as a couple,
by necessity discreetly, and worked side-by-side, Jansson
sketching and painting 'Bitti' in several portraits. Then, at
a Christmas party in 1955, Jansson met Tuulikki Pietilä, to
whom she became increasingly close. The American-born

A portrait of Britt-Sofie Fock seated
at her typewriter, 1954.

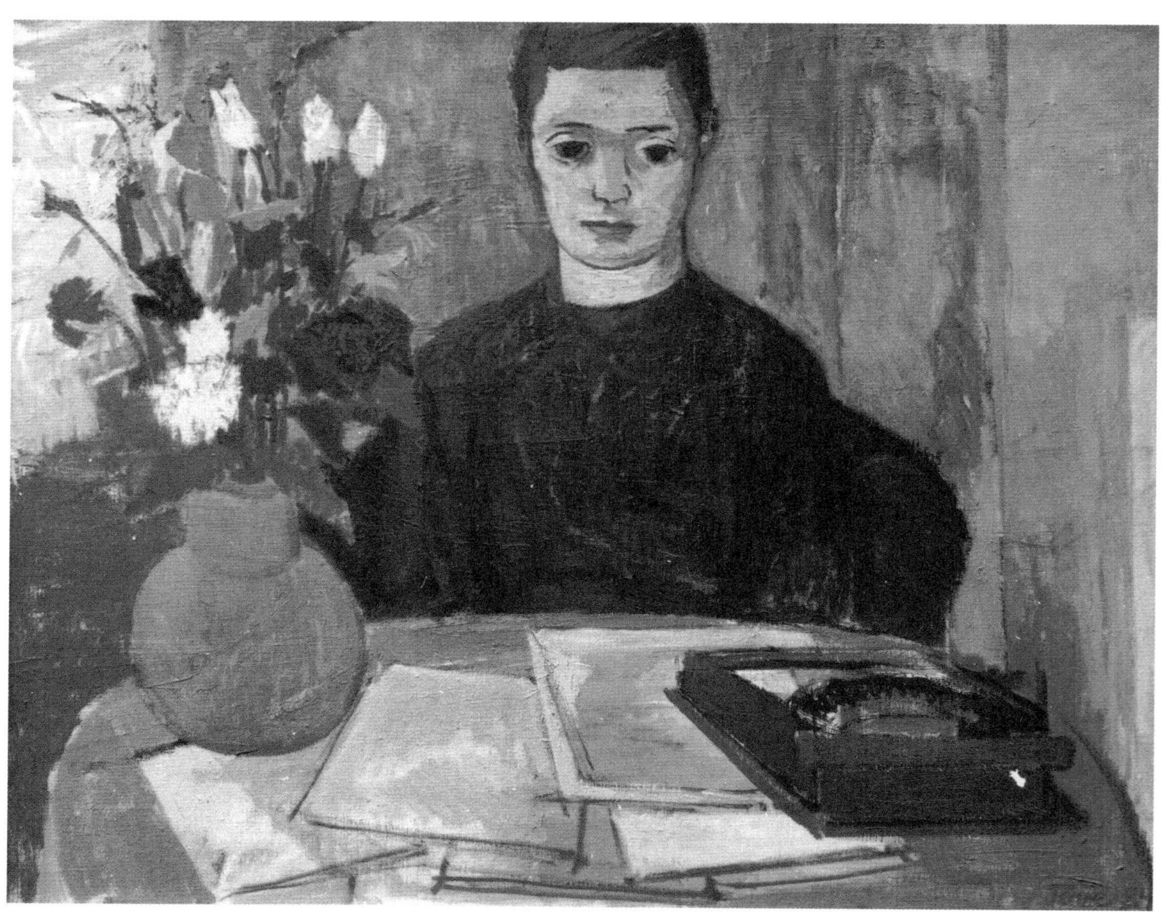

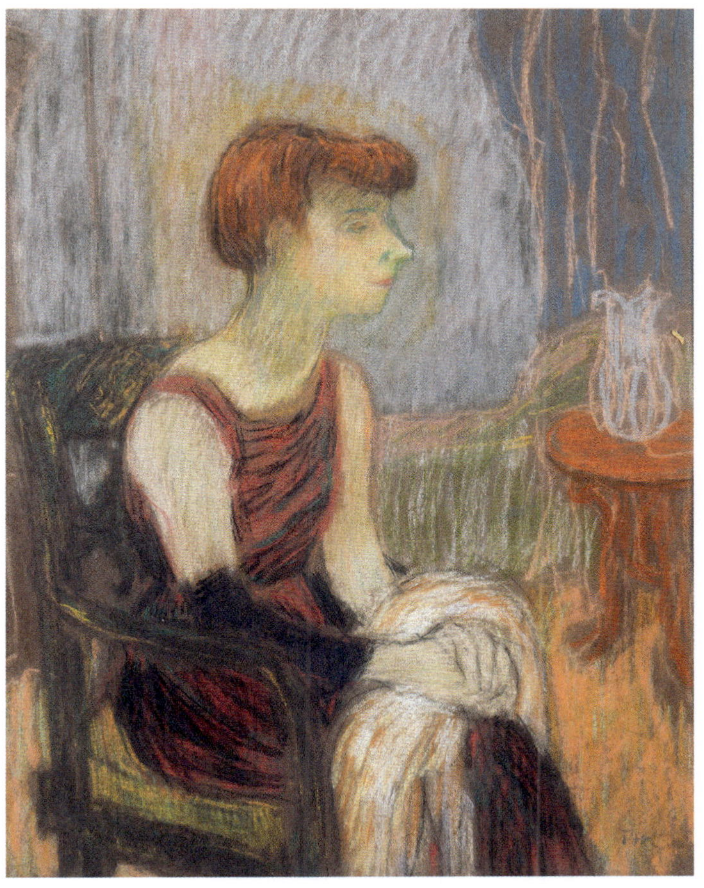

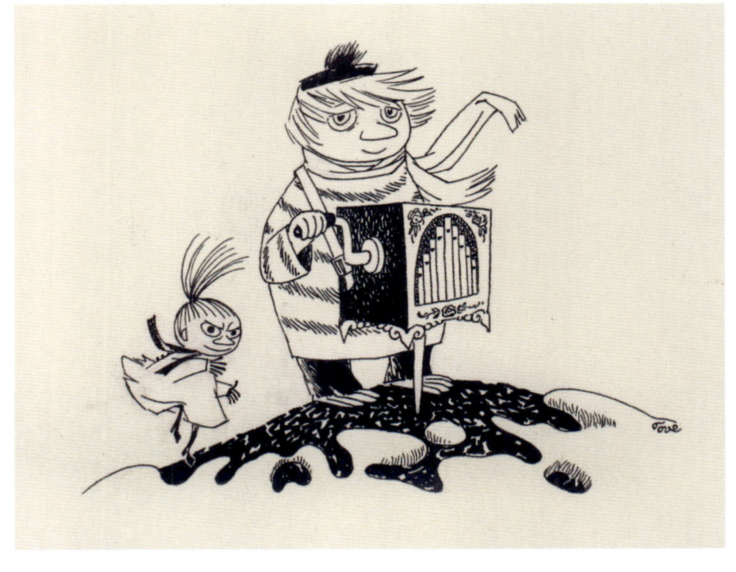

ABOVE
An early portrait of Tuulikki Pietilä in pastels, showing the influence of Toulouse Lautrec.

RIGHT
Tuulikki 'Tooti' Pietilä helped inspire 'Too-ticky', here playing her barrel organ in *Moominland Midwinter*, 1957.

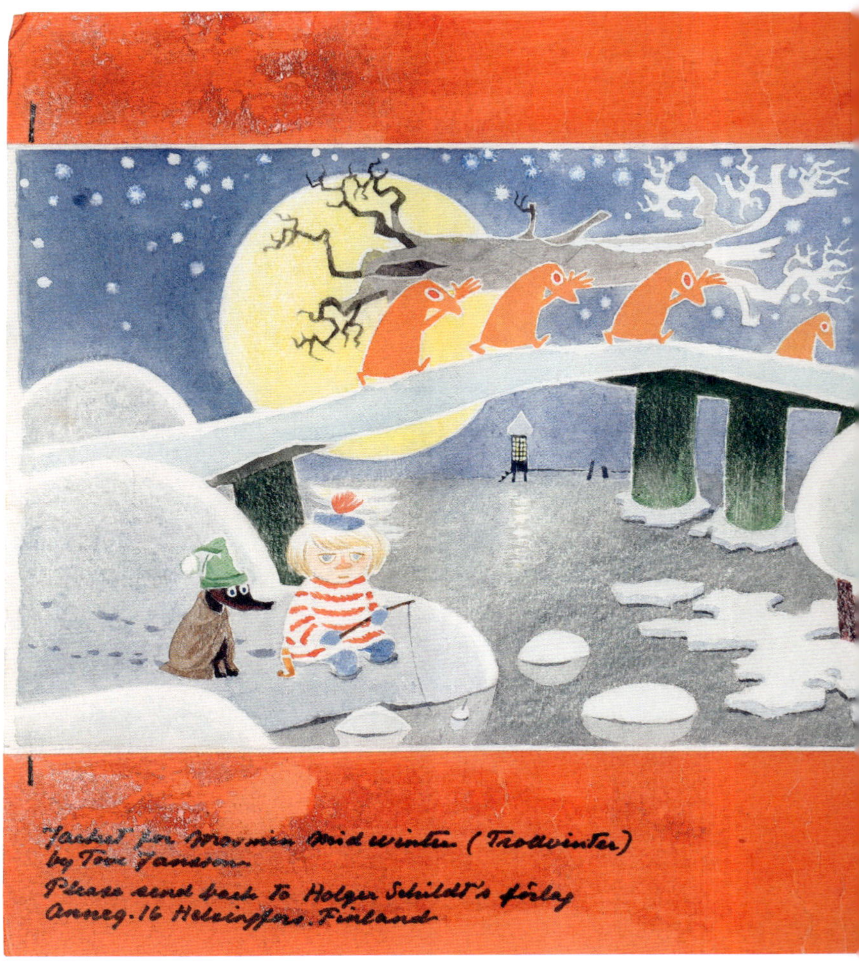

Finnish graphic artist was two-and-a-half years younger, an ex-Konstfack student like Jansson, and already a successful graphic artist and engraver. Jansson nicknamed her 'Tooti' and took inspiration from her to introduce the character 'Too-ticky' in *Moominland Midwinter*. The couple would share the next forty-five years together.

Throughout the 1950s, as well as producing large public murals and wall paintings, Jansson made new works for her third solo gallery exhibition. Further

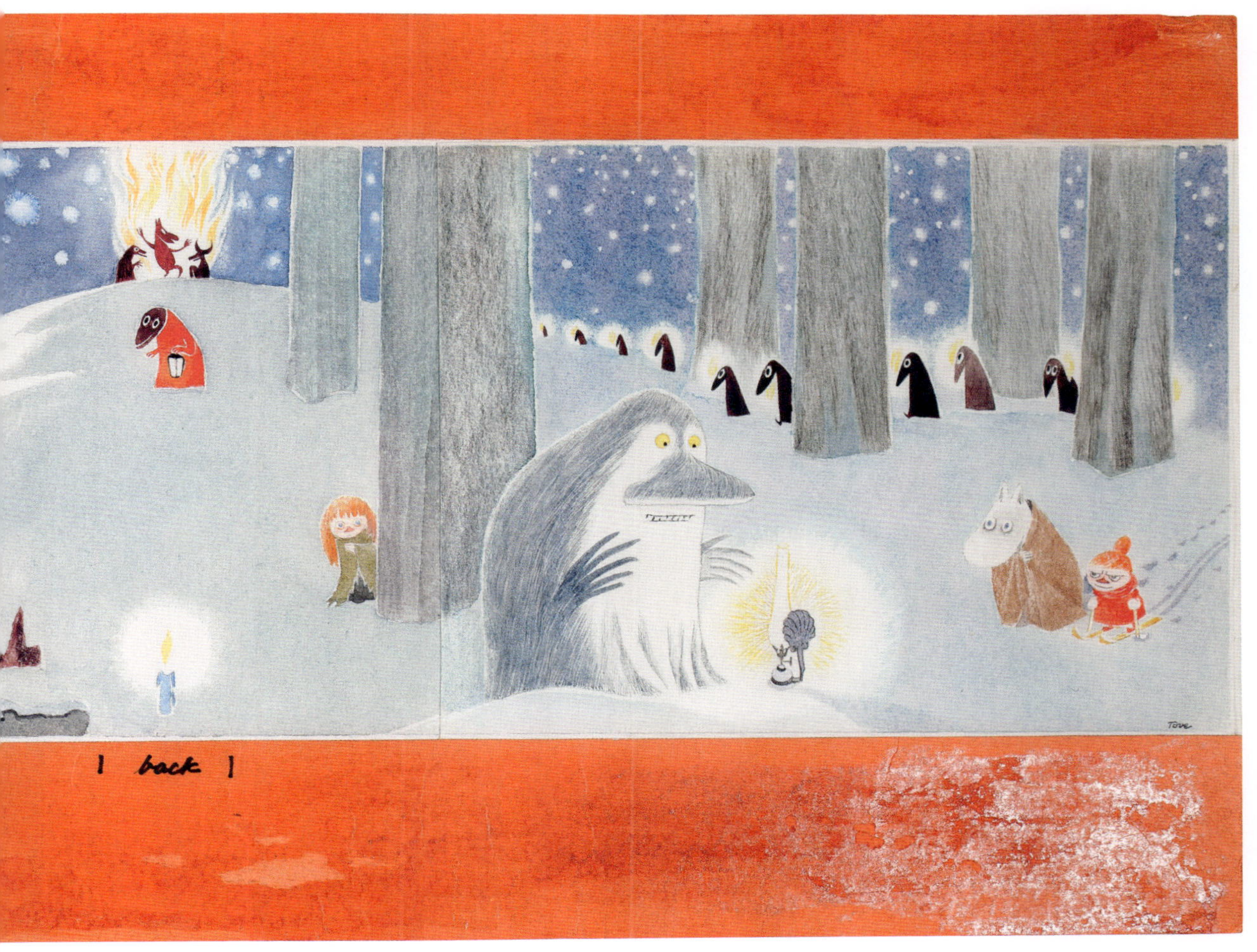

painting, however, mostly had to wait amid the escalating, profitable Moomin boom. One of its most unlikely and presumably well-paid spin-offs was a Moomin picture book in the form of a brochure to encourage children to join the Föreningsbanken's savings club. In 1954, the bank commissioned Jansson to paint a three-metre-wide (9⅞ ft) utopian canvas entitled *Fantasia*. Two years later, she was hired again, this time to write and draw ten black-and-white press advertisements, each an episode of a serial featuring

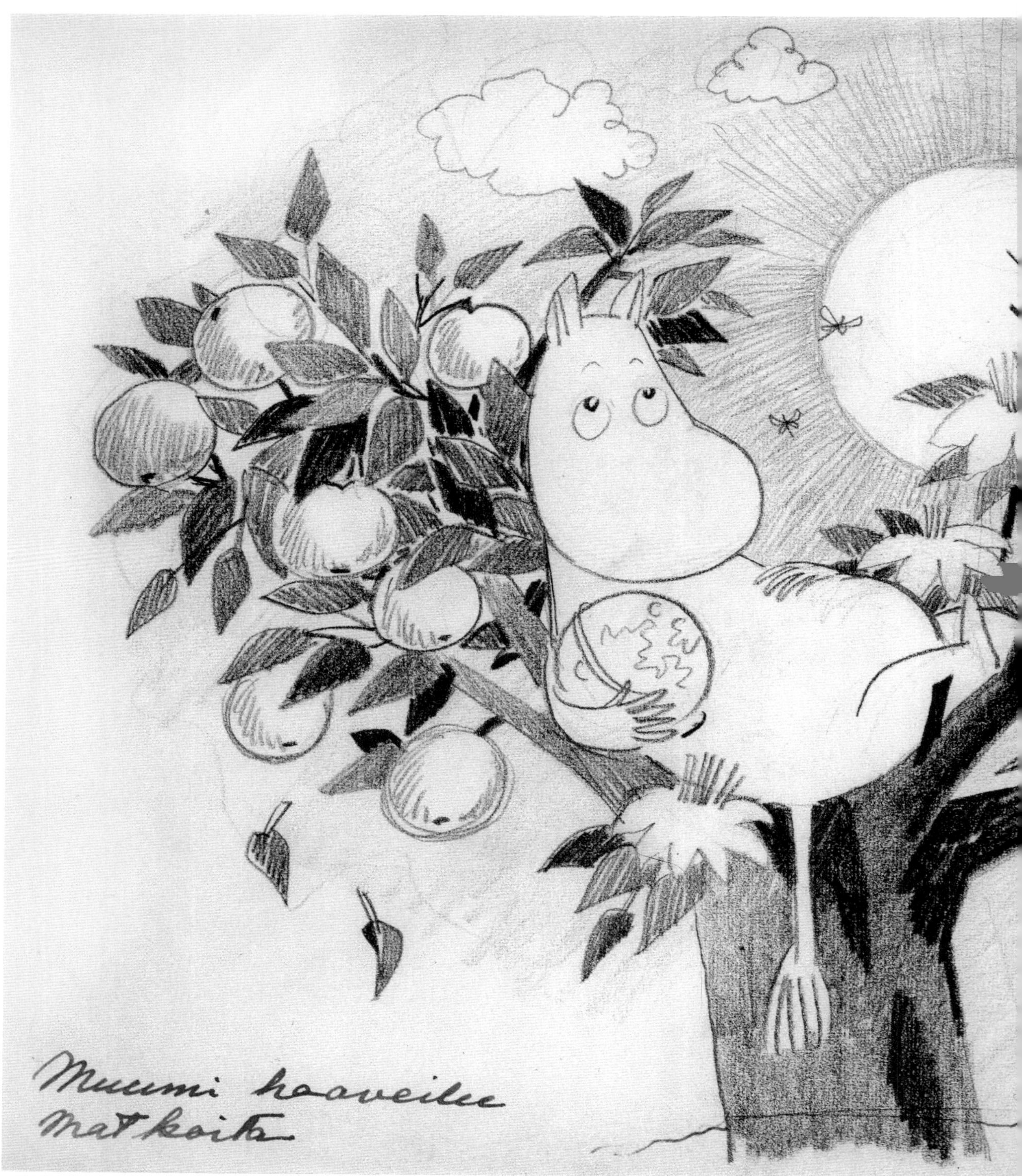

Muumi haaveilee
matkoita

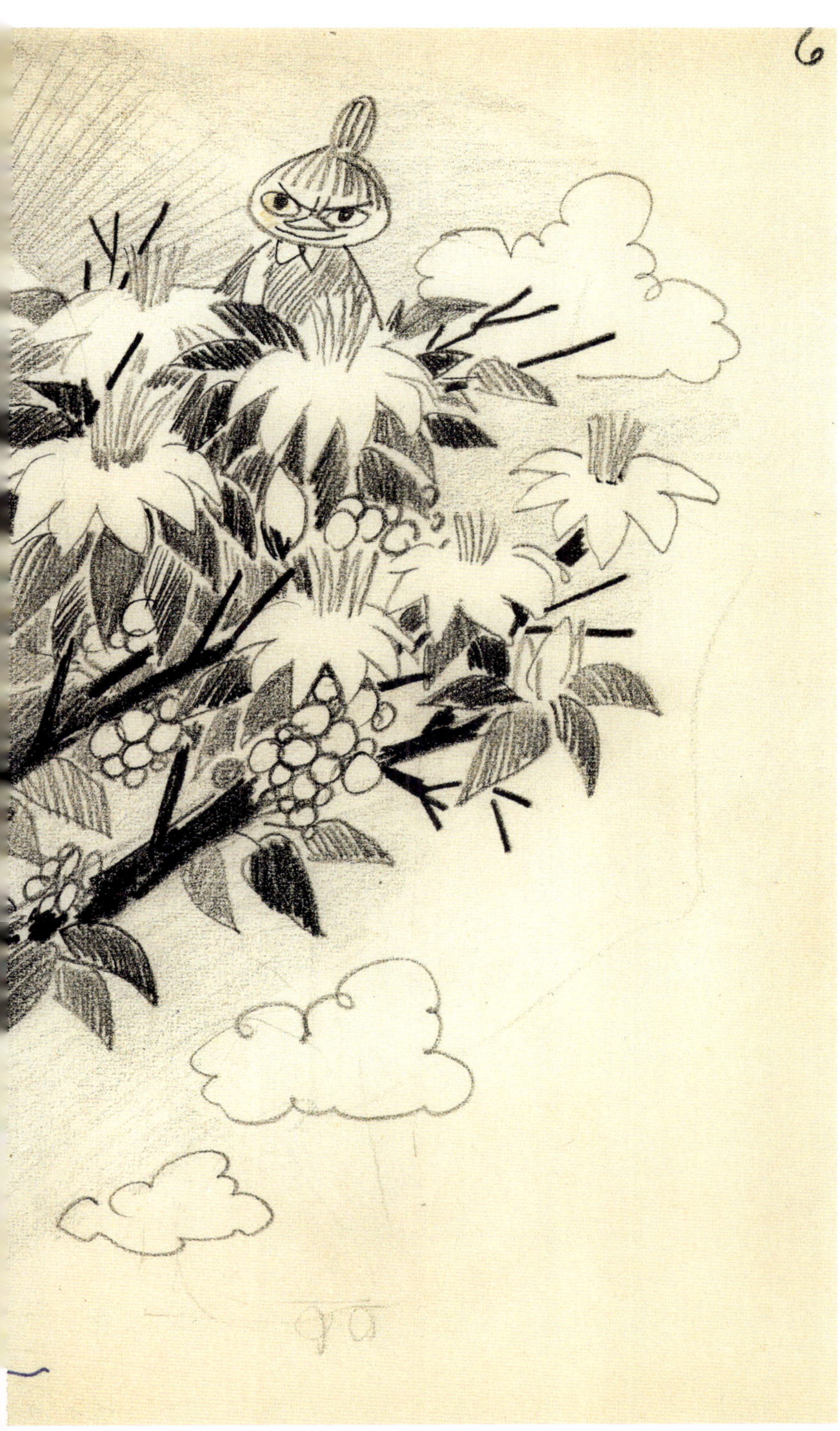

LEFT

Sketch in pencil for a
Föreningsbanken advertisement
of their children's savings account,
reprised in the promotional
booklet, 1956.

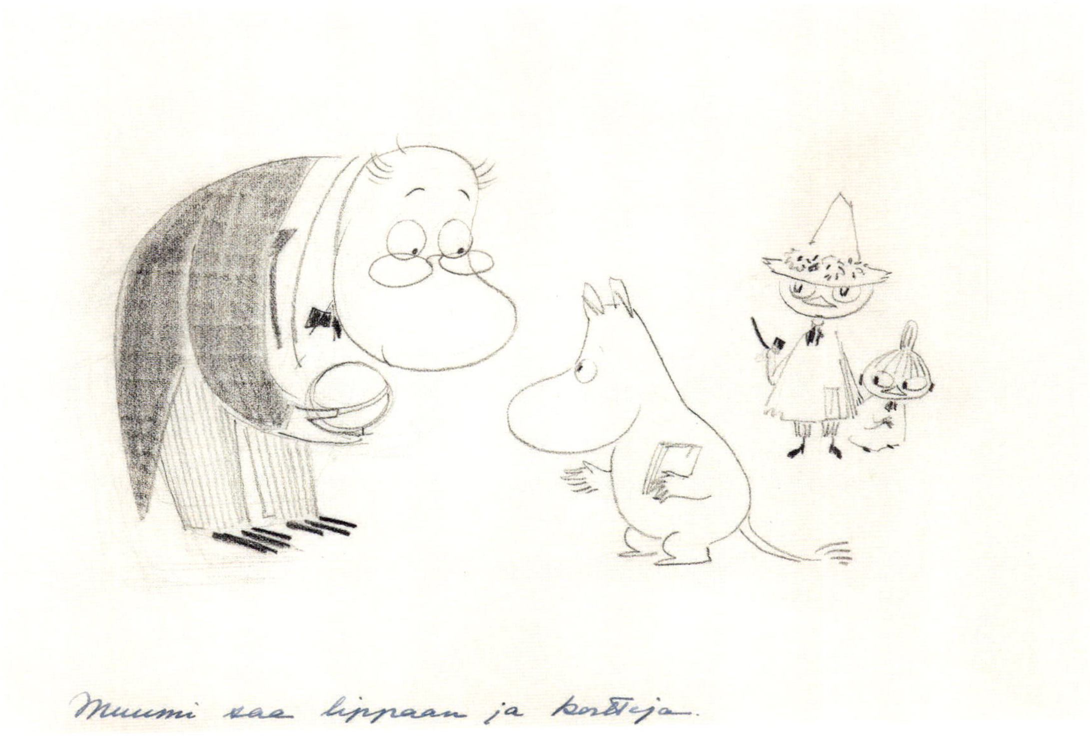

her cast and a new character, a Hemulen called 'The Bank
Uncle'. In a story written to the bank's brief, Moomintroll
has to earn money by delivering flowers in order to deposit
the 500 marks for the bank's blue-and-gold 'money globe' to
save up for a gift for Snorkmaiden. He even goes to school,
where, helped by the bank's free picture-cards, he excels
in geography. Despite the constraints of the commission,
Jansson drew splendidly, topping most pages with a large
scene and a little frieze across the bottom, all in pen and
ink. When they were reprinted as a booklet, she added
an enticing colour cover, showing Moomintroll on top of
the world, envisaging his global success, while Little My
reclined within the petals of a red rose, a recurring motif
of Jansson's.

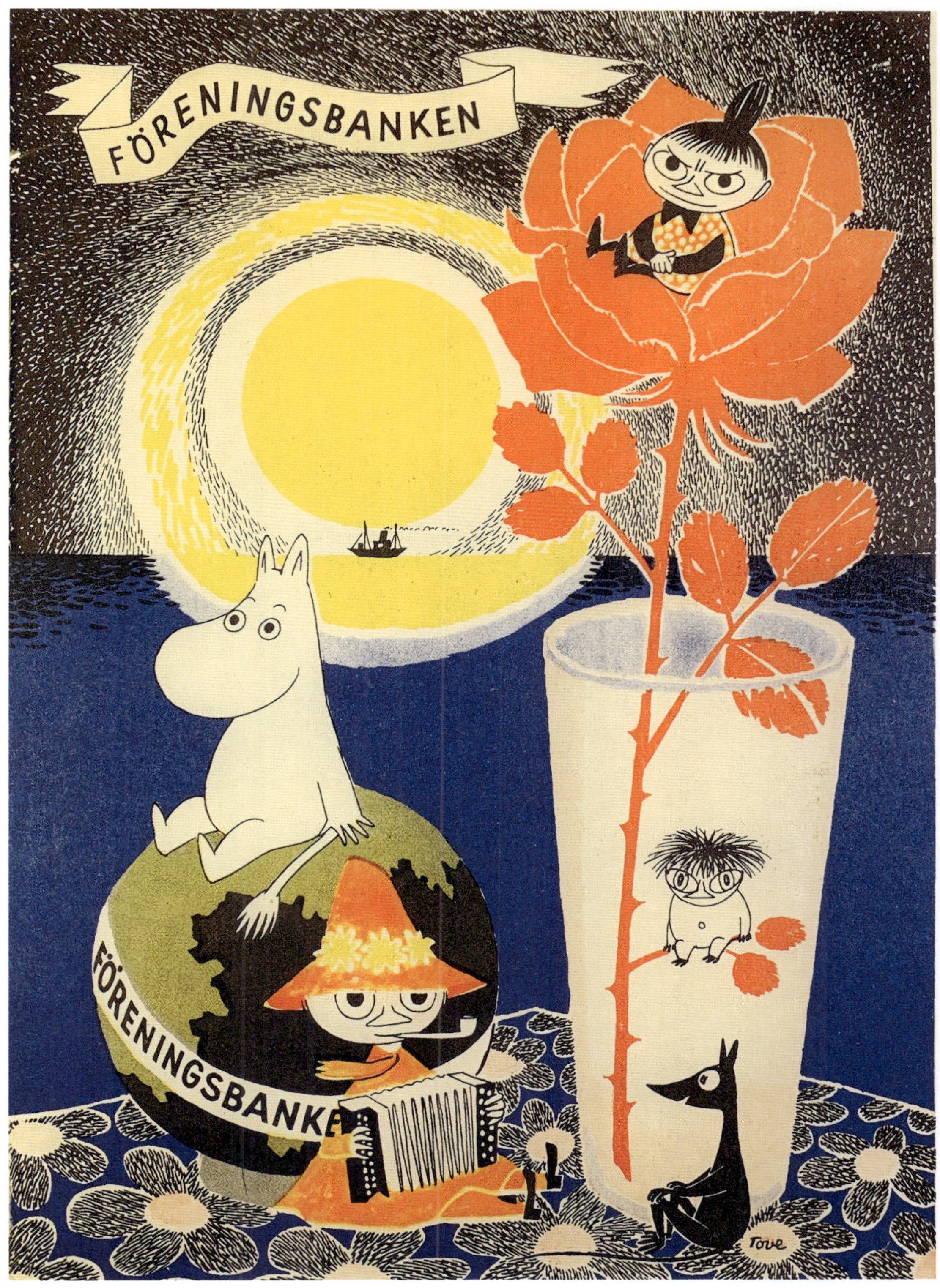
FÖRENINGSBANKEN
FÖRENINGSBANKEN
Tove

Illustrating the classics

To demonstrate her versatility beyond the Moomins, Jansson
jumped at three invitations to 'have a go at the classics' and
illustrate books by Lewis Carroll and J.R.R. Tolkien, authors
who, like her, drew as well as wrote their stories. In 1958,
she embarked on Carroll's absurd poem *The Hunting of the
Snark* (1876), which was 'as far as I know, never illustrated
before', and was finally receiving a Swedish translation.
In fact, it had been illustrated since its first edition by
Henry Holiday, followed by others, notably Mervyn Peake.
Unaware of her predecessors, Jansson knew how youngsters
enjoy being 'spellbound by what's unspoken and disguised'
and 'delight in the gruesome and macabre'.[7] She exaggerated

Illustration for the front cover of
The Hunting of the Snark, 1958.

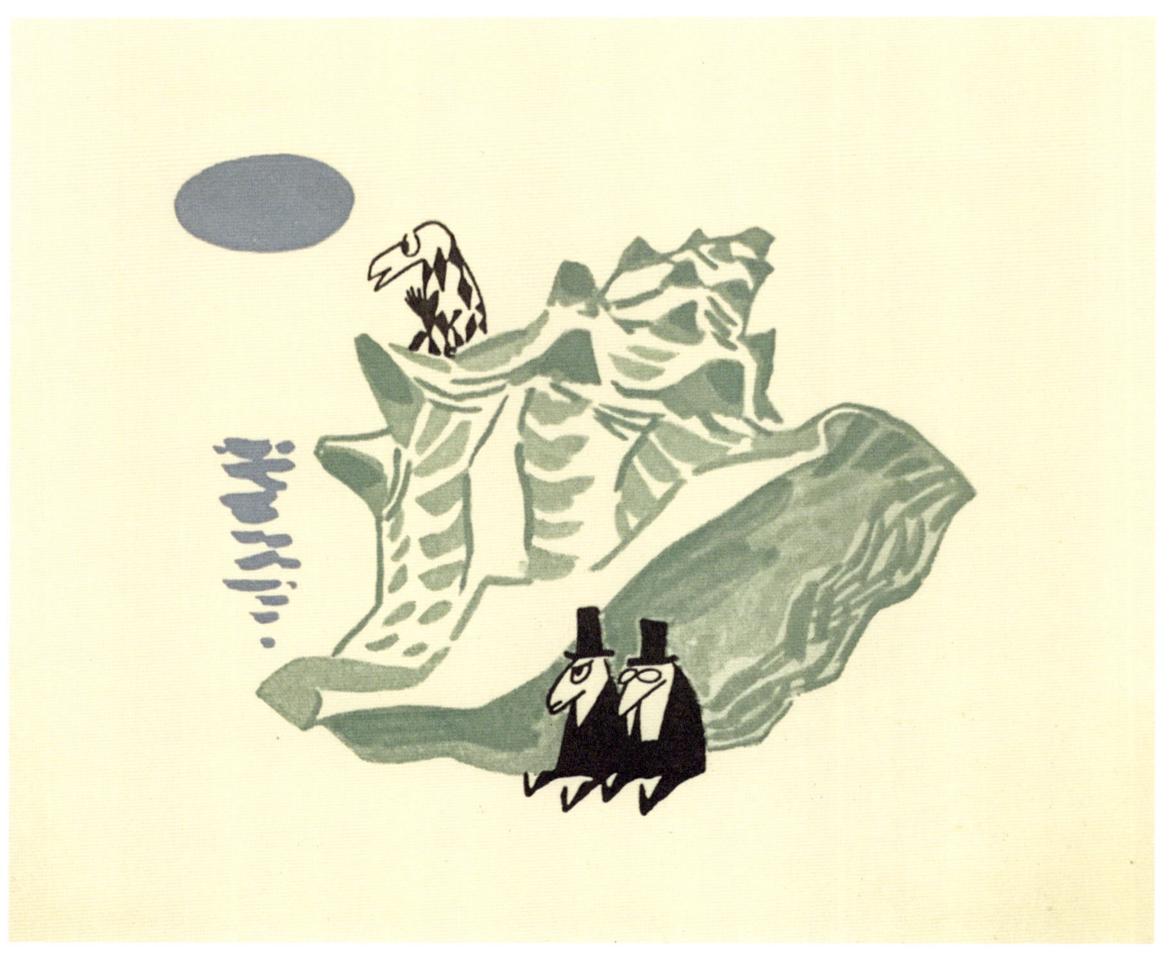

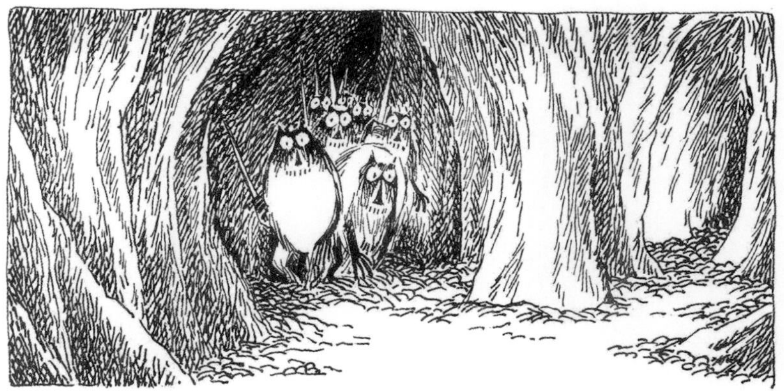

A sketch for an illustration in
The Hobbit, 1962.

Trial versions of Bilbo Baggins
sitting by the fire for *The Hobbit*,
1962.

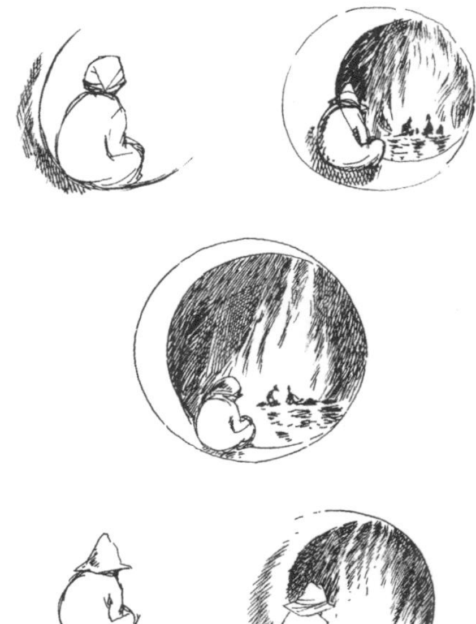

the difference in scale between the small, vulnerable crew
and the monsters, who are barely hidden within their
gargantuan surroundings.

Tolkien's *The Hobbit* in 1962 marked a more conscious
effort 'to free myself of Moomin-style lines and carefully
filled-in surfaces'. Jansson strove for still greater
spontaneity (or the appearance thereof) by drawing figures
repeatedly, some up to sixty times, 'till it looked fairly free'.
Rather than staying literal, she crafted her own impressions
of the landscapes, often turbulent and overwhelming, and
reinterpreted Tolkien's characters. Her Gollum towered
monstrously large, to the surprise of Tolkien himself, who
realized that he had never clarified Gollum's size and so
amended the second edition to describe him as 'a small,
slimy creature'.

Any illustrator of *Alice in Wonderland* faces the
monument of Tenniel's defining imagery, also an influence
on Jansson. When a Swedish translation in 1966 demanded
new illustrations of Carroll's cast, she asked the publisher,
'Can I draw them in a horror style? The way I saw them
when I was little.' Although she was still constrained by the
commission, her sixty-two images, fifty black and white in
ink and twelve glowing in colourful brushstrokes, conveyed
the book's heightened reality. By maturing her Alice to a
pre-adolescent girl and spotlighting parts of the text that
Tenniel had never tackled, she invited readers into another
Wonderland that was both Carroll's and her own, recalling
her childhood frissons.

The Moomin boom

By the dawn of the 1960s, Jansson's 'Moomin-minded'
philosophy was being widely discussed among local students
and literati. Among her champions was Lars Bäckström, a
Swedish poet and critic, who included an essay in praise of
Jansson in his first collection in 1959. For this she drew the
cover, which seems to represent not only Bäckström's theme

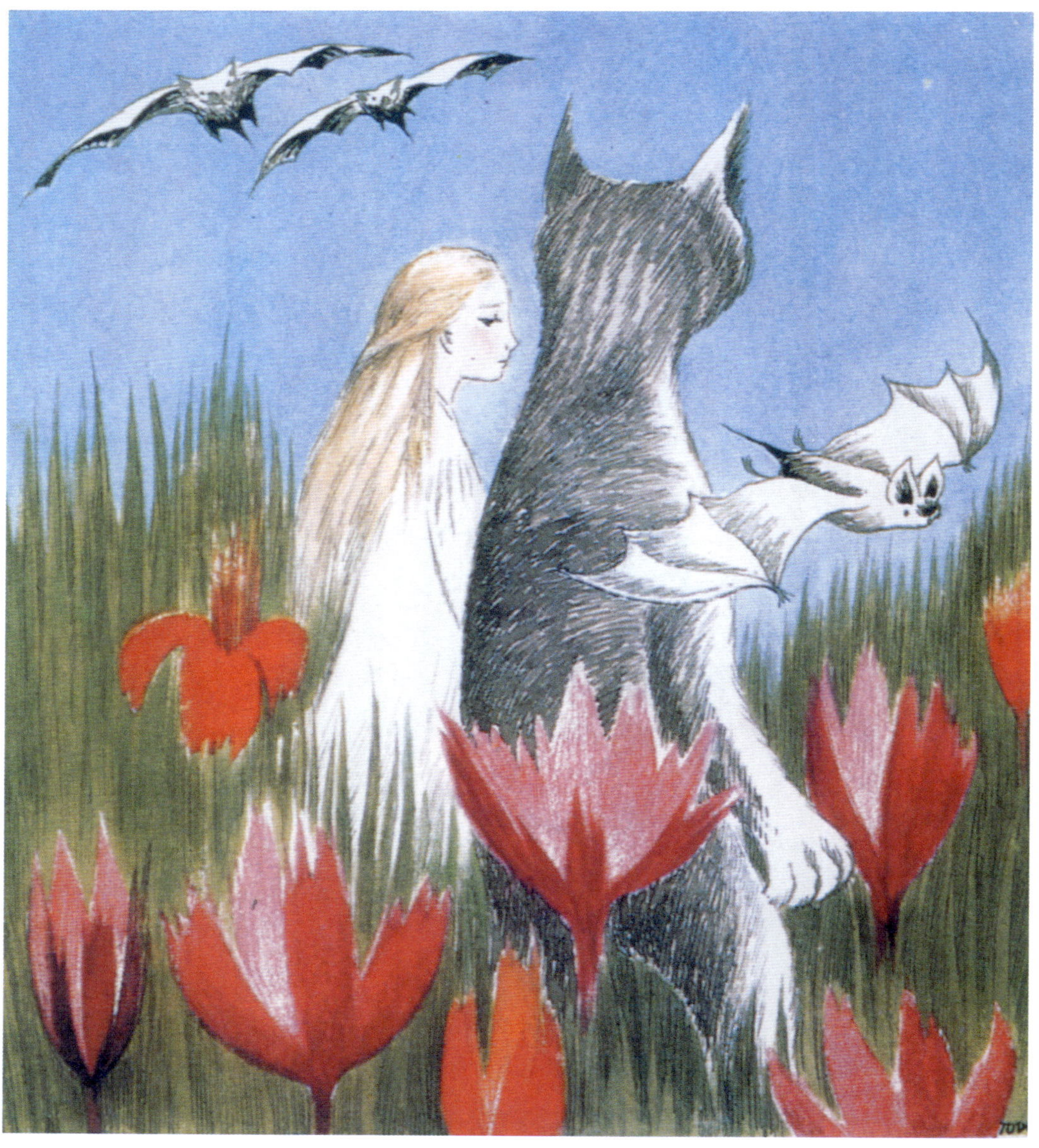

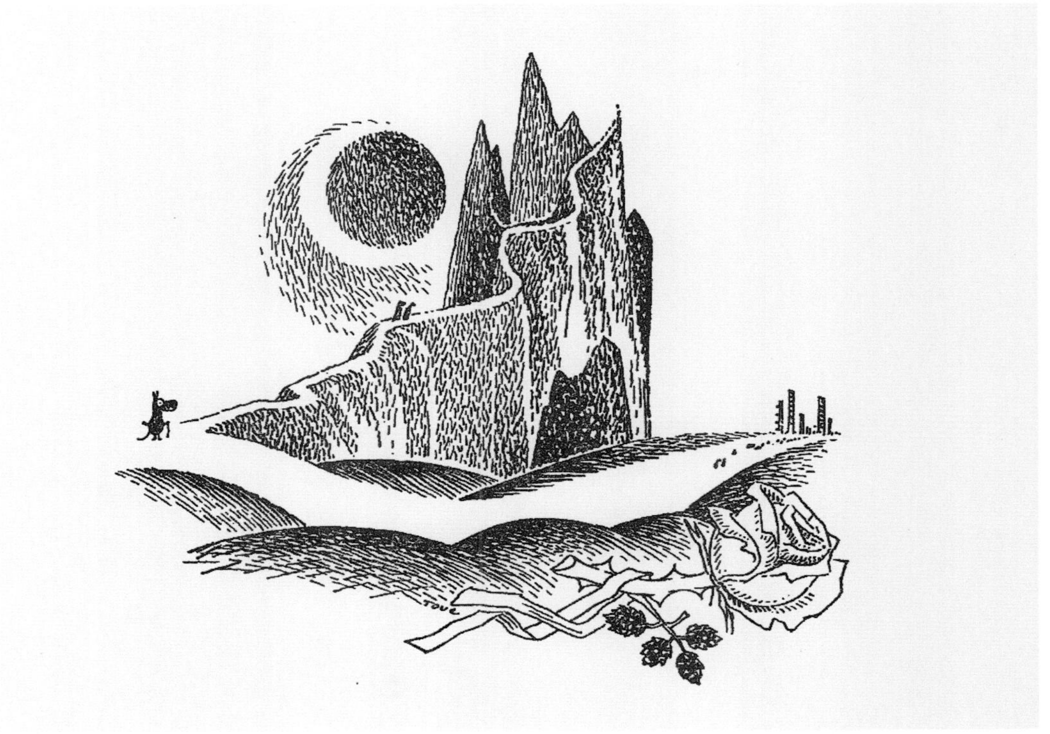

OPPOSITE

A mixed-media Alice and the Cheshire Cat from *Alice in Wonderland*, 1966.

ABOVE

Illustration for the front cover of Lars Bäckström's edited essay collection, *Under Välfärdens Yta: Litterärt under femtitalet* (*Beneath the Veneer of Well-Being: The Literary in the Fifties*), 1959.

but also the forks in the road of Jansson's life and creativity. She shows a Moomin, wide-eyed with his walking cane, deciding whether to take the perilous path up to a sublime peak, with only three others ahead of him, or join the crowds on the flat highway, pouring into a man-made metropolis. It summarizes the dilemma between following the crowd or choosing one's own way and accepting, even embracing uncertainty. In the foreground reclines her symbolic 'wind rose' in bloom. After the first four months of 1960, Jansson was delighted: 'I've done more paintings than the previous ten years'. But so many opportunities and choices lay ahead, not only in the Moomins' worldwide popularity, but also in a possible career as a writer for adults. How does someone so gifted choose only one road?

Jansson's last three Moomin novels presage her shift in ambition and audience by addressing adults as much as children. *Tales from Moominvalley* was her first collection of short stories, nine in all, in which Jansson taps into her depression and self-suppressed anger by examining her individual characters' sometimes troubled psychology and relationships. Her allegory of 'The Invisible Child' perfectly visualizes the erasing effects of a lack of love on a child's development and identity. Jansson had just become an aunt again, and she dedicated the book to her niece Sophia, the newborn daughter of Lars and his wife, the singer Nita Lesch.

Jansson dedicated her penultimate Moomin novel, *Pappa och havet* (*Pappa and the Sea*), non-specifically 'to some father'. It was evidently in memory of Faffan, who had died

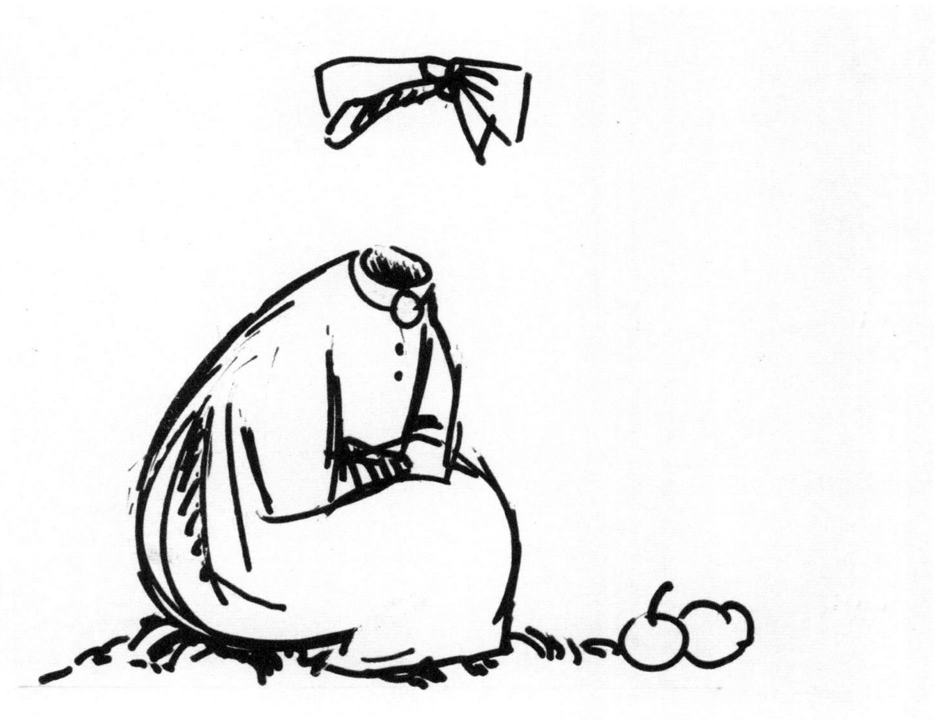

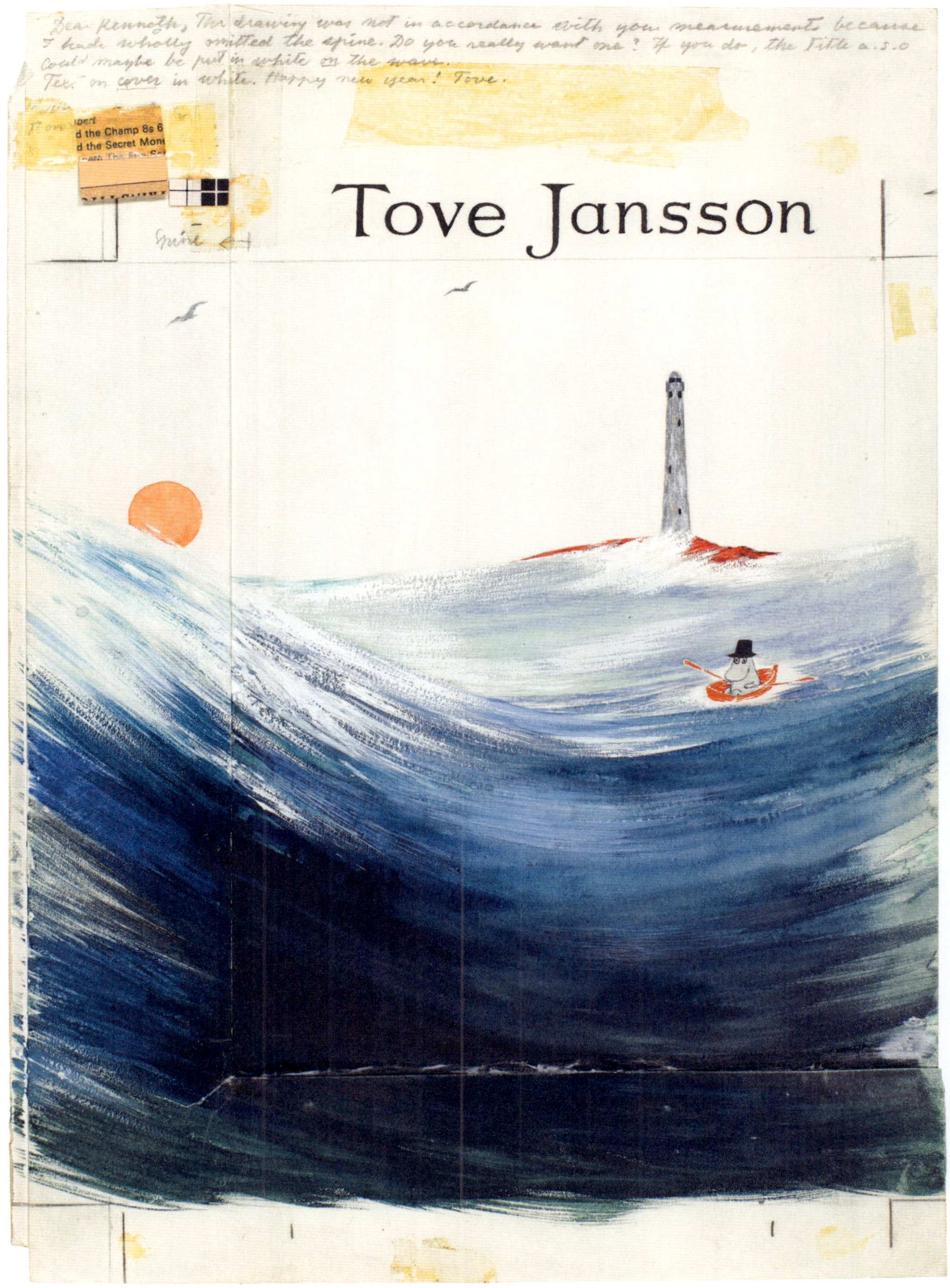
Dear Kennoth, The drawing was not in accordance with you mesurements because I had wholly omitted the spine. Do you really want one? If you do, the Title a.s.o Could maybe be put in white on the wave.
Tex." on cover in white. Happy new year! Tove.
Tove Jansson

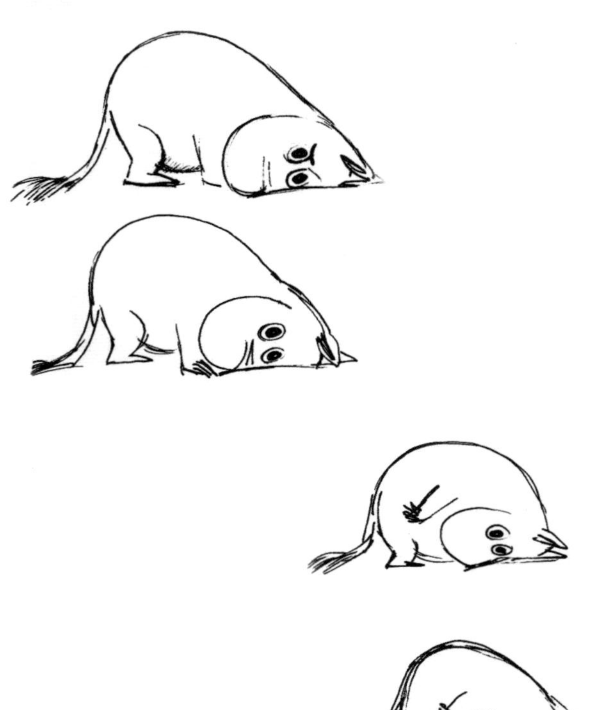

LEFT AND BELOW
Four trial sketches of
Moominpappa with his ear to
the ground, and the final version
published in *Moominpappa at Sea*.

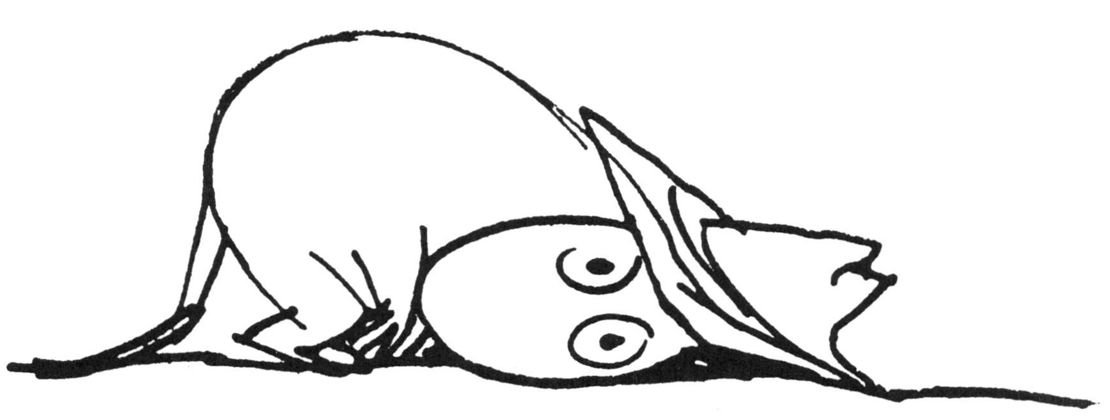

in 1958, and again she used storytelling as an outlet for repressed feelings. In a letter to Bäckström, she described it as 'a condensing of my own Grokes, and the bare bones of it are a kind of search for my sculptor father who died many years ago'. The English title *Moominpappa at Sea* adds a double meaning about the manly paterfamilias, who gets out of his depth after he uproots his family to live in a remote island lighthouse. When striving for a figure's precise expression and body language, Jansson would redraw it over and over. Four sketches of a turning point towards the end of the novel reveal her thinking, as she tried to define Moominpappa with his ear to the ground, so 'he could hear the island's heart beating'. Her final version is different again, showing him with a hat on his head, his eyes wide with wonder: 'Everything is alive.' A sculptor's daughter had found her father again.

The 1960s would crescendo in an even greater Moomin craze. Luckily, Jansson could rely on her brother Lars' help, from handling the daily strips to dealing with licensing proposals, 'at least five calls from abroad every day.' To cope, ahead of the launch in 1969 of their co-written, live-action series on Swedish television, the siblings set up a registered company, Moomin Characters. The same year, the first Moomin drawn animation series proved a big hit on Japan's only television channel, though they were not approved in advance, nor for later broadcast outside Japan. Jansson was amazed: 'I hadn't realized just how important TV is to people'.

Nevertheless, amidst all the commercialization, Jansson would also draw the Moomins for causes she supported, big and small. In 1960, twenty students in Lund, Sweden, donated their earnings from a day's work at a factory to foreign aid, and their 'Operation Dagsverke' (Operation Day's Work) spread. In 1964, she was one of sixteen writers and artists invited to contribute a new piece, their 'day's work', to the students' fundraising anthology. She drew Moomintroll for the cover in Peruvian dress, in honour of one of the beneficiary countries. Jansson also drafted five proposals for fifty-penny Finnish stamps, Ham's speciality, but they went no further, as she felt the figures were 'too small'.

Dagsverket

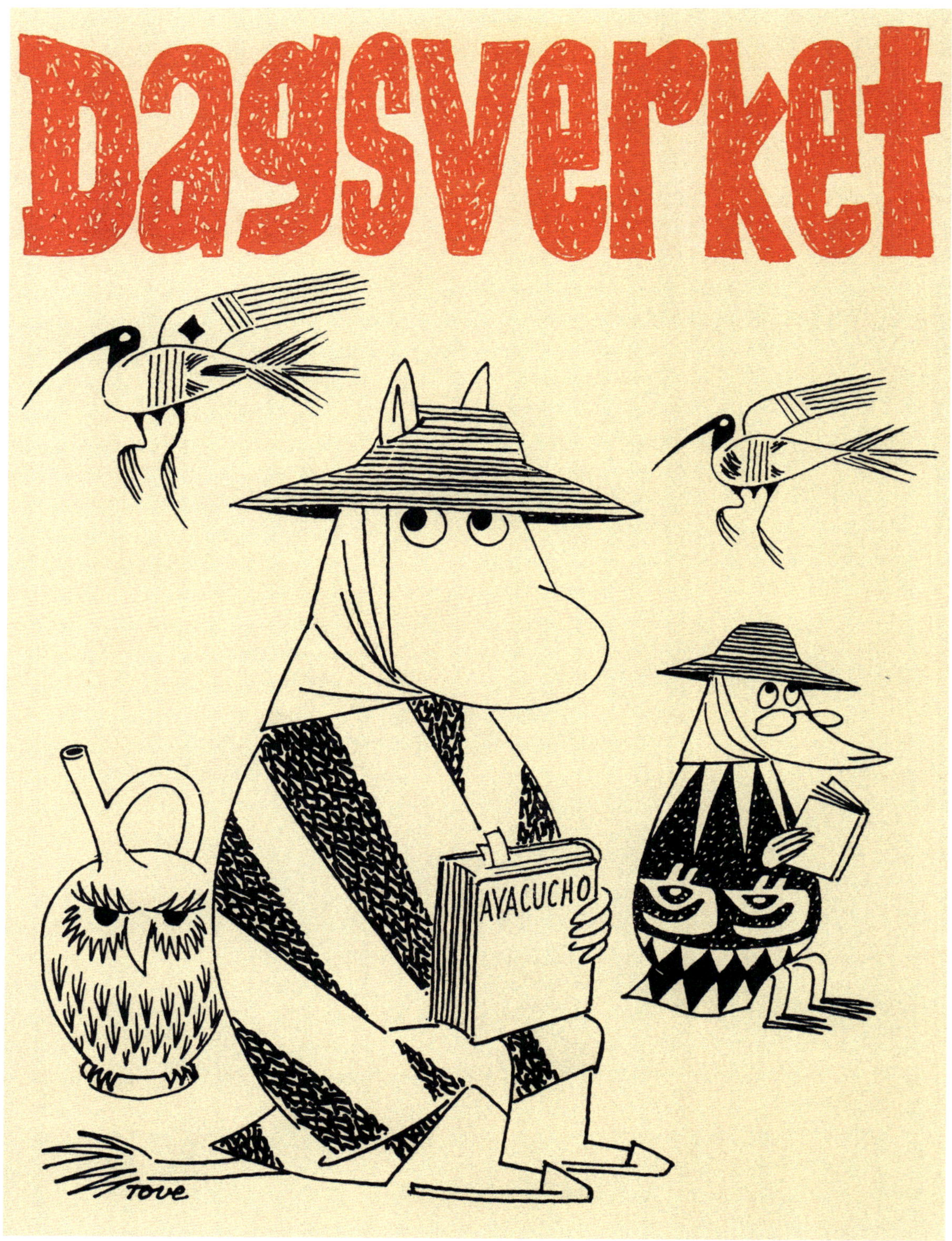

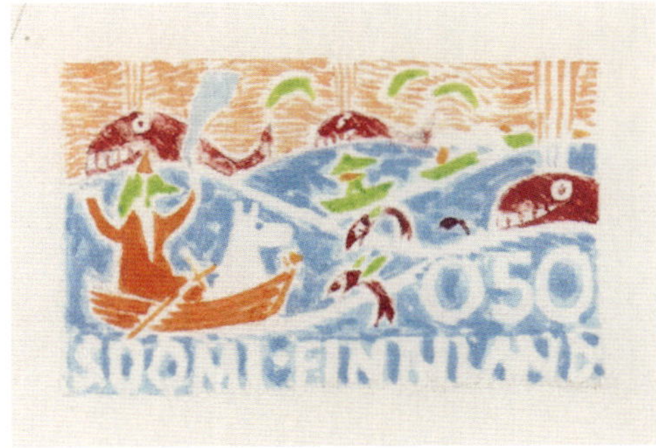
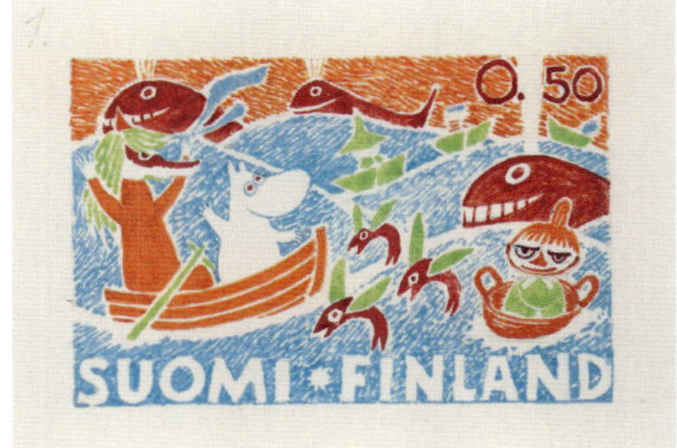
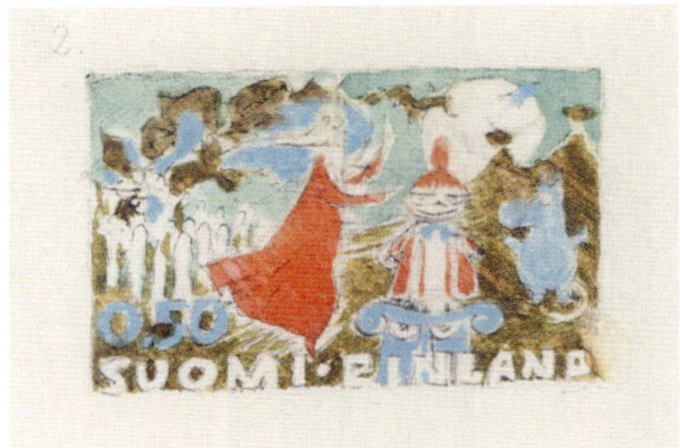
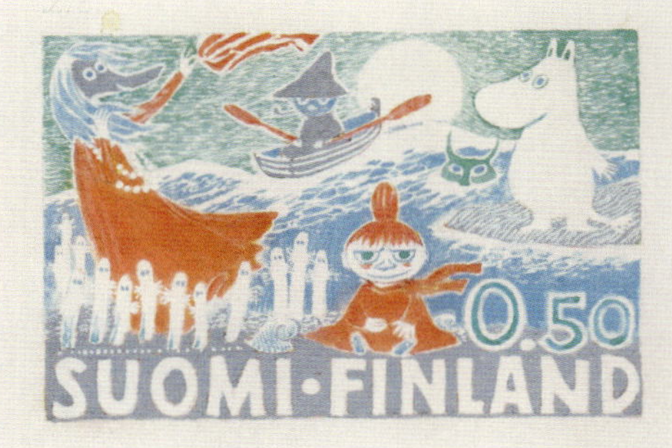

OPPOSITE

A Peruvian-themed cover of the *Dagsverket* fundraising anthology, 1964. Ayacucho is the capital city of the Ayacucho region in southern Peru.

ABOVE AND RIGHT

Three pairs of rough and more refined designs as part of a possible set of Finnish postage stamps. The first Moomin stamps would be released in Finland in 1992, using previously published colour illustrations.

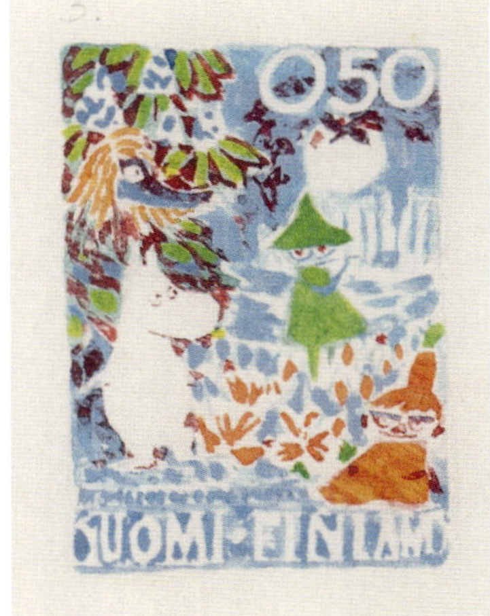
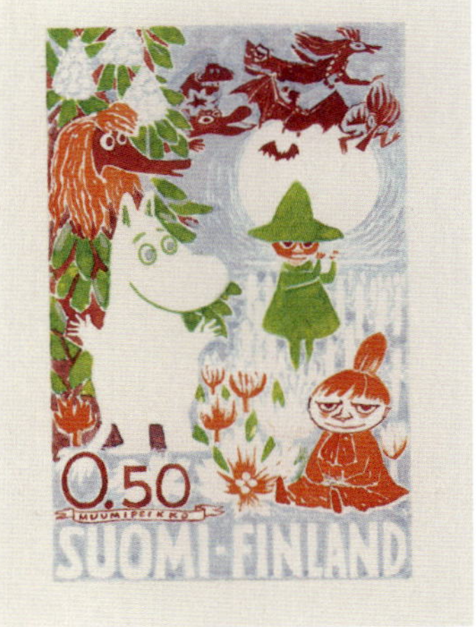

'Life is not peaceful'

'Life is not peaceful' was Snufkin's calm reply to a ruffled
Hemulen's plea for peace and quiet, and this proved true
for the Jansson family. In 1968, Nita Jansson (née Lesch),
Tove's sister-in-law, died at only thirty-eight, leaving behind
Lars and their daughter Sophia, aged six. For the youngest
member of the family, aunties Tove and Tuulikki, as well as
Grandma Ham, helped fill the unspoken absence, including
magical stays on their island. Only when Sophia insisted
in her late teens could they explain that her mother 'came
from a very tragic background. Then there was the war.
She developed a drinking problem and died young.' With
hindsight, Sophia understood how 'somebody so unhappy
was difficult for them to talk about openly'.[8] In 1970, Tove
Jansson lost her mother, again expressing this profound loss
through her work, first in *Sent i November* (*Moominvalley
in November*), the month known in Finland as 'the month
of death'. Jansson contrasts how Snufkin, her narrator Toft
and other cast members await the missing Moomin family's
return to Moominvalley, leaving the resolution out of view
and out of time. She knew this was her last Moomin novel.

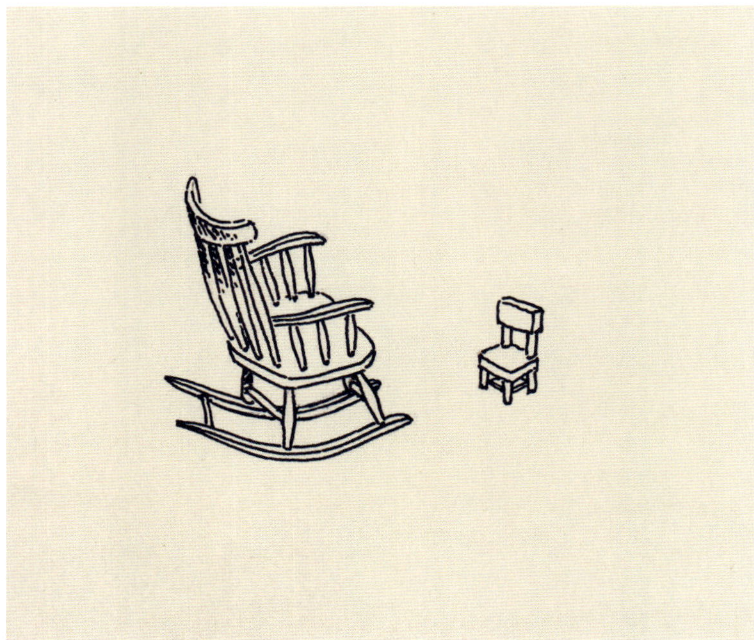

A poignant vignette from *Sent
i November* (*Moominvalley in
November*), 1970.

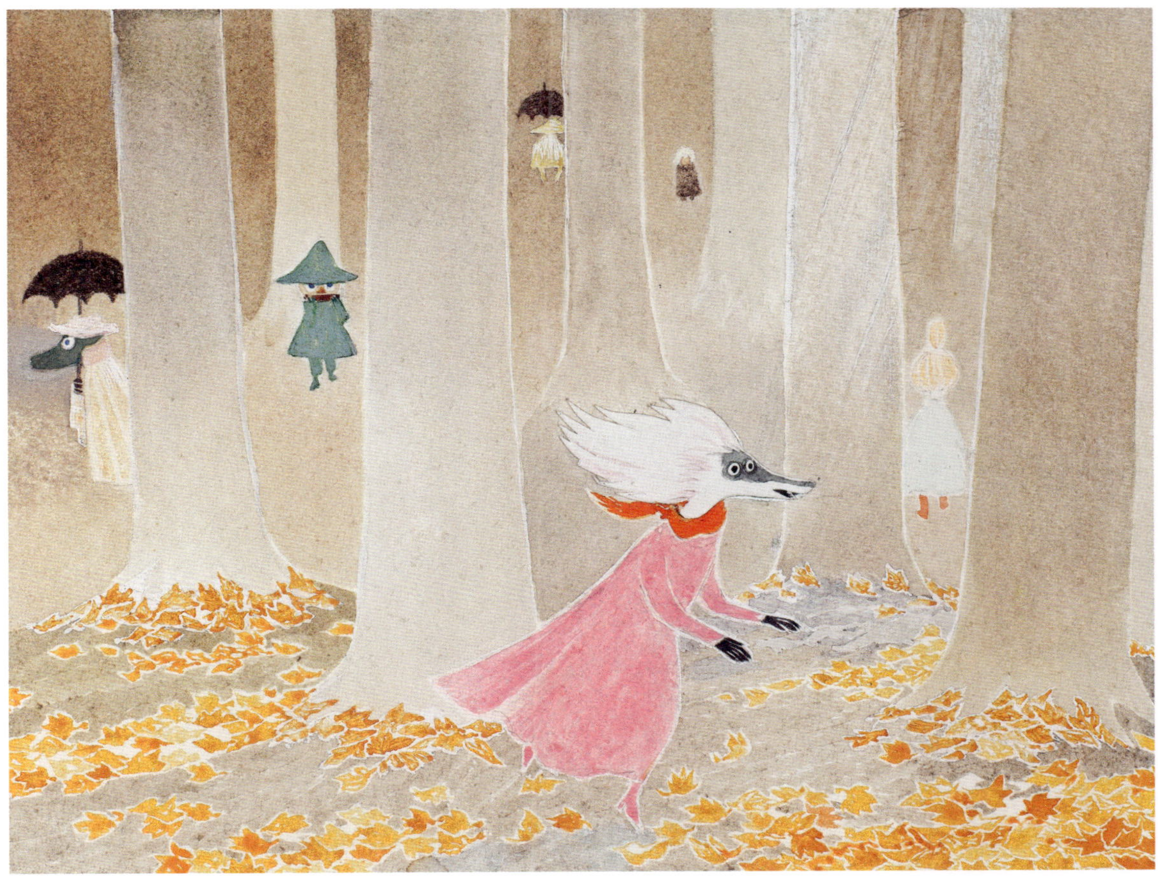

A preparatory version of the cover for *Sent i November* (*Moominvalley in November*), 1970.

Jansson's mother had once suggested to her the theme of an elderly grandmother and a little girl. In 1972, this became *The Summer Book*, in which Jansson found a way to reconnect with the mother she missed terribly by both recreating and imagining how Ham and Sophia had kept each other company during their island holidays. As the oldest and the youngest, the book's Grandmother and the girl of six – Sophia's age when her mother died – discuss their contrasting viewpoints on what living and dying mean. Ham had died in July, but in the book's closing chapter, 'August', she lives through that liminal 'border' month and witnesses summer slip into autumn. To signal that this book was not intended for children, Jansson subtitled it 'A Novel', but in 1976 her German publisher persuaded her to add seventeen illustrations, eight of them full-page.

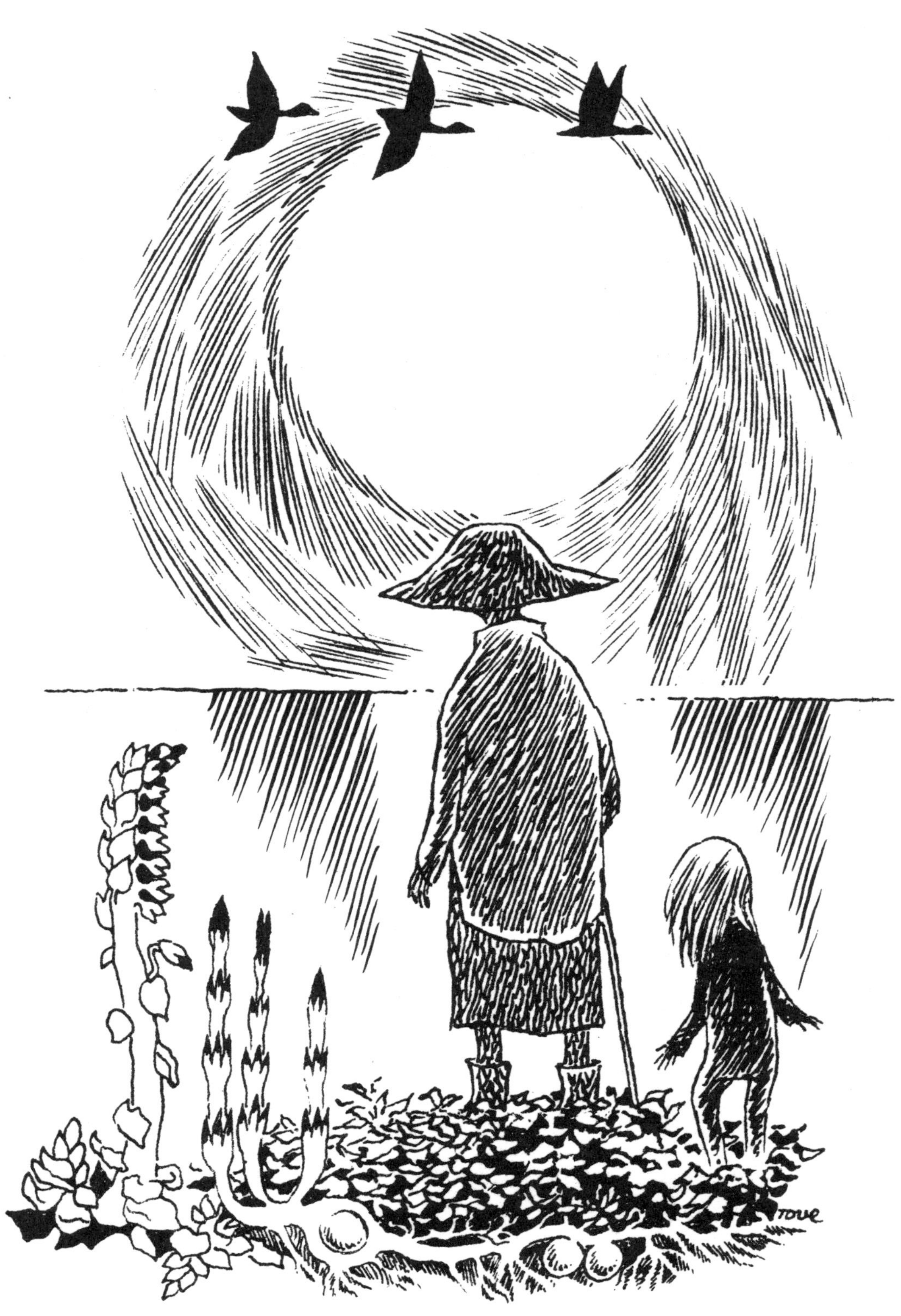

She draws both characters always from behind or at a distance, behind a book or even as clouds, so they stay faceless and universal. Widely translated and awarded, *The Summer Book* confirmed Jansson as a world-class writer for adults. From her first novel, *Sculptor's Daughter*, in 1968, to her last short stories in *Messages* in 1998, autobiography, more or less disguised, underpinned much of this thirty-year mature blooming, alongside wise, sometimes dark psychological insights. She returned to the island setting for her last novel, *Fair Play*, in 1989, this time home to two ageing women who make their daily lives fulfilling, weathering irritations, jealousies and artistic struggles through the blend of fairness and playfulness that give the book its title.

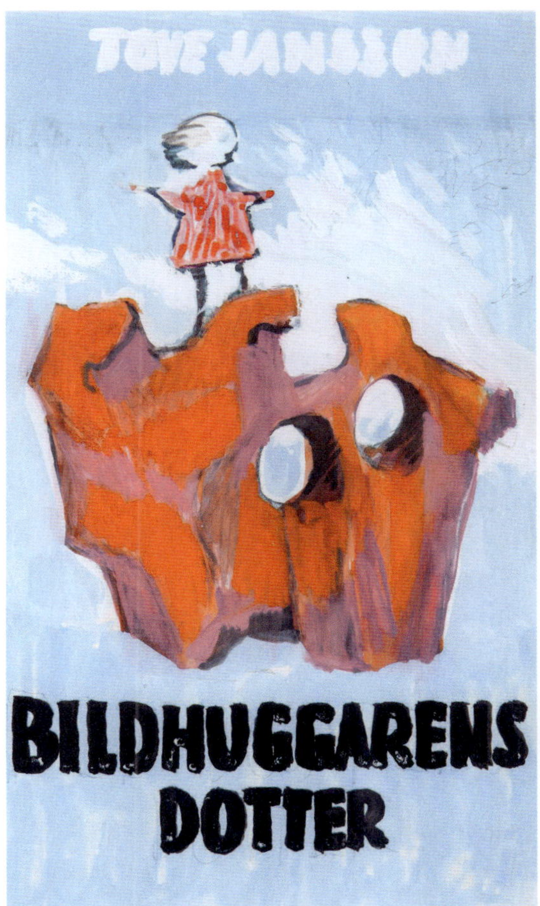

OPPOSITE

A full-page illustration for the 1976 German edition of *The Summer Book*.

RIGHT

A sketch in oils for the cover of *Sculptor's Daughter*, 1968.

Final collaborations

She may have finished her series of Moomin novels, but Jansson was far from finished with her creations, especially when they stirred such stimulating collaborations. When the versatile Finnish composer Ilkka Kuusisto approached her in 1974 about basing his first children's opera on *Moominsummer Madness*, she dived in, writing an hour-long libretto in which she relocated the story from a floating theatre to a floating opera house. Her lyrics inspired Kuusisto to combine diverse types of music, from Moominpappa's oratorios to the Hattifatteners' electronica. She designed the costumes, assisted by Hans Kling, who installed microphones inside the Moomins' headpieces so that they could keep them on while singing. Jansson devised the programme to resemble Moominmamma's handbag, the pages printed as cards tucked inside. It enjoyed thirty-four performances for the Christmas season at the Finnish National Opera in Helsinki, and continues to be revived.

Meanwhile, Moominvalley, last left Moomin-less, was still calling to Jansson and her public. In her final solo children's picture book, *Den farliga resan* (*The Dangerous Journey*), in 1977, she found her way back, personified as the young adventure-seeker Susanna. When this bored, Alice-like lead tries on a fresh pair of glasses, she realizes she can see and shape the world differently, and sets out to explore it. Alone at first, she soon meets a Hemulen, his timid dog Sorry-oo and Thingumy and Bob, joined by Sniff and Too-ticky, all en route to a Moomin party. To refresh how she worked, Jansson reversed her usual method, beginning not by writing her rhyming narrative, but by illustrating double pages with vigorous watercolours of fantastical and fearsome terrains for her voyagers to struggle through. Several landscapes allowed Jansson to hark back to Beskow and Bauer, her favourite Swedish fairytale illustrators, and she included unmistakable Japanese motifs such as the Hemulen's hat and smock, the flock of cranes and the kite Too-ticky flies above the party.

Jansson appreciated the significance, for herself and her readers, of the eventual reunion with the much-missed Moomin family, as her planning stages reveal. At first,

Design in gouache and ink for a poster advertising the Moomin Opera, 1974.

A preparatory version in gouache and pencil of the first double-page illustration in *The Dangerous Journey*, c. 1976.

A preparatory version in watercolour and pencil of the second double-page illustration in *The Dangerous Journey*, c. 1976.

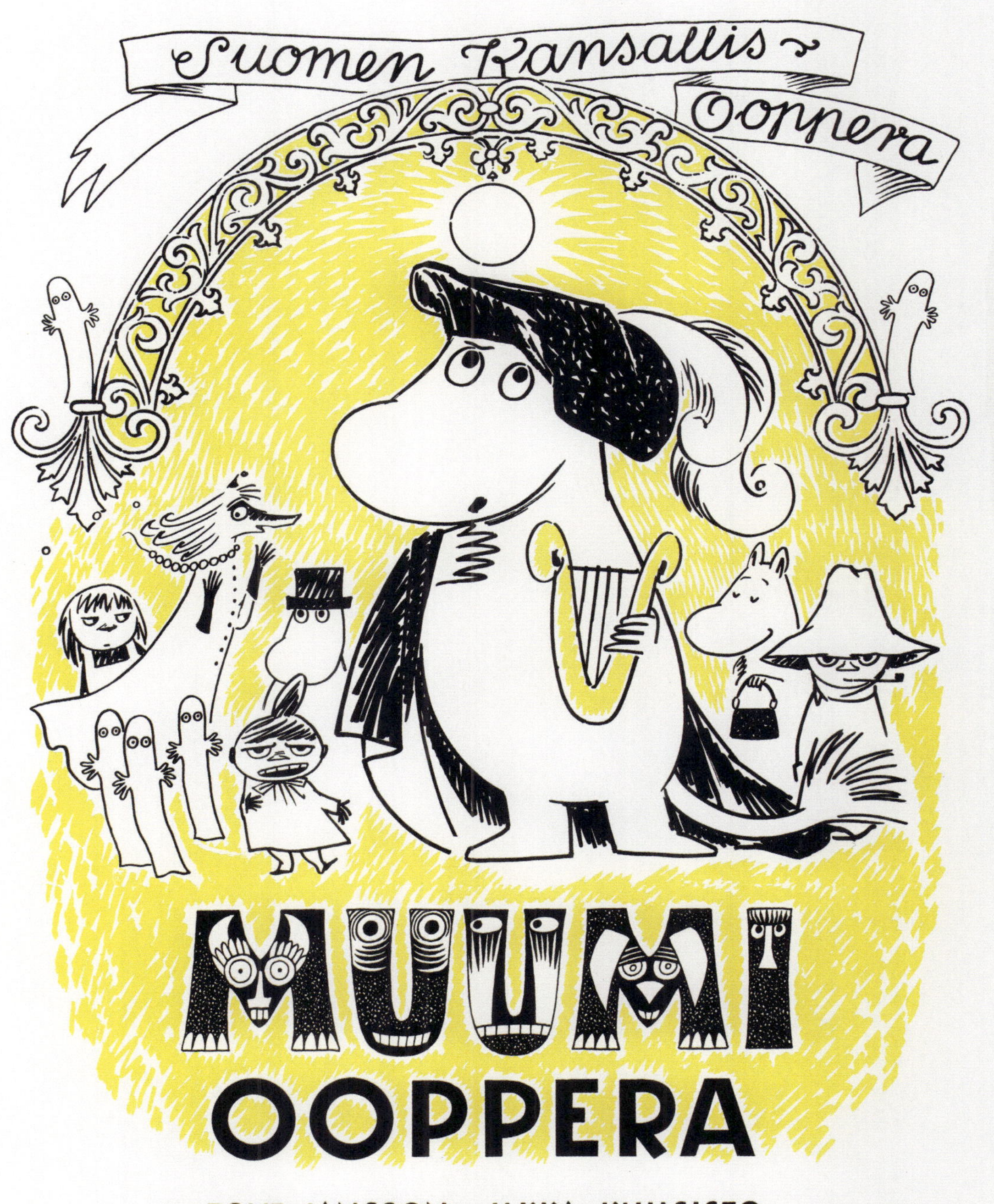

Suomen Kansallis-Ooppera
MUUMI
OOPPERA
TOVE JANSSON   ILKKA KUUSISTO
HEIKKI VÄRTSI

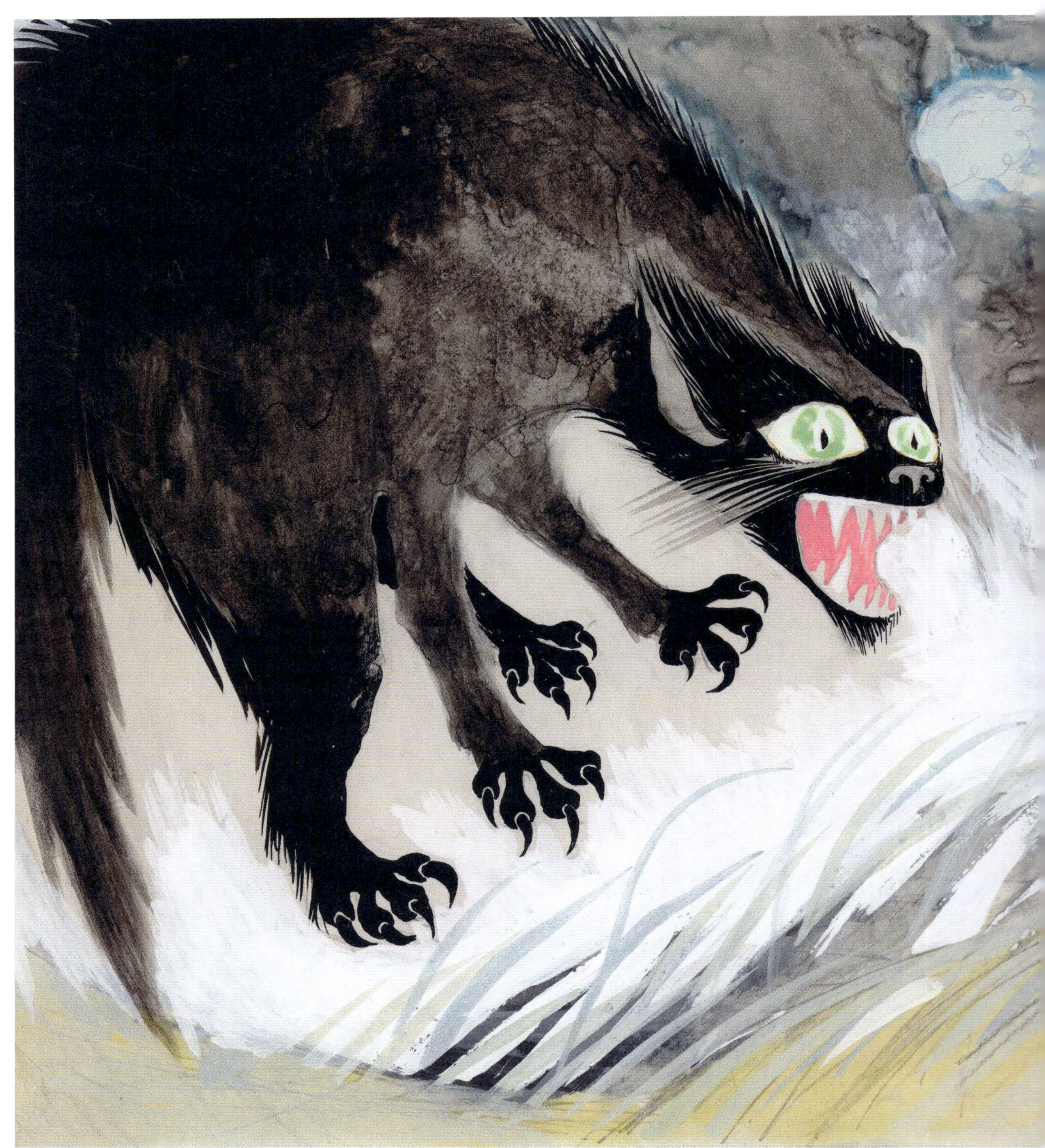

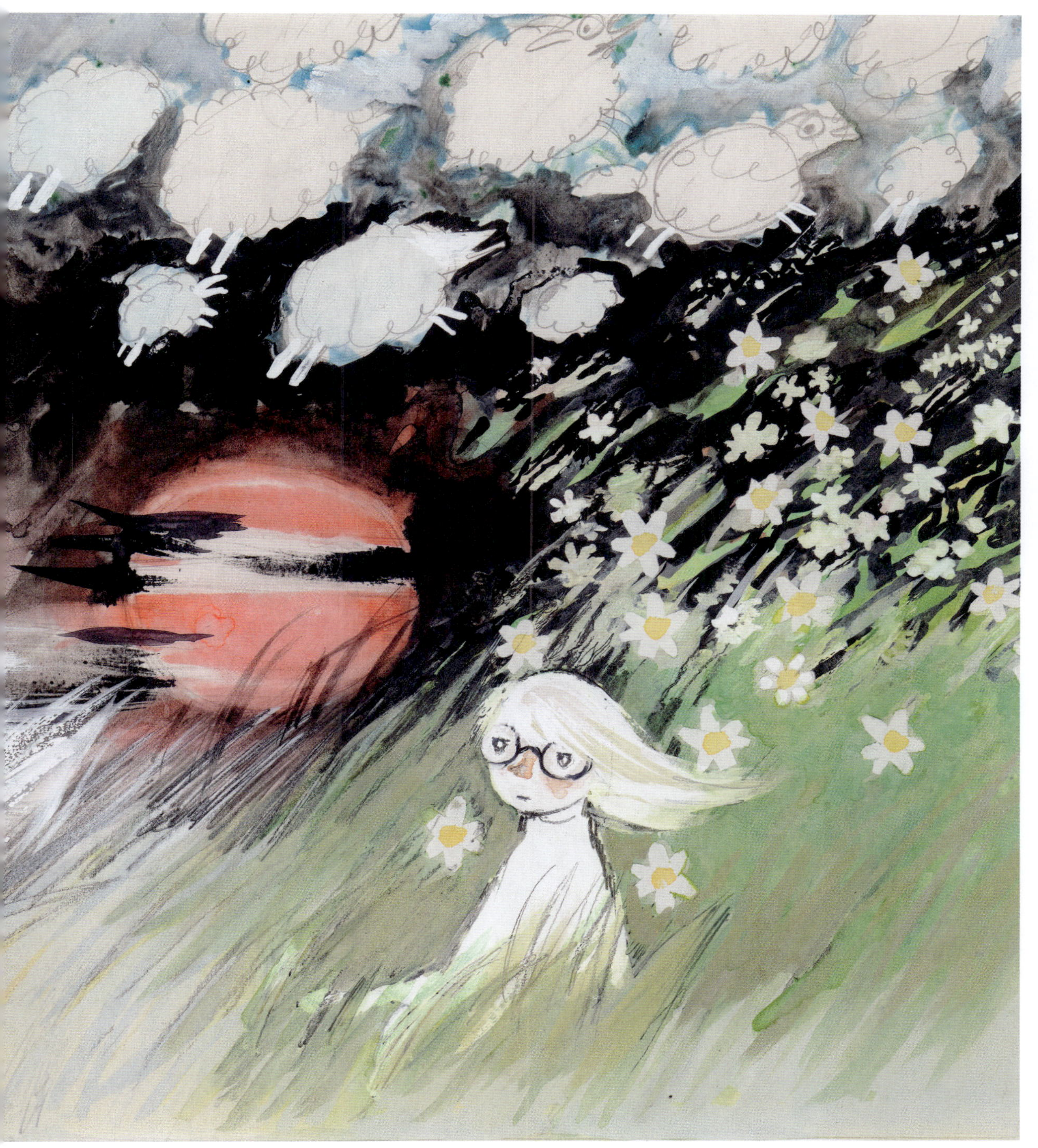

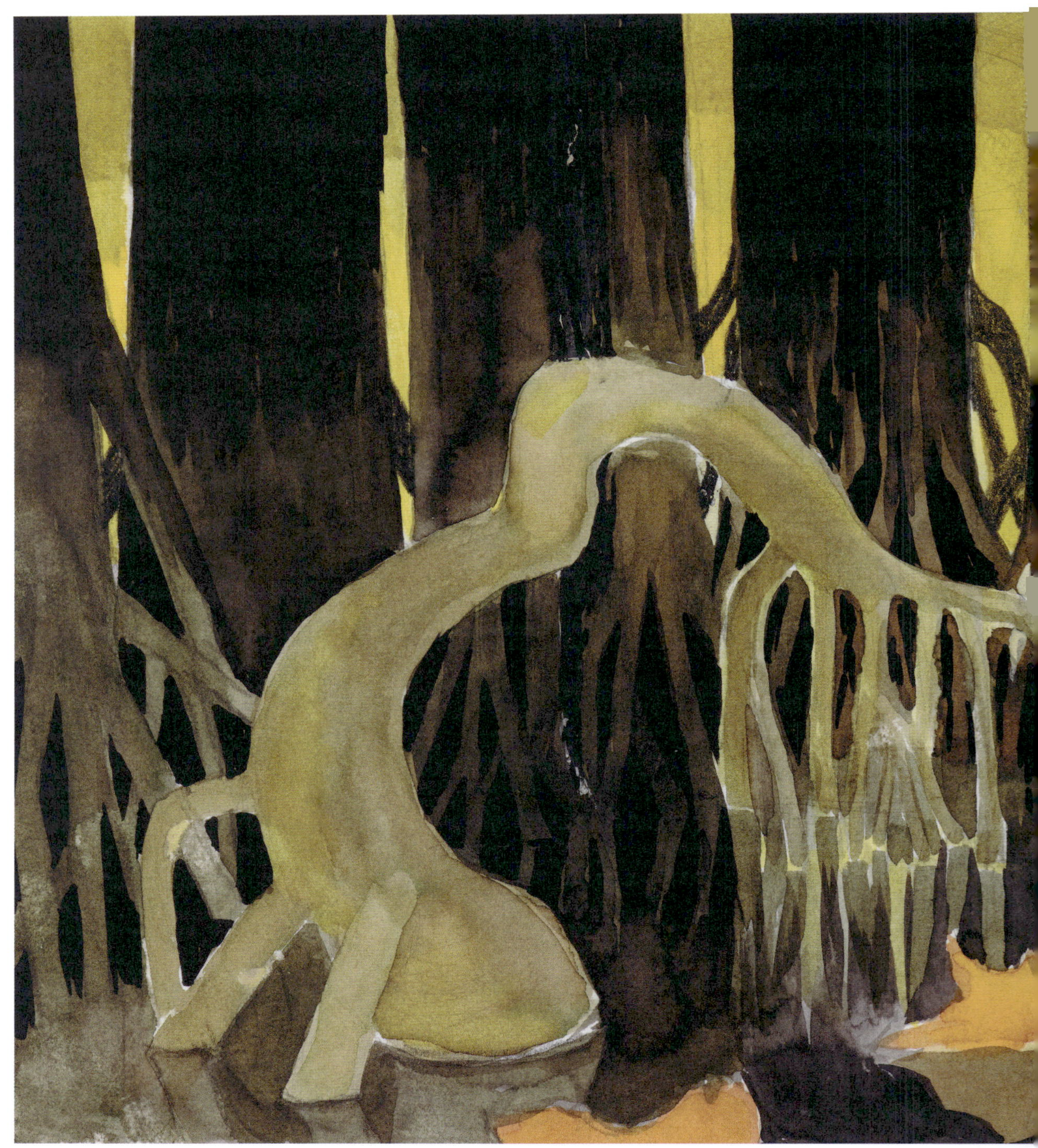

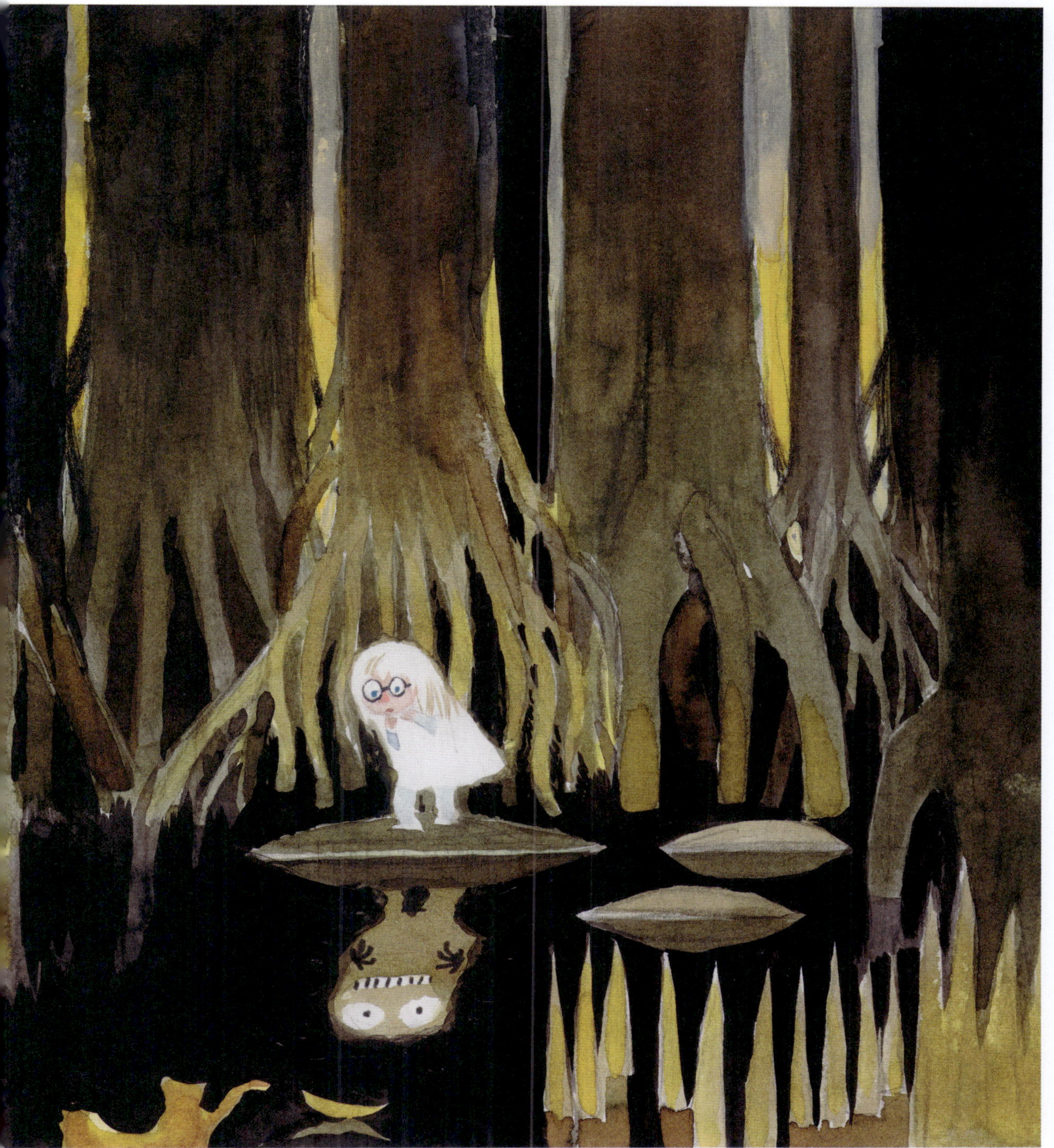

Hemulen stands large, centre-left, but in the published composition, Jansson sidelines him to the balloon's basket, so that Susanna heads the group. She also removed Moominmamma's apron and Moomintroll's trousers to show them *au naturel*. Jansson does not leave readers with a 'happily ever after' ending, but keeps it open by sending Susanna home, reunited with her cat and ready for the joys and uncertainties of the adventure of life.

Another collaboration began modestly in 1958, when Pentti Eistola, a doctor and close friend of Jansson and Pietilä, showed them a miniature model he had made of the Moominhouse. Enthused, Pietilä took to carving wooden figures of Moomin characters, and in 1976, Jansson, Pietilä and Eistola decided to construct a more elaborate version together. Over three years, they built organically, without drawings, in a multitude of architectural styles. Their Moominhouse rose to five storeys of over two metres (6½ ft) high, different from Jansson's rounded original, though its main tower was still painted blue and white. Inside, models of her main characters occupied its many furnished rooms. This Moominhouse starred in several museum exhibitions and provided the actors and locations, photographed by her brother Per Olov, for a spooky new short story and guided tour written by Jansson. In *Skurken i Muminhuset* (*Villain in the Moominhouse*; unpublished in English, but translated for a reading in London as *An Unwanted Guest*), Moomintroll and Little My visit everyone to find a mysterious intruder, who turns out to be Stinky from the first comic-strip tale. Pietilä and Jansson went on to make forty-one additional tableaux of scenes from the books. With the Moominhouse, these found a permanent home in Tampere, where Pietilä's architect brother Reima proposed they could be housed in the spacious unused basement to the city's new library, which he had designed. This, accompanied by other donations, would become the world's only Moomin Museum.

Latterly, Jansson's life as an illustrator tapered, with the exception of a collection of her Moomin song lyrics with music and covers for most of the books she wrote. During her final years, a trembling hand meant that Jansson drew less and less, but she never stopped writing back to

The Moominhouse, photographed by Per Olov Jansson for the cover of *Skurken i Muminhuset* (*Villain in the Moominhouse*), 1980.

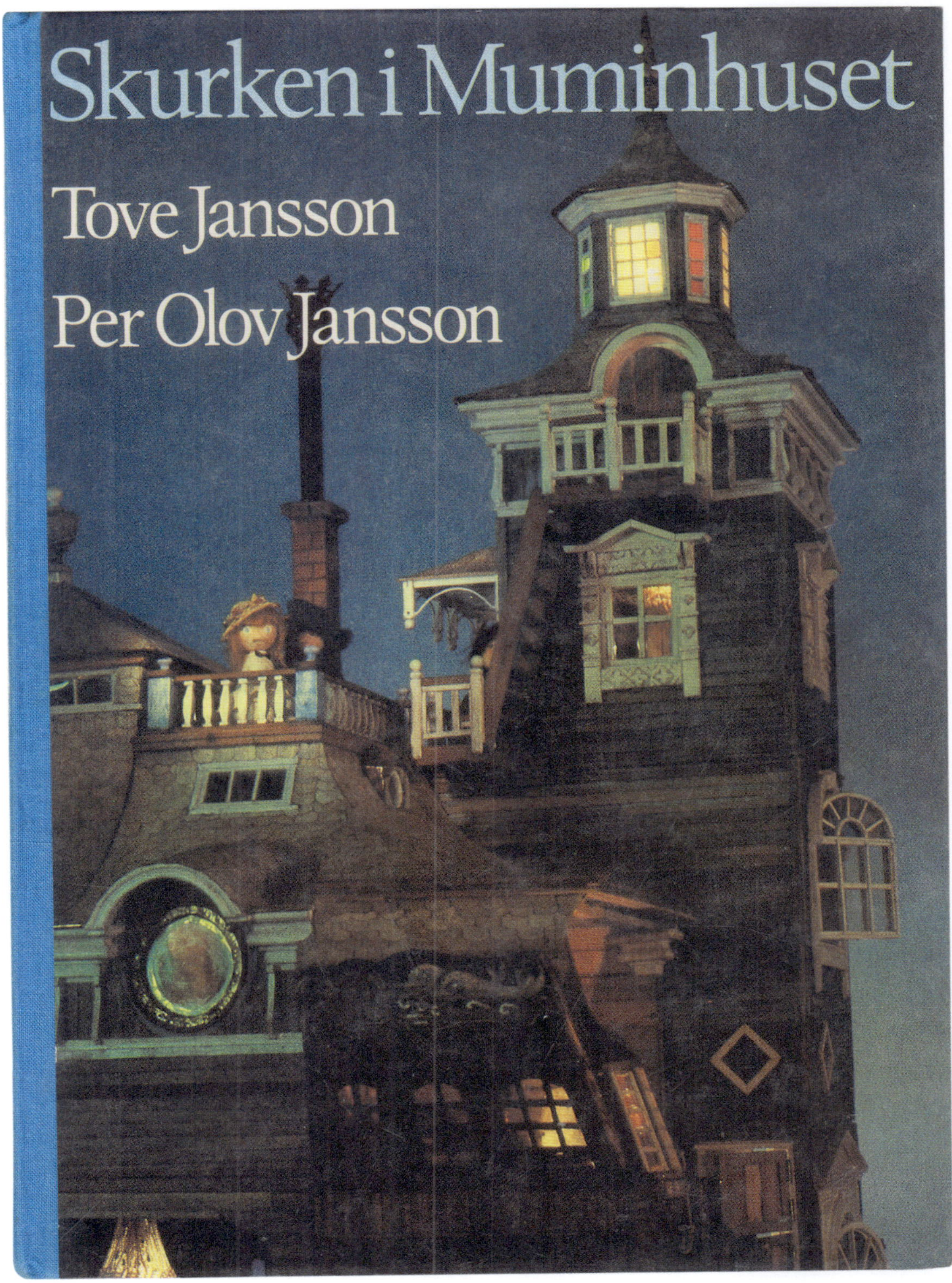
Skurken i Muminhuset
Tove Jansson
Per Olov Jansson

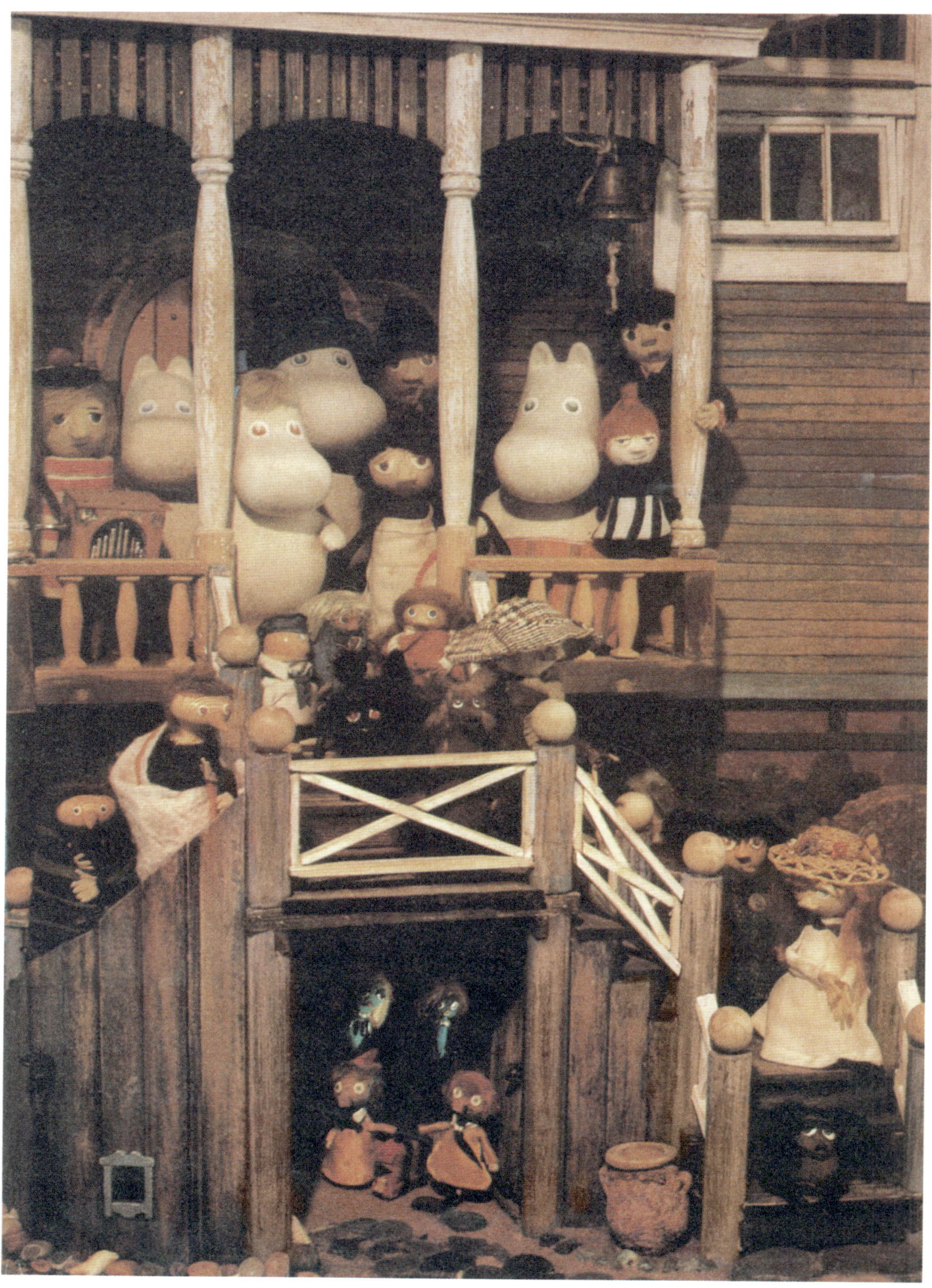

OPPOSITE

An interior photograph from
Skurken i Muminhuset (*Villain in
the Moominhouse*), showing many
of the carved figurines made by
Tove Jansson and Tuulikki Pietilä.

RIGHT

Among the later merchandise
was a Moomin colouring book, for
which Jansson developed a bold,
simplified line.

BELOW

A Little My paper doll and six dress
designs in watercolour.

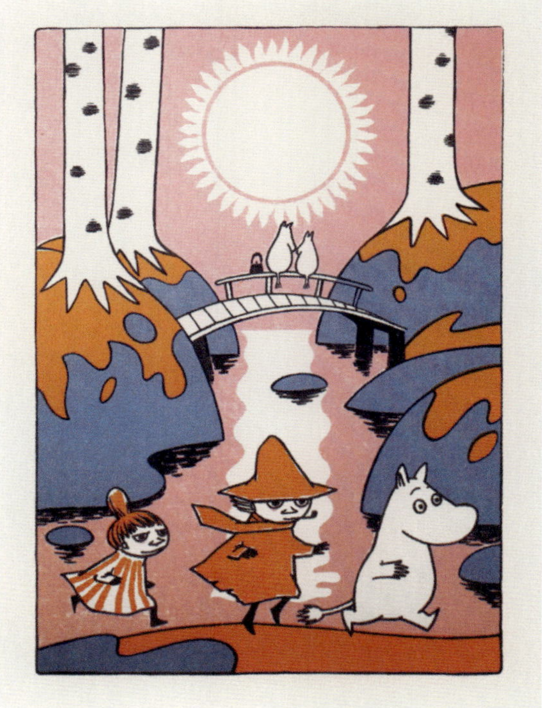

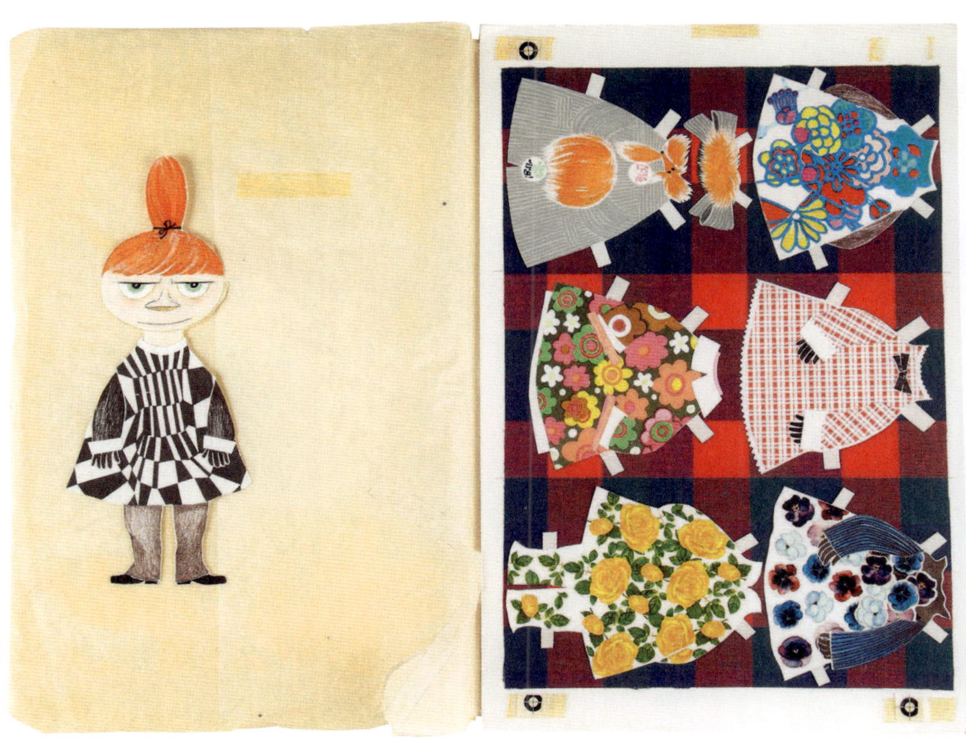

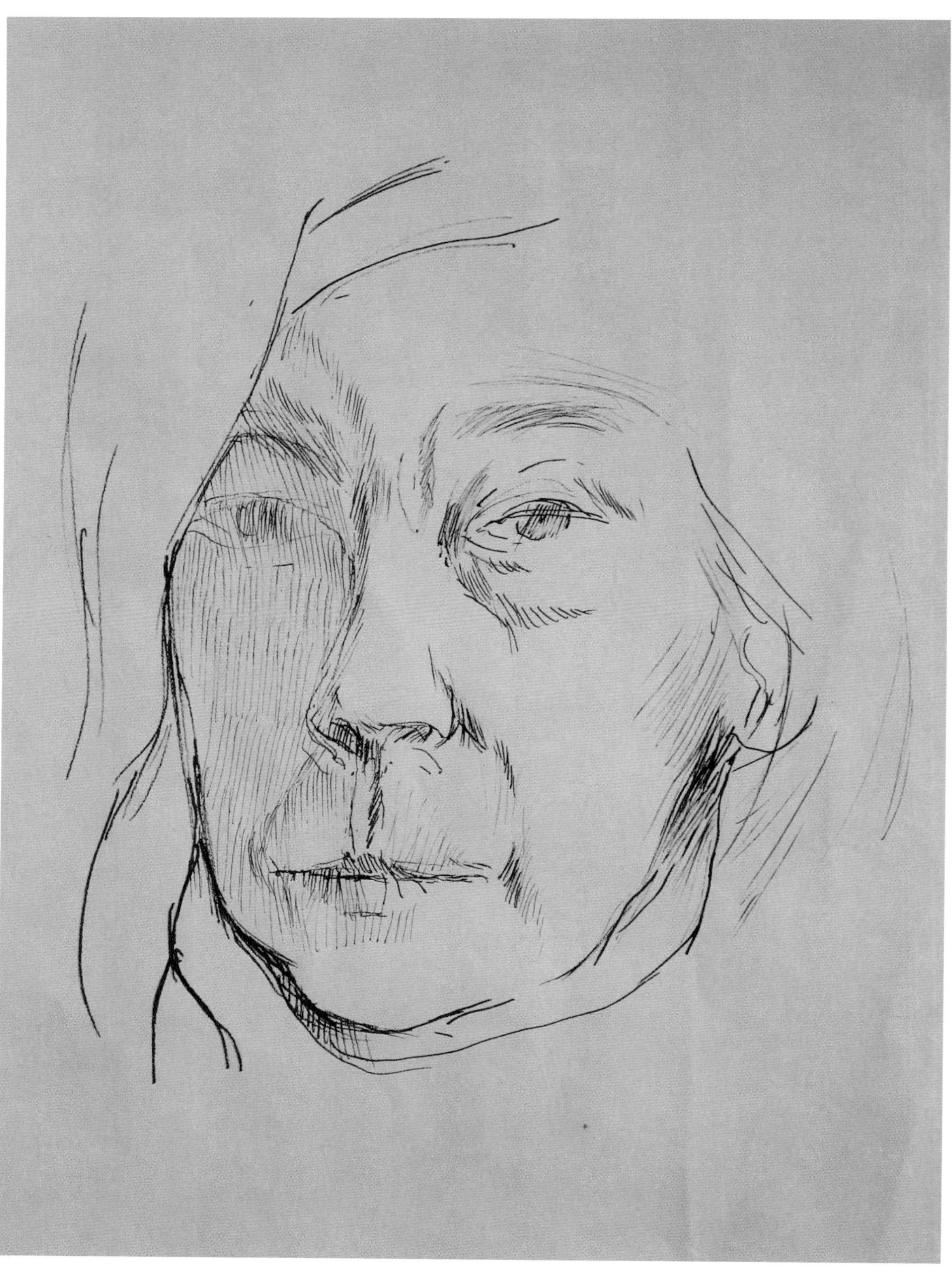

her readers. Pietilä illustrated her last and most personal novel, *Anteckningar från en ö* (*Notes from an Island*), in 1996. In 2000, Lars, her youngest brother, died of lung cancer; less than a year later, it also claimed Tove. Yet her legacy resonates even stronger in this uncertain century. In her celebration of nature, creativity, diversity and self-realization, Jansson's multiple lives continue to enrich the world profoundly. As her Moomintroll once observed contentedly, and she exemplified, 'How very different people are.'

OPPOSITE

A late self-portrait in ink.

BELOW

Around the family table on Klohvarun, with Tove Jansson standing, her mother Ham seated to her right, and opposite her, from left, Per Olov Jansson's wife Saga, their daughter Ingegerd and her nanny Anja Velroos. Photograph by Per Olov Jansson, *c.* 1950.

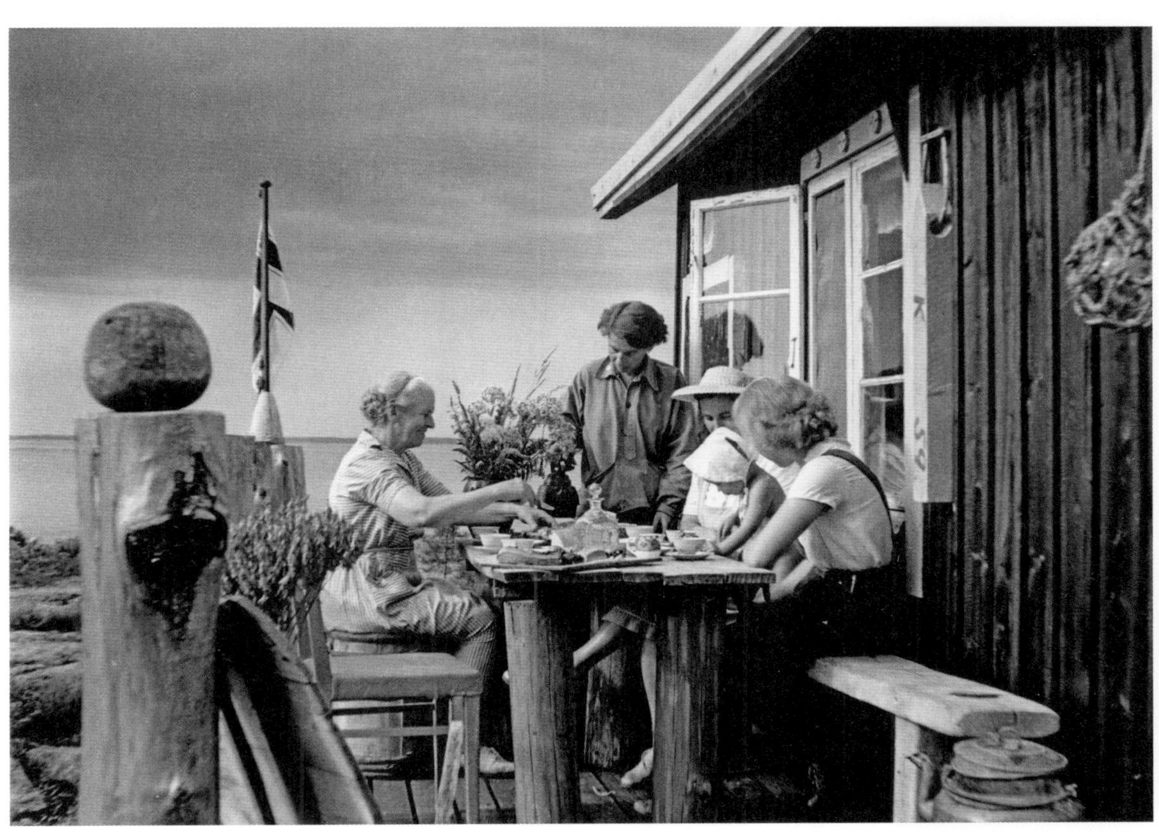

1. 'The Patter of Tiny Hoofs', *The Times Literary Supplement*, 21 November 1958, xiv.
2. *Sagan om verkligheten: den ärliga Elsa Beskow* (Stockholm: BLM, 1959; transl. Design House Sweden, 2014)
3. Tuula Karjalainen, *Tove Jansson: Work and Love* (London: Penguin Books, 2014), p. 73.
4. *Pen+ Magazine* (Tokyo: Media House Mook, June 2017).
5. *What Happened Next? The Book about Moomin, Mymble and Little My* may well have inspired the French artist Maurice Henry or his publisher, who contracted him on 30 July 1952, close to the release of Jansson's book, to create a 'Petite Mythologie' to include 'holes in the paper'. What eventually appeared in 1955 was more of a Surrealist, psychological dream journey, with holes in half of its sixty-four pages, yet the influence of Jansson's innovations on Henry's *Les Métamorphoses du Vide* seems probable. See Jacques Desse, 'Métamorphoses du Vide, métamorphoses du livre' in *Metámorphoses du Vide* (Brussels: Éditions du Sandre, 2018).
6. At Associated Newspapers's headquarters, Jansson was assigned the office of Wally Fawkes, a.k.a. the strip cartoonist 'Trog', who was 'away for a month, possibly at a nerve clinic'. This was probably conjecture, based on her being told that Fawkes had to go to Switzerland. In fact, Fawkes, who was also a jazz clarinetist, had seized the chance to rehearse with a Swiss band playing in Geneva for Sidney Bechet. To cover his absence, Fawkes had recruited fellow cartoonists to produce a 'stockpile' from his outlines, which explains why Jansson also mentioned warnings from 'tired cartoonists' to 'be sure to have stock-material so you don't get behind, otherwise you'll go crazy....' Fawkes had worked with a series of writers since 1949 to produce the furry, snouted Flook for the *Daily Mail*, where its change from fantasy to savvy social commentary proved highly popular, a recipe Sutton hoped to emulate with Moomin. See Adam Smith, 'Looking Back at Flook: An Interview with Wally Fawkes', *The Comics Journal*, 11 September 2013 <http://www.tcj.com/looking-back-at-flook-an-interview-with-wally-fawkes/>
7. Tove Jansson, 'Den lömska barnboksförfattaren' ('The Deceitful Children's Author'), *Horisont* 2, 1961
8. Interview with Sophia Jansson, *Guardian*, 3 July 2010 <https://www.theguardian.com/lifeandstyle/2010/jul/03/moomins-tove-jansson-sophia>

Tove Jansson's quotations come from:
Tuula Karjalainen, *Tove Jansson: Work and Love*, trans. David McDuff, Sort Of Books, 2014
Boel Westin, *Tove Jansson: Life, Art, Words*, trans. Silvester Mazzarella, Sort Of Books, 2014
Boel Westin and Helen Svensson (eds), *Tove Jansson: Letters from Tove*, trans. Sarah Death, Sort Of Books, 2019

Books with a * are published in English by Sort Of Books. Where the English title differs significantly from the Swedish, both translation and published title are included in the entry.

The Moomin books

*Småtrollen och den stora översvämningen (*The Moomins and The Great Flood*), Söderström & Co., 1945

*Kometjakten (*Comet in Moominland*), Söderström & Co., 1946

*Trollkarlens hatt (*The Hobgoblin's Hat*; published in English as *Finn Family Moomintroll*), Holger Schildts förlag, 1948

Muminpappans bravader skrivna av honom själv (*The Exploits of Moominpappa, Written by Himself*), Holger Schildts förlag, 1950; revised and republished as *Muminpappans memoarer (*The Memoirs of Moominpappa*), 1968

*Hur gick det sen? Boken om Mymlan, Mumintrollet och Lilla My (*What Happened Next? The Book about Mymble, Moomintroll and Little My*), Holger Schildts förlag, 1952

*Farlig midsommar (*Moominsummer Madness*), Holger Schildts förlag, 1954

*Trollvinter (*Moominland Midwinter*), Holger Schildts förlag, 1957

Moomin newspaper strip collections, later volumes with or by Lars Jansson, 1957–1975, first volume in Swedish, Holger Schildts förlag, 1957; first volume in English, Allan Wingate; complete series in ten volumes, Drawn & Quarterly, 2006–2015

*Vem ska trösta Knyttet? (*Who Will Comfort Toffle?*), Holger Schildts förlag, 1960

*Det osynliga barnet och andra berättelser (*The Invisible Child and Other Stories*; published in English as *Tales from Moominvalley*), Holger Schildts förlag, 1962

*Pappan och havet (*Moominpappa at Sea*), Holger Schildts förlag, 1965

*Sent i november (*Moominvalley in November*), Holger Schildts förlag, 1970

*Den farliga resan (*The Dangerous Journey*), Holger Schildts förlag, 1977

Skurken i Muminhuset (*Villain in the Moomin House*; known in English as *The Unwanted Guest*), with photos by Per Olov Jansson, Holger Schildts förlag, 1980

Visor från Mumindalen (*Songs from Moominvalley*), with Lars Jansson and Erna Tauro, Holger Schildts förlag, 1993

Other illustrated books

Sara och Pelle och Neckens bläckfiskar (*Sara, Pelle and the Water-Sprite's Octopuses*), printed under the name Vera Haij, Bildkonst, 1933

Writings for adults

*Bildhuggarens dotter (*The Sculptor's Daughter*), Holger Schildts förlag, 1968

*Lyssnerskan (*The Listener*), Holger Schildts förlag, 1971

*Sommarboken (*The Summer Book*), Holger Schildts förlag, 1972

Solstaden (*Sun City*), Holger Schildts förlag, 1974

*Dockskåpet och andra berättelser (*The Doll's House and Other Stories*; published in English as *Art in Nature*), Holger Schildts förlag, 1978

*Den ärliga bedragaren (*The True Deceiver*), Holger Schildts förlag, 1982

Stenåkern (*The Stone Acre*), Holger Schildts förlag, 1984

*Resa med lätt bagage (*Travelling Light*), Holger Schildts förlag, 1987

*Rent spel (*Fair Play*), Holger Schildts förlag, 1989

*Brev från Klara och andra berättelser (*Letters from Klara*), Holger Schildts förlag, 1991

*Anteckningar från en ö (*Notes from an Island*), with illustrations by Tuulikki Pietilä, Holger Schildts förlag, 1996

Meddelande. Noveller i urval 1971–1997 (*Messages*), Holger Schildts förlag, 1998

Selected illustrations for other writers' books

Jag (*I*) by Ella Pipping, with Signe Hammarsten-Jansson, Söderström & Co., 1937

Nalleresan (*Teddy's Journey*) by Solveig Schoultz, Wahlström & Widstrand, 1944

Bröderna Borgs bedrifter (*The Exploits of the Borg Brothers*) by Carolus Sjöstedt, Taidekorttikeskus, 1947

Snarkjakten (*The Hunting of the Snark*) by Lewis Carroll, Bonniers, 1959

Bilbo: En Hobbits Äventyr (*The Hobbit*) by J.R.R. Tolkien, Rabén & Sjögren, 1962

Alice i Underlandet (*Alice in Wonderland*) by Lewis Carroll, Bonniers, 1966

Selected reference works

Ardagh, Philip, and Frank Cottrell-Boyce, *The World of Moominvalley as created by Tove Jansson*, Macmillan Children's Books, 2017

Cottrell-Boyce, Frank, Paul Gravett, Tuula Karjalainen and Boel Westin, *Tove Jansson – Desire to Create and Live*, exh. cat., Förlaget, 2016

Karjalainen, Tuula, *Tove Jansson: Work and Love*, trans. David McDuff, Particular Books, 2014

McLoughlin, Kate, and Malin Lidström Brock (eds), *Tove Jansson Rediscovered*, Cambridge Scholars Publishing, 2007

Tölvanen, Juhani, *Muumisisarukset Tove ja Lars Jansson: Muumipeikkosarjakuvan tarina (*Moomin Siblings Tove and Lars Jansson: The Story of the Moomin Comics*), WSOY, 2000

Tomihara, Mayumi, *Garm – The People's Watchdog: Tove Jansson and Finland-Swedish culture's definitive caricature magazine*, Seidosha, 2009; English edition, 2014

Westin, Boel, *Tove Jansson: Life, Art, Words*, trans. Silvester Mazzarella, Sort Of Books, 2014

Westin, Boel, and Helen Svensson (eds), *Tove Jansson: Letters from Tove*, trans. Sarah Death, Sort Of Books, 2014

Moomin: The Art and The Story, exh. cat., MACG, 2019

1914 9 August, Tove Marika Jansson is born in Helsinki, then-Grand Duchy of Finland, Russian Empire.

1928 *Sara och Pelle och Necken's Bläckfiskar* accepted for publication by Tilmanns. The book is not published until 1933.

1929–53 Undertakes various commissions for the satirical magazine *Garm*, beginning at the age of fifteen, and ending with the magazine's closure.

1930–33 Leaves Brobergska samskolen, a Swedish school in Helsinki, to study arts and crafts at Tekniska skolan, Stockholm, Sweden.

1932 Begins taking on a wide range of commissions from book publishers, magazines and newspapers.

1933–36 Attends the School of Fine Arts, Helsinki, Finland.

1938 Attends L'École d'Adrien Holy, Paris, France, during which time she also spends two weeks at L'École des Beaux-Arts.

1939 Begins writing *Moomintroll and the Great Flood*; Moomins start to appear increasingly across her commissions and personal work.

1943 First solo painting exhibition, at Taidesalonki gallery, Helsinki.

1944 Moves into her turret studio at Ullanlinnankatu, Helsinki, which she kept until her death in 2001.

1945 *Småtrollen och den stora översvämningen (Moomintroll and the Great Flood)* is published.

1945 Completes her first mural commission for the canteen of the Strömberg factory, Helsinki.

1946 *Kometjakten (Comet in Moominland)* is published. It is followed by editions in Sweden (1947) and Britain (1951).

1946 Meets Vivica Bandler.

1947 Makes her first comic strip for the Socialist daily newspaper *Ny Tid*, commissioned by Atos Wirtanen.

1947 Jansson and her brother Lars rent a small island in the Gulf of Finland and build Vindrosen, where Jansson will live and work in the warmer months.

1947 Paints two frescos in Helsinki Town Hall.

1948 *Trollkarlens Hatt (The Hobgoblin's Hat)* is published; it is re-released two years later in English as *Finn Family Moomintroll*.

1949 Writes and designs first Moomin play, *Mumintrollet och kometen (Moomintroll and the Comet)*, which premieres at Svenska Teatern, Helsinki.

1950 *Muminpappans bravader skrivna av honom själv (The Exploits of Moominpappa)* is published.

1952 *Hur gick det sen? Boken om Mymlan, Mumintrollet och Lilla My (What Happened Next? The Book about Moomin, Mymble and Little My)*, Jansson's first children's picture book, is published.

1952–59 Signs a seven-year deal with Associated Newspapers, London, for a Moomin comic strip, originally intended to appear in the *Daily Mail*. From 1960 to 1975, Lars takes over the commission.

1952 Awarded Svenska Dagsbladet prize for Finland-Swedish literature.

1954 20 September, Moomin comic strip debuts in the *London Evening News*.

1955 Meets the graphic artist and teacher Tuulikki Pietilä, who would become her lifelong partner.

1956 New range of Moomin products promoted in two main department stores in Stockholm and Helsinki.

1957 The first and only compilation of Jansson's comic strips is published in English.

1958 Tove and Lars set up Moomin Characters as a general partnership. In 1977, it becomes a limited company.

1958 Tove writes and designs the set for *Troll i kulisserna (Troll in the Wings)*, her second play, directed by Vivica Bandler, which premieres at the Little Theatre in Helsinki.

1958 22 June Viktor 'Faffan' Jansson, her father, dies.

1959 Illustrates an edition of Lewis Carroll's *The Hunting of the Snark*.

1962 Illustrates an edition of *The Hobbit* by J.R.R. Tolkien.

1962 *Det osynliga barnet och andra berättelser (Tales from Moominvalley)* is published.

1964 Tove and Tuulikki build a cottage on the small, remote Klovharun island, in the Finnish archipelago, where they will spend their summers from 1965 to the 1990s.

1966 Illustrates an edition of *Alice in Wonderland* by Lewis Carroll.

1966 Receives the Hans Christian Andersen award for children's literature.

1968 *Bildhuggarens dotter (Sculptor's Daughter)*, her first novel for adults, is published.

1968 A documentary about Jansson, *Mumin och havet (Moomin and the Sea)*, is made for SVT, Swedish public television.

1969 Tove and Lars's co-written live-action series *Mumintrollet* debuts on Swedish television.

1969 The animation series *Mūmin*, never approved by Jansson, debuts in Japan.

1970 Signe 'Ham' Hammarsten, her mother, dies.

1970 Last Moomin book, *Sent i November (Moominvalley in November)*, is published.

1971–72 Takes eight-month, round-the-world trip with Tuulikki Pietilä.

1972 *Sommarboken (The Summer Book)* is published.

1972 Awarded the Mårbacka Prize by the Swedish Academy.

1973 *Mumintrollen* becomes an annual Christmas TV event in Sweden.

1974 Writes a libretto and designs the costumes, posters and programme for a Moomin Opera, with music by Finnish composer Ilkka Kuusisto for the Finnish National Opera. It premieres in December.

1976 Awarded the Pro Finlandia Medal for artists and writers.

1976–79 With Tuulikki and Pentti Eistola, creates a large, elaborate model of the Moominhouse.

1977 *Den farliga resan (The Dangerous Journey)* is published.

1978 Donates her manuscripts and other work to the Åbo Akademi, Turku, who award her an honorary doctorate.

1979–80 The Moominhouse is exhibited in Bratislava and Helsinki.

1980 *Skurken i Muminhuset (Villain in the Moominhouse)*, illustrated with Per Olov Jansson's photographs of the Moominhouse model, is published.

1980 Moomin exhibition opens at the National Museum, Stockholm, and tours Sweden.

1980 Awarded Helsinki culture prize.

1986 Donation of work to and major solo exhibition at Tampere Art Museum, Finland.

1993 *Visor från Mumindalen (Songs From Moominvalley)*, a songbook collaboration with Lars Jansson and Erna Tauro, is published.

1994 Awarded the Swedish Academy's Stora Priset.

1996 *Anteckningar från en ö (Notes from an Island)*, illustrated by Tuulikki Pietilä, is published.

2001 27 June, dies after a long illness, in Helsinki, Finland, and is buried in Hietaniemi cemetery. The Jansson family memorial includes a statue made by her father, Viktor Jansson.

First, I dedicate this book to my fine Finnish friend and Moominologist Juhani Tolvanen for his essential assistance and wisdom. I am also very grateful to Sophia Jansson and Hanna Ahlström at Moomin Characters; Tove Jansson's biographers Boel Westin and Tuula Karjalainen; and Jens Andersson, Anna Öjdahl Bodén and Peter Bodén, Bukowskis Auction House, Timothy Clark, Maria Didrichsen, Adrian Edwards and Stuart Gillies at The British Library, Hagelstam Auction House, Ville Hänninen, Dr Nicholas Hiley at the British Cartoon Archive at the University of Kent, Roisin Inglesby at The William Morris Gallery, Nat Jansz and Mark Ellingham at Sort Of Books, Clarissa Köhler at Handelsgillet i Helsingfors r.f., Erik Kruskopf, Mhairi Muncaster, Kana Murase, Fumio Obata, Anthony O'Neill, Huib van Opstal, Jane de Silva and Alison Williams. My sincere thanks as well to Roger Thorp, Julia MacKenzie, Kate Edwards, Mohara Gill, Alex Finch and all at Thames & Hudson, and in particular designer Therese Vandling and picture research sleuth Fredrika ('Sher-') Lokholm. And last, but never least, Dylan Horrocks, cartoonist and lifelong Tove Jansson connoisseur, who spotted in Reinhold Reitberger and Wolfgang J. Fuchs' seminal book *Comics: Anatomy of a Mass Medium* (1972) a solitary panel from a 'Moomin' newspaper strip, which spurred him to trace those almost-forgotten gems and help them return to print in English.

CREDITS

2 Photo Bukowskis. © Moomin Characters™

4, 8a, 10–11, 42l, 42r, 43a, 43b, 44, 45a, 45b, 46, 47, 48, 49, 50, 51, 55, 58, 59, 60, 61, 62, 65a, 65b, 71a, 71bl, 71br, 73b, 76–77, 78, 84, 85, 86, 90, 91, 93, 95, 96–97, 98-99, 103a, 103b © Moomin Characters™

7, 8b, 12, 14, 17, 18, 19, 23, 25, 30, 31, 32, 33, 35al, 35ar, 35b, 37, 40–41, 72, 104 © Tove Jansson Estate

9, 13, 105 © Per Olov Jansson

20, 21 © Tove Jansson, 1933, Moomin Characters™

27 © Garm Estate. © Tove Jansson Estate

28 Photo Bukowskis. © Tove Jansson Estate

29 Photo Jens Östman, Kungliga Biblioteket. © Tove Jansson Estate

39 © Tove Jansson, 1945, Moomin Characters™

52, 53 © Tove Jansson, 1948, Moomin Characters™

56 © Tove Jansson, 1952, Moomin Characters™

63 Courtesy Jane de Silva. © dmg media licensing, London, © Moomin Characters™

64, 66, 67, 68 © dmg media licensing, London, © Moomin Characters™

70 Handelsgillet. © Tove Jansson Estate

73a Photo Hagelstam & Co. © Tove Jansson Estate

74–75, 112 © Tove Jansson, 1957, Moomin Characters™

79 Photo Jens Andersson. © Moomin Characters™

80 Photo Jens Andersson. © Tove Jansson, 1959

81a, b © Tove Jansson, 1962

82 © Tove Jansson, 1966

83 Courtesy Juhani Tolvanen. © Tove Jansson Estate

88 Photo Jens Andersson/Peter Bodén. © Tove Jansson Estate

89 Photo Hagelstam & Co. © Moomin Characters™

92 © Tove Jansson, 1972, Moomin Characters™

101, 102 Photos Jens Andersson. © Tove Jansson, 1980, Moomin Characters™ © Per Olov Jansson

CONTRIBUTORS

Paul Gravett is a widely published writer specializing in international comics. His books include *Graphic Novels: Stories to Change Your Life, Comics Art, Mangasia: The Definitive Guide to Asian Comics* and *Posy Simmonds (The Illustrators)*. He also curates exhibitions about comics, which have included retrospectives of the work of Tove Jansson, Charles Schulz and Posy Simmonds. www.paulgravett.com

Quentin Blake is one of Britain's most distinguished illustrators. For twenty years he taught at the Royal College of Art, where he was head of the illustration department from 1978 to 1986. Blake received a knighthood in 2013 for his services to illustration and in 2014 was admitted to the Légion d'honneur in France.

Claudia Zeff is an art director who has commissioned illustration for book jackets, magazines and children's books over a number of years. She helped set up the House of Illustration with Quentin Blake, where she is now Deputy Chair. Since 2011 she has worked as Creative Consultant to Quentin Blake.

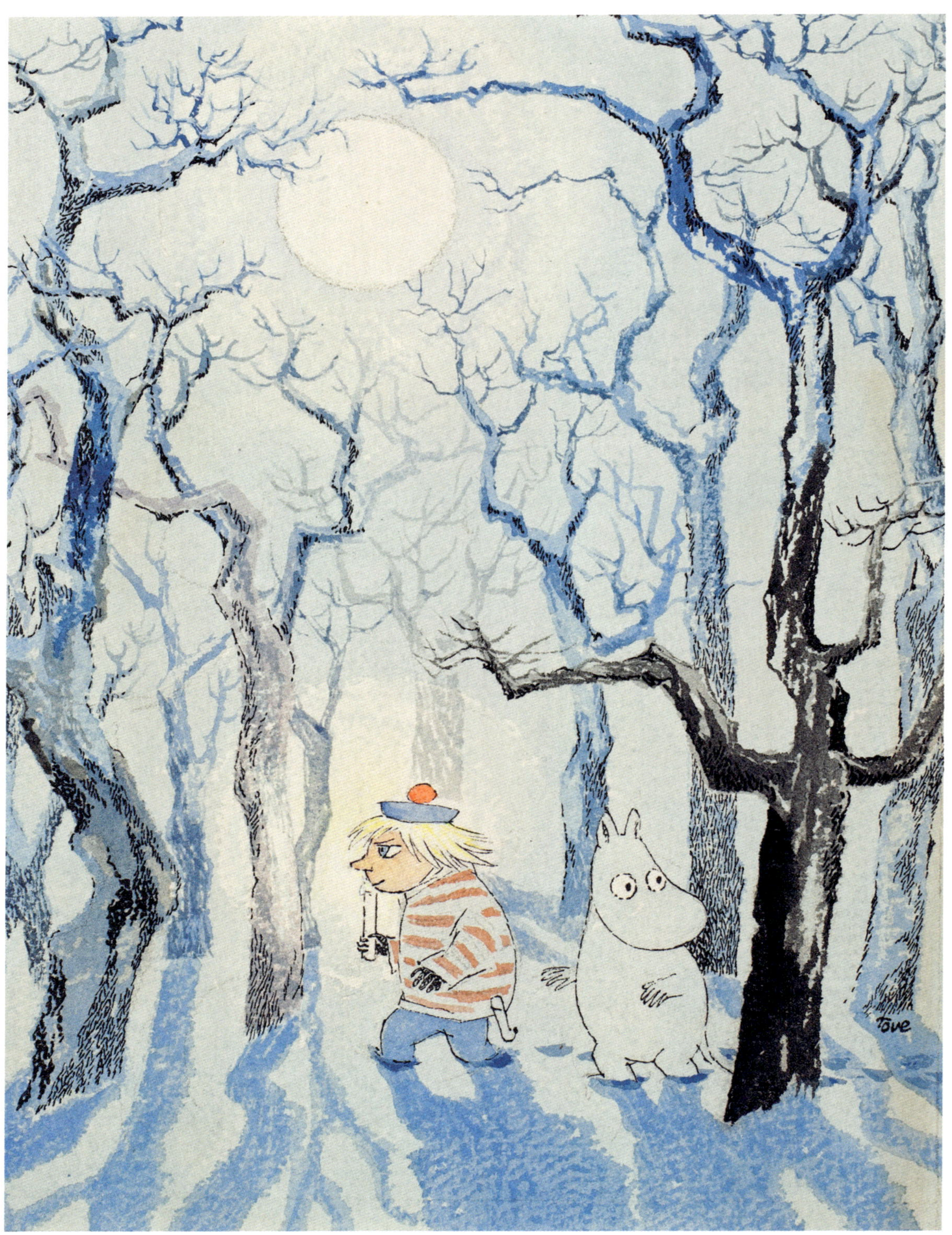

tove